# THE FOUNDATIONS OF DISTANCE EDUCATION

# the
# foundations of
# Distance
# Education WITHDRAWN

## Desmond Keegan

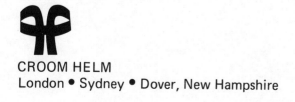

CROOM HELM
London • Sydney • Dover, New Hampshire

© 1986 Desmond Keegan
Croom Helm Ltd, Provident House, Burrell Row,
Beckenham, Kent BR3 1AT
Croom Helm Australia Pty Ltd, Suite 4, 6th Floor,
64-76 Kippax Street, Surry Hills, NSW 2010, Australia

British Library Cataloguing in Publication Data
Keegan, Desmond
    The foundations of distance education.
    1. Distance education
    I. Title
    371.3    LC5800
    ISBN 0-7099-1547-0


Croom Helm, 51 Washington Street, Dover,
New Hampshire 03820, USA

Library of Congress Cataloging in Publication Data

Keegan, Desmond.
    The foundations of distance education.

    Includes index.
    1. Distance education.  I. Title.
LC5800.K43   1985    378'.03     85-21274
ISBN 0-7099-1547-0

Printed and bound in Great Britain by
Biddles Ltd, Guildford and King's Lynn

# CONTENTS

FOR

MARTIN

AND

PATRICIA

# ACKNOWLEDGEMENT

I wish to pay tribute to the camaraderie that exists in distance education. The hospitality I received while carrying out the research documented in this book and the way doors were thrown open with an invitation to probe and evaluate was universal and genuine. It is my hope that the book will strengthen the endeavour of administrators in distance systems to implement good practice in whatever country they work and whether their institutions are publicly supported or privately sponsored.

For relatively lengthy periods I was the guest of a number of institutions. Working in another context one inevitably learns much of the personal interaction and institutional tensions that are characteristics of all groupings in society. My gratitude for their generous welcome goes to a number of institutions in Australia, to the Open University of the United Kingdom at Milton Keynes, the Fernuniversität-Gesamthochschule in Hagen, the Télé-université, Université du Québec, at Québec and Montréal and the Open Learning Institute at Richmond, British Columbia. It would sadden me greatly if anything of a confidential nature were found in the text. Four friends and colleagues in different countries have read this book in manuscript form and commented on it: Greville Rumble of the Open University of the United Kingdom, Arthur Cropley of the University of Hamburg, Börje Holmberg of the Fernuniversität in Hagen and Ian Mc. D. Mitchell of the South Australian College of Advanced Education, Adelaide. I have gained much knowledge and understanding from their feedback; clearly I accept full responsibility for what I have written. This mention is their only recompense for many hours of intensive study. Professor John Sparkes of the Open University of the United

# ACKNOWLEDGEMENT

Kingdom gave considerable help with the first chapter. Thank you.

Many of the ideas in the book have been published before, notably in an article 'On defining distance education' in the first issue of <u>Distance Education</u> (1980), in the monograph <u>Six distance education theorists</u> published in Hagen in 1983 and in the material prepared in 1982 for the course team for the first unit of the Graduate Diploma in Distance Education of the South Australian College of Advanced Education. Few of the formulations, however, remain the same because research in education is cyclic not static. If research on a living reality like distance education is to be valid, one's concept of it constantly changes as one seeks to grasp it ever more precisely and present one's findings to others.

Finally I must acknowledge the patience of my publisher Croom Helm and David Croom in particular. The book was 90% written in March 1984 when my appointment as Director General of the Italian Distance University Consortium was announced. There can be few things more disruptive when trying to finish a book than transporting one's family, library and oneself from Australia to Italy. Due to this the manuscript reached Croom Helm twelve months later than planned. To my secretary, Janina Sadowska, goes much of the credit for finally getting it to the publishers.

The quotation on pages 215-216 is published by authorisation of UNESCO and the diagrams on pages 198, 238 and 239 by permission from Croom Helm Ltd.

Desmond Keegan

Nemi, Italy

# ABBREVIATIONS

The following abbreviations are used from time to time especially in lists of references:

| | |
|---|---|
| CMA | Computer marked assignment |
| CU | Conventional university |
| DIFF | Deutsches Institut für Fernstudien, Tübingen |
| DTU | Distance teaching university |
| FeU | Fernuniversität-Gesamthochschule, Hagen |
| ICDE | International Council for Distance Education |
| OU | Open University |
| OUUK | Open University of the United Kingdom |
| TMA | Tutor marked assignment |
| UNE | University of New England, Armidale, Australia |
| UNED | Universidad Nacional de Educación a Distancia |
| UNISA | University of South Africa, Pretoria |
| ZIFF | Zentrales Institut für Fernstudien-forschung, Fernuniversität, Hagen. |

PART ONE: THE CONCEPT OF DISTANCE EDUCATION

CHAPTER ONE

THE STUDY OF DISTANCE EDUCATION


<u>It is the development of distance education as
an academic discipline that will have the most
profound effect on its practice in the future.</u>
<u>Eric Gough, 1984</u>


## Context

In the 1980s distance education emerged as a standard component of the provision of education in
many national systems.  In contrast with conventional education which is oral and group-based,
distance education shatters the interpersonal communication of face-to-face provision and disperses
the learning group throughout the nation.

By harnessing industrialised processes to
education and responding to the growth of privacy
and loss of the sense of community which are characteristics of post-industrial society, distance
education has opened access to study towards all
levels of qualification to the working adult -
the student who continues to contribute to the
nation's Gross National Product throughout the
length of his or her study programme.

In 1983 Sewart of the Open University (UK)
could write:

> The last decade has seen a phenomenal growth
> in distance education and the integration
> of this method of education into the standard
> educational provision in a large number of
> countries to such an extent that it is now
> no longer possible to think solely in the
> traditional sense of face-to-face contact.
> (1983:5)

For long the cinderella of the education spectrum,
distance education emerged in the 1970s with a
changed image.  It has recently come of age after
a chequered and often criticised first one hundred
years.  Furthermore, its future seems assured because of the growing privatisation of life in many

3

developed Western societies and the incapacity of on-campus programmes to cope with even minimal educational opportunity elsewhere.

The improvement of distance education in the 1970s was both qualitative and quantitative. It can be attributed to:

°　the development of new communications technology (Bates 1982; Ruggles 1982)

°　a growing sophistication in the use of printed materials (Daniel and Stroud 1981)

°　improved design of instructional materials (Holmberg, 1981)

°　improved provision of support services for students studying at a distance (Sewart, 1978)

°　the foundation in 1969 of the Open University (UK) at Milton Keynes and the subsequent foundation of a series of similar structures in both developed and developing countries (Rumble and Keegan, 1982).

Despite the euphoria of claims like Sewart's it is clear that distance education is little known and little studied. Even a cursory reading of educational literature shows that distance systems are usually ignored. It merits not a paragraph in most volumes of educational philosophy, in guides to administrative practice or in analyses of didactic strategy.

When it is not ignored, it can be seen - in the harsher funding atmosphere of the 1980s - as an unwanted competitor, especially in those countries where cohorts of on-campus students are diminishing. The time has come for taking stock. Not all the portents are favourable. Writing in 1984, the Australian distance educator, Gough, proposed that 'it is the development of distance education as an academic discipline that will have the most profound effect on its' practice in the future'. (1984:25)

This book is an attempt to contribute to such a philosophy.

Aims

In this context the book has three aims:

°     to provide a guide to the literature, theory and practice of distance education

°     to provide a guide to good practice in distance education both for distance educators and for those who are studying this sector of education for the first time

°     to contribute to the foundations of distance education as a new discipline within education.

The book attempts to respond to the call made over a decade ago by Moore, then of the University of Wisconsin at Madison and today at the Open University (UK):

> As we continue to develop various non-traditional methods of reaching the growing numbers of people who cannot, or who will not, attend conventional institutions but who choose to learn apart from their teachers, we should direct some of our resources to the macrofactors:
>
> -   describing and defining the field
>
> -   discriminating between the various components of this field
>
> -   identifying the critical elements of the various forms of teaching and learning
>
> -   building a theoretical framework which will embrace this whole area of education (1973:661).

Moore's call went largely unheeded. A theoretical framework to embrace this whole area of education has yet to be erected. This is particularly grave because distance education purports to make available a parallel provision of education to that of conventional schools, colleges and universities. Unlike other methods of teaching or modes of operation with which they are sometimes bracketed, distance systems claim to provide a complete educational coverage, equal in quality and status to that of conventional provision, which encompasses every stage of the educational process from application, enrolment and counselling through to examination and certification many years later.

5

Most research in this field has been practical rather than theoretical. While research on the practice of distance education is important and fundamental it is incidental and peripheral to a firmly-based theory of distance education. A theory is something that eventually can be reduced to a phrase, a sentence or a paragraph and which, while subsuming all the practical research, gives the foundation on which structures of need, purpose and administration can be erected. A firmly based theory of distance education will be one which can provide the touchstone against which decisions - political, financial, educational, social - can be taken with confidence. Such a theoretical basis would replace the ad hoc way of responding to 'crisis' situations which normally characterises this field of education.

## Premises

In attempting to provide a guide to theory and practice in distance education the following assumptions are made:

1.  Distance education is a coherent and distinct field of educational endeavour: it embraces programmes at a distance at primary and secondary, technical and further, college and university levels in both public and private sectors. It has existed for somewhat over 100 years and is to be found today in most countries.

2.  Distance education is more than a teaching mode or method. It is a complete system of education. It can provide a complete educational programme for both children and adults outside of, and distinct from, conventional, oral, group-based provision. It has its own laws of didactical structure and its own quasi-industrial administrative procedures.

3.  Distance education is a form of education fraught with problems for administrators, teachers and students. It is characterised by the fragility of the non-traditional in education. These difficulties concern the quantity, quality and status of education at a distance. Good practice in distance education seeks to provide solutions for these

inherent difficulties.

4. Distance education is a needed component of most national educational systems.

The study does not seek to promote distance education, rather it seeks to analyse it from as neutral a standpoint as possible and present it with both its strengths and weaknesses under-lined. In doing this an attempt is made not to limit the research to the English-speaking tradition in education because the contribution of the English-speaking countries is only a part of a much more complex whole. Much of the basic research in the period 1960-1970 was done in German; the basic institutional model is probably French; in recent years much progress has been reported from Spanish-speaking countries; this book is a much altered version of a series of lectures first delivered in Italian.

## Methodology

Considerable thought was given to evolving a meth-odology for presenting the reader with a guide to both theory and practice in this field of edu-cational activity.

A methodology was needed that would lead to knowledge and understanding. It had to be capable of describing and defining the field of distance education; it had to discriminate between the insti-tutional types, the didactic strategies, the varying media that constitute this field; it had to be able to identify both those forms of teaching and learning which are seen as constituent of distance education and those that lie outside it.

In order to be successful as a guide, the methodology chosen had to be able to take account of the context and complexity of the field and to get to the real phenomenon of distance education and nòt some 'scientific' abstraction. It had to cover one hundred years of history and the world-wide activity of the present time.

As well as charting the fragile theoretical underpinnings that scholars have supplied to date, the aim was to provide a guide to good practice: to help administrators make sensible decisions, to help practitioners choose good models, to help the managers of distance systems decide on methods and media. Scientific research is ill-at ease in the context of a guide. The controlled experiment, which is the lynch-pin of science's insistence on the reproducibility of data, involves ensuring that the normal variability of the environment is kept within specified limits. It is exactly the variability of the environment that a good guide should reflect.

Further, the nature of scientific research, in which one attempts to analyse educational problems in terms of distinct causal theories, is out of place in an area where management rather than pedagogy is the key problem encountered. When the management of quasi-industrial processes is central to an educational system what is needed is not normative scientific study of special approaches to pedagogy but problem-based case studies that can provide guides to good practice. Happily, narrow scientific research is not the only way to knowledge and understanding, other methods can lead to valid explanations of the complex world of distance systems.

## Procedure

The methodology adopted attempts to be synergistic, that is, it attempts to find a way to cope with the complexity of the educational environment and the inter-connectedness of human and institutional relationships. Another element that synergistic theories and methodologies seek to encapsulate is experience. It is of particular importance in this study: we are concerned here with the experience of the dedicated distance education tutor, the experience and common sense of the practiced administrator, and it is important that such experience should not be eliminated by the methodology chosen.

In its actual execution, the study developed in four stages with extensive feedback mechanisms linking the various periods of research.

## Stage 1

A Delphi-like approach was first used for a review of the literature. In the first instance this was to classify the varied terminology used at that time in the field, and then to see whether any cohesion could be found in the multiplicity of educational phenomena encountered. The bulk of the literature analysed was in English, but the considerable literature in German both from the Federal Republic of Germany and the German

Democratic Republic was not ignored. Efforts were
made to gather literature in French and Spanish
as well, although the results were relatively
meagre.

## Stage 2

Distance education, however, does not exist in
a vacuum: it has been in action for over one hundred
years. It was imperative, therefore to see and
participate in the institutions concerned. In
the period 1978-1979 visits were carried out to
sixty-two institutions that had been encountered
in the literature. Included were institutions
large and small, public and private in Australia,
India, United Kingdom, Netherlands, Italy, Ireland,
France, German Democratic Republic, Hungary, Federal
Republic of Germany, Canada and the United States
of America.

The institutions ranged from correspondence
schools at primary and secondary levels to open
universities. Many were to be eliminated from
the study at a later date as being general non-
traditional programmes rather than a part of distance education as it came to be defined.

The institutional visits were at first structured around a framework for the analysis of distance education institutions developed by Kaye
and Rumble (1981:293) at the Open University (UK).
This formula proved too complex in practice, and
was replaced by a formula developed specially for
the study.

## Stage 3

Initial hypotheses about the nature and structure
of the groupings of educational phenomena encountered in the literature were constantly refined
by feedback from the institutional case studies.
This led to a period of synthesis in which patterns
and hypotheses were developed for the field as
a whole. Considerable care had to be exercised
at this stage because of anomalies which had been
discerned between the literature search and the
institutional case studies. With reference to
the choice of non-print media, especially broadcast
television, it quickly became evident that a dis-
turbing amount of published research was exaggerated
or inaccurate and that some of the researchers
appeared not to have visited the institutions,
nor even the countries, on which they were reporting.

As a result of this analysis an attempt was made to clarify the conceptual structure and terminology of the field in an article 'On defining distance education', and a first sketch of the field as a whole was published in Germany under the title On the nature of distance education. This provoked further feedback both in published work and in private communications.

## Stage 4

As a final stage more extensive visits of up to three months in length were undertaken to a number of the institutions in Europe and North America which had emerged as central to the concept of a discipline of distance education.

## Initial findings

As the work progressed it became clear that systemic similarities of a marked kind were present in all the institutions that fell within the definition of distance education being formulated. These similarities were the more remarkable as they cut sharply across the sectoral boundaries within which education is normally administered. They were characteristic of government primary and secondary correspondence schools, of private foundations (whether non-profit or profit-oriented), of government distance technical or further education colleges, and of open universities. Among these characteristics were:

° the absence of classrooms, lecture rooms, seminar rooms and tutorial rooms;

° the presence of, or access to, comprehensive printing and materials production facilities;

° the absence of a library, or of places for student study, if there was a library;

° the central location of the warehouse;

° the absence of cafeterias, playgrounds, recreation facilities, drama and music amenities;

° the use of buildings which often resembled industrial offices, warehouses or factories;

° the fact that many of the institutions acted

as post offices.

These divergencies marked the institutions off from institutions structured for conventional, oral, group-based education in a striking and decisive way. In the case of a distance education department of an existing college or university, many of the characteristics noted were present, other things being equal, in the distance wing of the conventional institution. Here was a largely unstudied grouping of educational institutions, globally represented and growing in influence annually.

## Analytical model

The study had not been in progress long before it became clear that as a theoretical focus for the whole area of education being investigated, the 1973 thesis by Peters, (pronounced Pay-ters) Die didaktische Struktur des Fernunterrichts. Untersuchungen zu einer industrialisierten Form des Lehrens und Lernens, (The didactical structure of distance teaching. Investigations into an industrialised form of teaching and learning) was by far the most satisfactory explanation yet formulated. Peters' comparative research on distance institutions of all types throughout the 1960s led to his characterisation of distance education as 'the most industrialised form of education'.
The conclusions of his study surprised many researchers who recoiled from the implications of the position that his comparative and theoretical analysis led him to enunciate:

> Anyone professionally involved in education is compelled to presume the existence of two forms of instruction which are strictly separable: traditional face-to-face teaching based on interpersonal communication and industrialised teaching which is based on an objectivised, rationalised, technologically-based interaction. (1973:313)

Peters had previously (1971) complained that the normal procedures of educational research had proved of little avail in the investigations of correspondence education:

> Correspondence instruction is the most

industrialised form of instruction and the usual theoretical criteria for the description of traditional instruction do not help very much in analysing correspondence instruction. (This) has suggested the introduction of new categories taken from those sciences investigating the industrial production process. It is, in fact, astounding to see how much better these criteria help to understand and describe the institutional process in correspondence instruction. Some of the suggested criteria are: division of labour (on the side of the teachers); mechanisation; automation; application of organisational principles; scientific control; objectivity of teaching behaviour; mass production; concentration and centralisation. (1971:225)

## Feedback model

It might be appropriate therefore to investigate the phenomenon of education at a distance by a methodology more widely used in industrial situations. Such a methodology is at hand in control theory, comprising a coherent set of strategies for arriving at prescribed goals. It is normally applied to systems that are a good deal simpler than educational and research systems, nevertheless it has valuable insights to offer.

A key concept in control theory is that of negative feedback. Applied to the educational process it draws attention to the benefits to be had in both teaching and learning when errors and inadequacies are pointed out and dealt with in some way likely to lead to their correction. Negative feedback processes are in contrast with both open-loop control systems and positive feedback systems, both of which however also have their place in education.

Negative feedback processes in education exemplify the conversational theory of learning, since they bring out that part of learning that is achieved by a continuous iteration of the process of absorbing new information, trying to use it and checking whether it was correctly used. In other words, concepts are recycled through the learning regions of the brain and gradually acquire sufficient richness of meaning for them in the end to be used with confidence to express the learner's own ideas. Such recycling of ideas can be achieved in a variety of ways. In residential universities it is achieved relatively easily through the use of libraries, tutorials, laboratories, discussion groups and exercises. In distance teaching special efforts need to be taken to achieve equivalent results. (Sparkes, 1976)

Open loop systems are more appropriate where facts, or surface knowledge, rather than ideas or concepts are involved. Successful learning can be expected from little more than one or two teaching sessions - at least with motivated students who have good memories. The system can be characterised by the diagram or model in Figure 1.1.

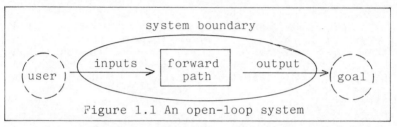

Figure 1.1 An open-loop system

An open-loop system does not contain a feedback path from output to input. The goal, namely knowledge, is obtained as far as practicable by ensuring that the inputs are correct and comprehensible. The term 'forward path' is borrowed from feedback theory. A good deal of learning can be achieved using simple instruction or by uncomplicated study.

Feedback systems are sometimes called closed-loop systems which explains why those without feedback are called open-loop systems. A diagram representing a closed-loop feedback system is shown in Figure 1.2.

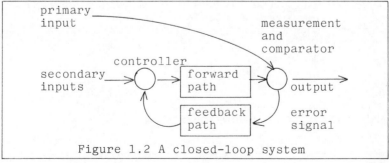

Figure 1.2 A closed-loop system

There are two kinds of input to this system. The primary input sets the goal; the secondary inputs are the various inputs to the learner (texts, T.V., audio).

The difference between the systems output and the goal is the 'performance' of the learner, and any error or inadequacy is fed back (as an error signal) to the input so that the secondary inputs can be controlled in such a way as to correct such errors. Crucial to such systems is the measurement or assessment of performance. For independent learners self assessment is clearly important, but in distance teaching much help can be given through assignments, self-help groups and tutorials.

Positive feedback loops are another name for vicious circles. They cause runaway behaviour. Any deviation from stability is emphasised and the system travels to some extreme position and stays there as long as the feedback remains, and perhaps even permanently. The system illustrated in Figure 1.2. becomes a positive feedback system if the secondary inputs are controlled to reinforce, rather than correct, the deviations from the goal detected by the measurements of the system's output.

Negative feedback acts in a negative sense and is potentially useful provided the feedback is properly tuned to the rest of the system. Negative feedback acts to remove the discrepancies and so enables us to achieve what we wish to achieve with greater accuracy. In addition the tuned system will automatically make corrections for any changes or disturbances with greater speed. By applying negative feedback in different ways it is possible to mould the dynamic behaviour to suit our specific requirements. However even negative feedback which is wrongly applied can cause temporary or permanent instability, sometimes with disastrous consequences.

A simple negative feedback loop is suitable as a paradigm for research in distance education and is illustrated in Figure 1.3.

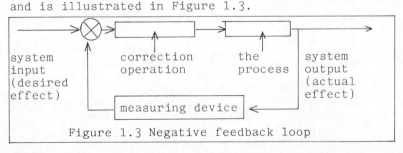

Figure 1.3 Negative feedback loop

The above loop is a control system and 'the process' is the educational research activity that we are trying to control, along with some or all of its related components. The overall performance of the system is dominated by the effectiveness of the feedback path.

Although in practical systems feedback paths and controllers may be non-human (the system is then said to be automatic), in distance education practice the controller is usually a human being, often the student himself or herself (although the use of, for instance, 'teaching machines' is theoretically possible). Thus, such models are essentially paradigms, or aids to the understanding of complex behaviour patterns.

Control theory provides a satisfactory methodology for studying the phenomena of distance education: it is synergistic, does not destroy the complexity of reality, can encapsulate experience and build on common sense. Such a method can help in finding patterns in distance education, and provide guides to good practice - administrative structures that ought to work. The evidence that the research has in fact got it right will, nonetheless, be mainly anecdotal. A successful use of a similar methodology is A.W. Bates' (1984) study of educational broadcasting, Broadcasting in education: an evaluation.

References

Bates, A.W. (1982) Trends in the use of audio-visual media in distance education systems. In Daniel et al (eds) Learning at a distance. A world perspective. Edmonton: Athabasca U./ICCE.
Bates, A.W.(1984) Broadcasting in education: an evaluation. London: Constable.
Daniel, J. and Stroud, M. (1981) Distance education: a reassessment for the 1980s. Distance Education, 2, 2, 146-163.
Gough, E. (1984) Towards a philosophy of distance education. In Smith, K. (ed.) Diversity down under in distance education. Toowoomba: Darling Downs Institute.
Holmberg, B. (1981) Status and trends of distance education. London: Kogan Page.
Kaye, A. and Rumble, G. (1981) Distance teaching for higher and adult education London: Croom Helm.

Moore, M. (1973) Towards a theory of independent learning and teaching. Journal of Higher Education, 44, 666-678.

Peters, O. (1971) Theoretical aspects of correspondence instruction. In Mackenzie, O. and Christensen, E.L. (eds) The changing world of correspondence study. University Park: Pennsylvania State U.

Peters, O. (1973) Die didaktische Struktur des Fernunterichts. Untersuchungen zu einer industrialsierten Form des Lehrens und Lernens. Weinheim: Beltz.

Ruggles, R. et al (1982) Learning at a distance and the new technology. Vancouver: ERIBC.

Rumble, G. and Keegan, D. (1982) General characteristics of the distance teaching universities. In Rumble, G. and Harry, K. (eds) The distance teaching universities, 204-224.

Sewart, D. (1983) Editorial. ICDE Bulletin, 1, 5.

Sewart, D. (1978) Continuity of concern for students in a system of learning at a distance. (Ziff Papiere 22) Hagen: Fernuniversität.

Sparkes, J.J. (1976) Feedback theory. (Technology Foundation Course Unit No. 1) Milton Keynes: Open University.

CHAPTER TWO

OPEN, NON-TRADITIONAL AND DISTANCE EDUCATION

When we studied the research in education we read, for example, that... 'the word instruction refers to the activity which takes place during schooling, and within the CLASSROOM setting'. It was clear that a vast number of adult learners were receiving instruction in non-group settings, and we concluded that educational theory which did not provide a place for such learning and teaching was incomplete, and unsatisfactory. Michael G. Moore, 1971.

## Background

When the research reported in this book began, analysis of distance education was characterised by confusion over terminology and by lack of precision on what areas of education were being discussed or what was being excluded. The confusion can be highlighted by listing the terms used in English for this field of education: 'correspondence study', 'home study', 'external studies', 'independent study', 'teaching at a distance', 'off campus study', 'open learning' and there may well have been more.

Allied to this was inconsistency about the boundaries that could be set to areas that had some similarities to distance education, either in philosophy or procedure, but which could not be identified with it. Among these areas of educational concern were: non-conventional education, open education, extra-mural studies, educational broadcasting, non-traditional education and the like.

The purpose of this chapter is to emphasise the importance of study of the non-conventional structures in education and then to provide a listing of the forms of non-conventional education which have similarities to distance education. The next chapter attempts to define distance education in a way which identifies it and isolates it for heuristic purposes from all other forms of education.

## Methodology

The research began by the analysis of a very large grouping of institutions that had non-conventional

17

or distance elements. The list included: public
and private correspondence schools, rural development projects, educational broadcasting networks,
open colleges and universities, external and distance departments of conventional institutions,
universities without walls, extra-mural and external
degree programmes, experiential learning and other
experimental structures.

The findings confirmed the results of an investigation of 'more than 2,000 items of literature
pertaining to educational programmes in which learners were not in face-to-face relationships with
teachers', carried out by Moore at the University
of Wisconsin a decade earlier. Moore presents the
result of his investigation:

> Teaching consists of two families of
> activity with many characteristics in
> common, but different in one aspect so
> important that a theory explaining one
> cannot satisfactorily explain the other.
> The first of these families, the
> older, better understood, more fully
> researched, includes all educational
> situations where the teacher is physically
> contiguous with his students, so that
> the primary means of communication is
> his voice, and in which (to use the econ-
> omists' terms) teaching is a 'service'
> that is 'consumed' simultaneously with
> its 'production'. The physical proximity
> of the learners with the teacher permits
> each to stimulate the other, consequently
> teaching of this kind is conceived as
> a process of 'social interaction'.
> The second family of teaching meth-
> ods, and the subject of our concern,
> includes educational situations dis-
> tinguished by the separation of the
> teacher from his learners, so that com-
> munication has to be facilitated by a
> mechanical or electronic medium. Teaching
> in this environment is 'consumed' at
> a time or place different from that at
> which it is 'produced', and to reach
> the learner it must be contained, trans-
> ported, stored and delivered. There may
> be interaction, between learner and
> teacher, but if so, it is so greatly
> affected by the delay resulting from
> the necessity to communicate across

> distance or time, that it cannot be an
> assured component of teaching strategy,
> as it may in classroom or group teaching.
> We refer to this as DISTANCE TEACHING,
> to distinguish it from 'contiguous teach-
> ing' where teacher and student are in
> physical proximity. (Moore, 1977:6)

## Conventional education

For the purpose of this study it was decided
to label as 'conventional education' the normal
on-campus provision at school, college or
university level. This is not the place to
attempt to define 'conventional education'.
For the purpose of this book the description provided by Kaye and Rumble is adequate:

> The term 'conventional education' is
> applied to formal classroom-based in-
> struction in a school, college or uni-
> versity setting, where teacher and
> students are physically present at the
> same time at the same place. (1979:22)

In educational literature this is regarded
as the 'normal' form of educational provision and
the complaint of Moore over a decade ago is that
he had found hundreds of references of the type
'the word instruction refers to the activity which
takes place <u>during</u> schooling, and <u>within</u> the <u>class-
room</u> setting'. In distance education writing,
one often finds the term 'face-to-face education'
used for normal provision. In this study an attempt
at further precision is made from time to time
with the use of the term 'conventional, oral, group-
based' education in place of 'face-to-face'.
As the research progressed it became clear
that distance education and conventional education
as defined by Kaye and Rumble could be established
as two mutually exclusive categories and that the
literature contained other major clusters of concepts that would repay further analysis. These
were non-tradition education, indirect education,
open education and educational technology.

## Non-traditional education

The relationship between non-traditional education
and distance education was addressed by Moore in
the early 1970s. His decision (1973:661) to place

19

distance education amongst the non-traditional forms of education is a far-reaching one. If accepted it would contribute to the fragility of this form of education and its continual lack of status in the eyes of many administrators and educationists in conventional institutions.

The presentation of 'non-traditional education' by the Carnegie Committee on Non-Traditional Education was published as <u>Diversity by design</u> (1973) under the editorship of Gould and may be considered comprehensive and normative. Gould writes:

> How to define non-traditional study accurately and comprehensively was a stumbling block we never quite hurdled to our satisfaction. The epigram 'Tradition is something you make up as you go along' could substitute the word <u>non-traditional</u> and be just as meaningful.
>
> Despite our lack of a completely suitable definition, we always seemed to sense the areas of education around which our interests centered. This community of concern was a mysterious light in the darkness, yet not at all mysterious in retrospect. Most of us agreed that non-traditional study is more an attitude than a system and thus can never be defined except tangentially. This attitude puts the student first and the institution second, concentrates more on the former's need than the latter's convenience, encourages diversity of individual opportunity rather than uniform prescription, and de-emphasises time, space, and even course requirements in favour of competence and, where applicable, performance. It has concern for the learner of any age and circumstances, for the degree aspirant as well as the person who finds sufficient reward in enriching life through constant, periodic, or occasional study. This attitude is not new; it is simply more prevalent than it used to be. It can stimulate exciting and high-quality educational progress, it can also, unless great care is taken to protect the freedom it offers, be the unwitting means to a lessening of academic rigor and even to charlatanism. (1973:5)

The relationship between traditional and non-traditional education, especially in the United States, has seen a re-establishment of traditional concepts in the 1980s where non-traditional structures blossomed briefly in the 1970s. Traditional American education for adults has consisted of residential colleges and universities in which carefully selected students between the years of 18 and 24 have enrolled in on-campus courses taught by individual teachers who lectured and led class-room discussion. Education was something to be acquired before one began the business of life. Students were expected to be unmarried and un-employed. This climate, built on the views of writers like Newman, Hutchins and Barzun has domi-nated American higher education for much of its history and has left little room for success for distance programmes.

For the purposes of this study, therefore, 'non-traditional learning' is a vast generalised term for a vague range of educational programmes that diverge from what is seen to be the norm.

## Indirect or mediated education

Education may be described as 'direct' or 'indirect' in accordance with the presence or absence of con-ventional, face-to-face communication. In the next chapter an attempt will be made to provide a defi-nition of distance education, which will show that all the other forms of indirect education listed, either never possess all the characteristics of distance education as defined or else do so only on occasion - so that care is needed by researchers to indicate when they consider these educational possibilities as forming part of distance education and when they do not do so.

The diagram contained in Figure 2.1, developed from an idea of Peters, may prove helpful to the reader.

The various mediated forms of education in the diagram all bear resemblances to distance edu-cation but lack one or more of the essential components of a distance education programme:

Education by letter. From Plato and Paul to Erasmus letters have been used for instructional purposes and the practice, doubtless, continues today. They lack the structuring of an educational institution that is a characteristic of distance education.

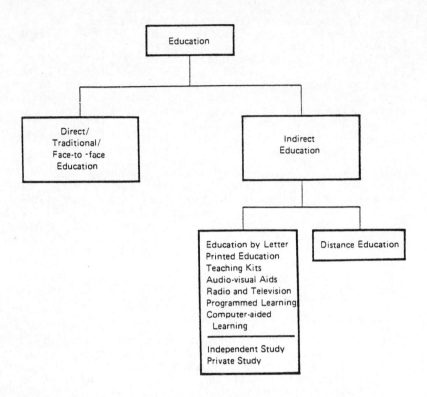

Figure 2.1 Relationship of distance education
to other forms of indirect education

Printed education. Pamphlets, books and teach-
yourself manuals fall into this category. The lack
of an educational organisation is again the major
factor which distinguishes these from distance
education, together with the impossibility of two-
way communication. It is clear that many people
learn a great deal from these means, even though
they may lack didactical structuring or even an
educational goal.

Teaching kits. In increasing use in face-to-face
teaching are kits of various kinds containing
samples, games and specimens on which students
are invited to work without supervision.

Audiovisual aids. When lecturers communicate with
students by means of audiovisual aids: slides,

film, audio and videotapes, they are teaching in-
directly. Although such aids can be used in distance education it is their use in face-to-face
education that is in question here.

Radio and television. Many people learn a great
deal from radio and television and sometimes those
media are used in distance education programmes.
Kenneth Clarke's Civilisation or Jacob Bronowski's
The ascent of man were not conceived as part of
an education programme. Nevertheless they have
become part of both on-campus and distance education programmes when offered for credit with
accompanying didactically structured assignment,
reading and assessment materials.

Programmed learning, is a form of indirect teaching
which has many similarities to distance education.
Both demand extensive preparation of learning materials, careful sequencing and tend towards the
individualising of learning.

Computer-aided learning is a form of indirect education and is used extensively in many conventional
teaching programmes.

Open education

There is extensive overlap between the use of the
term 'open education' and distance education. The
decision of the United Kingdom Government in the
mid-1960s to rename the 'University of the Air'
to the 'Open University' popularised the term
'open'. It is found in the titles of the distance
teaching universities in Pakistan, Sri Lanka,
Thailand and Venezuela, and in the titles of the
multi-level distance colleges such as the Open
Learning Institute of British Columbia and the
Open College of Technical and Further Education
of South Australia. However, the terms are not
synonymous. Writing from a Latin American background Escotet distinguishes them clearly:

> Open education is particularly charac-
> terised by the removal of restrictions,
> exclusions and privileges; by the ac-
> creditation of students' previous experi-
> ences; by the flexibility of the manage-
> ment of the time variable; and by sub-
> stantial changes in the traditional re-
> lationship between professors and

23

> students. On the other hand, <u>distance education</u> is a modality which permits the delivery of a group of didactic media without the necessity of regular class participation, where the individual is responsible for his own learning. (1983: 144)

Keegan and Rumble (1982:12) argue that the open universities should be termed 'distance teaching universities'. McKenzie, Postgate and Scupham in their 1975 book <u>Open learning</u> define 'open learning' as follows:

> Open learning is an imprecise phrase to which a range of meanings can be, and is, attached. It eludes definition. But as an inscription to be carried in procession on a banner, gathering adherents and enthusiasms, it has great potential. For its very imprecision enables it to accommodate many different ideas and aims and the two terms of the phrase carry with them emotional overtones that evoked a wide response in the 1950s and 1960s when it came into use, particularly at the later secondary and post-secondary levels. (1975:21)

'Open learning', therefore, is a term that is not to be used in an administrative context; its context is, rather, theoretical and describes, for instance, colleges with 'open' administration policies or a special spirit. Open learning can, in fact, be carried on under both face-to-face and also distance conditions. Many of the distance teaching universities, for instance, have closed and rigid structures, are inflexible and slow to respond to community educational needs, have cut-off dates for computer marked assignments and fixed assessment patterns. They design learning materials that narrow the curriculum and leave little room for interpretation outside the direction provided by the course designers. Thus, while some basic ideas are shared by both open learning and distance education, the terms are not synonymous.

## Educational technology

As has already been emphasised, educational technology plays a major role in distance education, but this term would become meaningless if it were forced to involve all forms of educational technology or education at a distance. A working definition of educational technology would probably include both the use of technology 'in education' and technology 'of education'. Educational technology is defined as 'a rational problem-solving approach to education. A way of thinking sceptically and systematically about learning and teaching'. (Elton 1978:41) Rigorously to be excluded from the concept of 'distance education' are all uses of educational technology in classrooms, lecture theatres or laboratories of conventional institutions, whether the technology be print-, audio-video-, or computer-based.

## Educational broadcasting

It is important to identify the place of distance education within the complex field of educational broadcasting (Bates: 1984). Following an idea of Bates on the case of education by moving image (i.e. film, video cassette, video-disc, broadcast and cable television) three forms of presentation can be identified, only one of which is a constituent of distance education:

  (i)   moving image for broadcast television.

  (ii)   moving image as resource material for use on video cassettes in the class and lecture room.

  (iii) moving images as a constituent of a package of distance learning materials (whether printed, broadcast or on cassette or disc).

Only the last falls within the range of distance education and as a consequence can be shown to have characteristics shared by other distance learning materials:

  (i)   it is part of a package. Producers are not therefore free to structure the programme at will but have to consult the other elements of the teaching package so that the video presentation of moving image will be complementary to the rest of the material.

  (ii)   two-way communication has to be provided.

25

The viewer does not seek to interact with a TV programme like <u>Sesame Street</u> or even with a film or video shown in a classroom (though the teacher may discuss it after it is shown). But a TV film or video cassette in distance education is a learning experience and interaction and feedback are paramount. Thus, unlike the other two categories, the distance education video may contain elements like 'Stop the tape here', 'Do the following assignment' and frequent deictic elements drawing attention to learning objectives and ensuring that the student does not watch the programme as if it were a television programme.

(iii) <u>the audience for a distance education programme is not guaranteed</u>. The producers of distance education materials have to search out and attract their audience in a way that educational technologists in other fields do not have to do. Research has shown that they often fail. Schwittmann (1982), has shown that time is the major deciding factor not only in the success or failure of a distance education course but also in the students' decision on what elements of the teaching package to study and which to bypass. Frequently it is the video cassette/broadcast television component of the distance course that is the first to be abandoned.

## Other forms of non-traditional education

A final grouping of non-traditional educational structures is listed here as a preparation for the attempt to define distance education in the following chapters. Some of these structures approximate closely to it.

<u>Extension programmes</u> are ways of extending the expertise of a university or college to new populations. The term can imply offering the same programmes as for full-time, daytime students by different means, at different locations or at different times. An <u>extra-mural</u> department usually has a similar function of extending the expertise of the university to a broader community.

Extended campus refers to provision of lectures at alternative locations often far from the official campus.

University Without Walls implies the design of an individualised programme based on a learning contract for students with clear learning objectives who cannot realise their whole educational aspirations through existing programmes. A University Without Walls programme can include experiential learning credits, ordinary lectures, distance education elements, learning from community sources or job-related activities, all of which can be evaluated towards a college or university degree.

Experiential learning programmes are those which give credit for prior learning which did not take place in a lecture room setting and was not sponsored by an education institution, but was acquired through work experience.

The external degree is a degree programme which can be completed in the following manner: a student entering the programme with the minimum entrance qualification can complete it with less than 25 per cent of the required work taking the form of campus-based classroom instruction. (Sosdian and Sharp, 1977:1)

The relationships between the various forms of education provision presented in this chapter might be summarised thus:

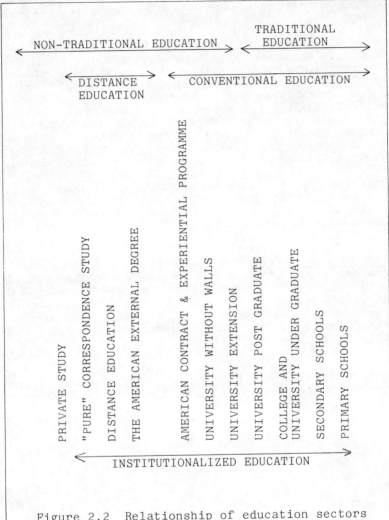

Figure 2.2   Relationship of education sectors

## References

Bates, A. (1984) _Broadcasting in education: an evaluation_. London: Constable.

Elton, L. (1979) Educational technology and the needs of higher education. _British Journal of Educational Technology_, 12, 3, 40-47.

Escotet, M. (1980) Adverse factors in the development of an open university in Latin America. _Programmed Learning and Educational Technology_, 17, 4, 262-270.

Gould, S. (1973) _Diversity by design_. San Francisco: Jossey Bass.

Kaye, A. and Rumble, G. (1979) _An analysis of distance teaching systems_. Milton Keynes: OU.

Keegan, D. and Rumble, G. (1982) Distance teaching at university level. In Rumble G. and Harry, K. (eds) _The distance teaching universities_. London: Croom Helm.

McKenzie, O., Postgate, R. and Scupham, J. (1975) _Open learning_, Paris: UNESCO.

Moore, M. (1971) Teaching the distant adult learner. cited, In Sewart, D., Keegan, D. and Holmberg, B. (1983) _Distance education. International perspectives_. London: Croom Helm.

Moore, M. (1973) Toward a theory of independent learning and teaching. _Journal of Higher Education_, 44, 661-679.

Moore, M. (1977) _On a theory of independent study_. Hagen: FeU.

Schwittman, D. (1982) Time and effort in distance study. _Distance Education_, 3, 1, 150-165.

Sosdian, C. and Sharp, L. (1978) Guide to undergraduate external degree programmes in the U.S. Washington: NIE.

Wedemeyer C. (1977) Independent study. In Knowles A.S. (ed) _The international encyclopaedia of higher education_. Boston: CIHED.

CHAPTER THREE

DEFINITION OF DISTANCE EDUCATION

_It is natural for man to desire to know._ Aristotle,
_323 B.C._

## Context

The purpose of this chapter is to

    °     enable readers to make their way through
    the maze of terminology encountered in
    the literature.

    °     formulate a definition of the area of
    education under study that will form
    the basis for discussion in this book.

The definition developed here is used as an instrument to eliminate from the discussion forms
of education which are not synonymous with it,
although they may have similarities to it.
The methodology used is based on the
contributions of acknowledged experts in the
field coupled with the use of feedback techniques. One of the advantages of seeing educational
research in the context of feedback techniques
is that it solves the constant problem of which
comes first: the research or the hypothesis? In
feedback theory, investigation is seen as a loop
process and one can commence at any appropriate
point in the loop in the attempt to deepen knowledge
and understanding.

## A description

The need to clarify terminology is immediate. No
progress can be made in formulating the theoretical
underpinnings of this area of educational endeavour
or in developing guides to good practice if there
is no agreement on the area of education under
discussion. This book proposes the adoption of

30

'distance education' as a generic term for the field of education under discussion. It may be described thus:

> 'Distance education' is a generic term that includes the range of teaching/learning strategies referred to as 'correspondence education' or 'correspondence study' at further education level in the United Kingdom; as 'home study' at further education level and 'independent study' at higher educational level in the United States; as 'external studies' in Australia; and as 'distance teaching' or 'teaching at a distance' by the Open University of the United Kingdom. In French it is referred to as 'téléenseignement'; Fernstudium/Fernunterricht in German; 'educación a distancia' in Spanish and 'teleducacão' in Portuguese.

This description lists the major terms used by distance education institutions in the English-speaking world and gives parallel terms for the major European languages. 'Distance education' subsumes a number of existing terms but not all are synonymous.

## Correspondence education/correspondence study

These terms have a long history in the education of children and adults at a distance. They still have their supporters who claim that nearly all distance education is still organised through the post and that both the public and prospective students recognise the terms.

'Correspondence education' is defined in the UNESCO volume Terminology of adult education as:

> Education conducted by the postal services without face-to-face contact between teacher and learner. Teaching is done by written or tape-recorded materials sent to the learner, whose progress is monitored through written or taped exercises to the teacher, who corrects them and returns them to the learner with criticisms and advice. (UNESCO, 1979)

The main problem with the term 'correspondence education' is that it cannot encompass the didactic

31

potential of this form of education in the 1980s and beyond: print-, audio-, video-, and computer-based possibilities must be reflected by the terminology chosen. Critics of the term tend to associate 'correspondence education' and 'correspondence study' with some of the less successful aspects of distance education in the past and to feel that these terms contribute to the still-questioned status of study at a distance in many countries. Even when distance education is print-based, the term 'correspondence education' is inadequate to describe Courses by Newspaper or systems with no postal component.

A term is, however, needed to designate the postal sub-group of the print-based forms of distance education in which student contact is not encouraged. It seems suitable to reserve the term 'correspondence education' for this purpose.

## Home study

Communications theory experts tell us that words grow tired and if they do, then 'correspondence study' is a tired word. It is significant that as early as 1926 when the directors of the correspondence schools of the United States came together to form an association, the title chosen was the National Home Study Council and not the National Correspondence Study Council.

'Home study' however has little claim to being an overall term as it is used mainly in the United States and is there confined to further education (technical and vocationally orientated institutions) and not higher education (universities and university-orientated colleges). The distance student may not, in fact, study at home or may study in part at home and in part at other centres.

## Independent study

The proponent of 'independent study' as an overall term for this area of education was Charles A. Wedemeyer, formerly of the University of Wisconsin at Madison:

> Independent study in the American context is generic for a range of teaching-learning activities that sometimes go by separate names (correspondence study, open education, radio-television teaching, individualised learning). In several

> European countries such systems are
> clustered under the term 'distance edu-
> cation' or are still perceived as separate
> programmes without any basic, generic
> relationship. (1977:2115)

This term is often used for distance education
programmes at higher education level in the United
States of America (Markowitz, 1983). The weakness
of this term is that it often indicates independence
from an educational institution; this is not the
case in distance education. Even in the United
States there is hesitancy about using the term
as it is often used for individual study programmes
containing periods of normal lectures organised
on a contract basis agreed to by a·student and
a faculty member.

## External studies

External studies is the term most widely used in
Australia. It describes well the ethos of distance
education as found in Australian universities and
colleges of advanced education: a form of education
that is 'external to' but not 'separated from'
the faculty staff of the institution. The same
staff have two groups of students, one on-campus,
the other external, and they prepare both groups
for the same examinations and awards.
'External studies' can have little claim to
general acceptance because of its limitation to
Australia and because of possible confusion with
programmes structured differently such as the
American external degree (see Chapter 2).

## Distance teaching or teaching at a distance

These two terms have been used as a characteristic
of this form of education for over a decade. Moore
described 'distance teaching' as:

> All those teaching methods in which,
> because of the physical separation of
> learners and teachers, the interactive
> (stimulation, explanation, questioning,
> guidance) as well as the preactive phase
> of teaching (selecting objectives, plan-
> ning curriculum and instructional stat-
> egies), is conducted through print,
> mechanical or electronic devices (1973:
> 669)

The term has grown greatly in popularity since the inception of the Open University (UK) which uses it for its academic journal, <u>Teaching at a Distance</u>. It is, nevertheless, inadequate for the field of education we want to define. Just as 'distance learning' would be too student-based as an overall term and would tend to ignore the role of the institution, so 'distance teaching' is too teacher-orientated and places all the emphasis on the institution.

## Distance education

Distance teaching and distance learning are only half the process we are seeking to describe. Distance teaching indicates well the process of course development by which a distance institution prepares learning materials for students. In the same way wide currency has been given to the term 'distance learning' or 'learning at a distance' for the process as seen from the student's perspective.

There is a peculiar necessity in distance systems that the perspective of student learning should be encompassed within the term chosen. 'Distance teaching' often does not teach. Costly distance teaching materials, prepared over months and sometimes years, often lie unopened and discarded in the homes of prospective students. The essential intersubjectivity that has often been seen as the essence of the education process has not occurred.

'Distance education' is a suitable term to bring together both the teaching and learning elements of this field of education. The relationship of 'distance teaching' and 'distance learning' may be shown thus:

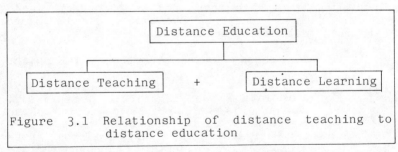

Figure 3.1  Relationship of distance teaching to distance education

A decade ago Rawson-Jones summed up the pros and cons of the term:

> I do not like the term 'distance edu-
> cation'. It seems to put an undue em-
> phasis on the distance between the teacher
> and the learner. But I cannot think
> of a better name for a multi-media edu-
> cational process in which the teacher
> and the students may never meet in a
> face-to-face situation. 'Distance teach-
> ing' seems too teacher-oriented and 'dis-
> tance learning' too student-based. Dis-
> tance education combines the two, so,
> in the absence of a better name for the
> process, I shall use it when appropriate.
> (1974:61)

Since then the term has gained in strength and
acceptance. It indicates well the basic characteristic of this from of education: the separation
of teacher and learner which distinguishes it from
conventional, oral, group-based education. It also
encompasses well the two characteristic operating
systems which later in this study will be shown
to be unique to distance education: the course
development subsystem (distance teaching) and a
student support subsystem (distance learning).
It is also a term for the future. Distance educators
in the past have held on to terms like 'correspondence' or 'home study' because, it was claimed,
they were comforting to students. There is every
evidence that citizens of the late 1980s and 1990s
will be able to cope with distance in a way previous
generations could never dream of. Students, too,
are coming to choose distance rather than back
off from it.
    At its 12th world conference in 1982
at Vancouver, British Columbia, the International
Council for Correspondence Education debated the
question of nomenclature for the form of education
under discussion. The Council decided to change
its name to the International Council for Distance
Education, thus giving international sanction to
the use of the term 'distance education'. An International Council does not change its name lightly
and when it does, it accepts that the advantages
of the change counter-balance the claims of the
previous title. It accepts the necessity of building on the advantages of the change and
living with the disadvantages. In the years since
the Vancouver meeting the acceptance of the term
has been rapid and energies that were previously

dissipated into terminological cul-de-sacs have
been directed towards a more unified structure.

Perhaps the main problem with the term is
that it tends to mask the fact that most students
in distance systems are metropolitan residents.
Only in Australia, Canada and some developing
countries does distance education belie its urban
origins in the United Kingdom, Sweden, Germany
and the United States to embrace vast distances
- and even in Australia and Canada 50% to 70% of
enrolments are normally from the major cities.
However, it is the distance between the teaching
acts and the learning acts that is crucial, not
the magnitude of the geographical separation of
teacher and learner.

In this chapter 'distance education' is chosen
as the most suitable term for this form of education and it is proposed as the only term for
international usage. Terms that are considered
synonymous with or constituents of it were considered earlier in this chapter; terms for fields
of education or educational strategies that are
similar to it but not to be regarded as synonymous
with it were considered in the last.

Terms such as 'correspondence study/education',
'distance teaching' or 'teaching at a distance'
will be used to refer to subsets of distance education or to specific elements such as the course
development part of the process.

'Home study' becomes an American equivalent
of 'distance education at further education level'
and 'independent study' the American term for 'distance education at higher education level', with
'external studies' being a term suitable for the
particular Australian structures.

## Languages other than English

'Distance education' is the normal equivalent of
the French télé-enseignement. Télé-enseignement
(teaching from a distance) has been an influential
term replacing the earlier enseignement par correspondance (teaching by correspondence) and figuring
in the titles both of the extensive French Government provision of distance education at all levels
through the Centres National de Télé-enseignement
(C.N.T.E.) and of the distance departments of conventional universities, the Centres de Télé-
enseignement universitaire (C.T.U.).

The problem with télé-enseignement is that
many do not realise that the root of 'télé' is

the Greek word têle 'from afar' 'from a distance' and does not refer to television.

'Distance education' is a satisfactory translation for both Fernstudium (distance study) and Fernunterricht (distance teaching) in German, though in some circumstances it may be necessary to translate Fernstudium as 'distance education at higher educational level' and Fernunterricht as 'distance education at further education level' because of the awkward status problems between the two terms in the Federal Republic of Germany, where the word Studium is usually reserved specifically for study at university level. In usage the split often seems to be 'Fernstudium' for publicly sponsored distance education and 'Fernunterricht' when distance education is privately conducted. This problem does not exist in the German Democratic Republic where Fernstudium is used interchangeably both for the higher education programmes at a distance organised from the Zentralstelle für das Hochschulfern-Studium des Ministeriums für Hoch- und Fachschulwesen in Dresden and for the technological education programmes from a similar institute in Karl-Marx-Stadt.

'Distance education' is the correct term for translating educación a distancia which has emerged as the dominant term in Spanish. It appears in the titles of the two open universities, Universidad Nacional de Educación a Distancia in Madrid and the Universidad Estatal a Distancia in Costa Rica.

## A definition of distance education

A clear idea of what is the subject of discussion is essential in a book on an area of study in which there has been much confusion about terminology. A clear definition is also important in the rather ill-defined areas of non-traditional education, open education and non-conventional education. It is important to be able to say whether distance education is to be regarded as the same as or different from University without walls, extra-mural studies, experiential learning, off-campus education, open learning, extended campus, the American external degree or university extension. The rest of this chapter seeks to establish a definition of distance education which will serve as a basis for the analysis in the rest of the study.

A satisfactory framework for definition in education is provided by the American educational philosopher Scheffler (1968), who presented the following scheme for different types of definition:

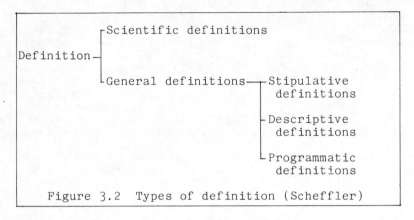

Figure 3.2   Types of definition (Scheffler)

Scheffler sees scientific definitions as being based on special knowledge which is used to construct a network of theory adequate to all available facts encompassed in the definition, whereas general definitions are statements that a given term is to be understood in a certain way for the space of some discussions or for several discussions. Scheffler claims there are three types of general definitions: stipulative, descriptive and programmatic. Stipulative definitions state that a given term is to be taken as equivalent to some other given term within a particular context. This is not the type of definition needed here as a stipulative definition does not claim to reflect the previously accepted usage of the defined terms. A general descriptive definition answers the question 'What does that term mean?'. It not only serves as a convention for usage in discussion but always in addition explains the defined terms by giving an account of its prior usage. A programmatic definition is a definition with a purpose, a programme: seeking to include additional items within a term or to exclude from a term elements which people had previously thought were included. In Scheffler's terms this study commences with a general descriptive definition and seeks to proceed by feedback and refinement towards a scientific definition. It seems appropriate to begin with a search of the literature for authoritative or accepted definitions and to analyse them for their common elements.

Distance education, however, has a hundred year history and the elements of a definition that can be established by this process do not therefore exist as abstractions; they must correspond to the reality. It is correct therefore to examine the definition in the context of existing institutions, then to consider more recent definitions before re-examining the definition established in the light of existing institutions. The process is then continued: it is cyclic and continuous. If the search of the literature is extensive and if the case-studies of institutions to which the nascent definition is applied are wide and varied, it should be possible within the confines of this chapter to produce a definition instrument capable of delineating all educational institutions either into the category 'distance education' and hence subjects within the scope of this book or of excluding them and consigning them to other studies.

Some important definitions

1.  G. Dohmen, (1967) The first definition is chosen from Dohmen, a director of the German Distance Education Institute (DIFF) at Tübingen in the Federal Republic of Germany:

> Distance education (Fernstudium) is a systematically organised form of self-study in which student counselling, the presentation of learning material and the securing and supervising of students' success is carried out by a team of teachers, each of whom has responsibilities. It is made possible at a distance by means of media which can cover long distances. The opposite of 'distance education' is 'direct education' or 'face-to-face education': a type of education that takes place with direct contact between lecturers and students. (1967:9)

From this early formulation may be highlighted:

°   the organisation of self study by an institution.
°   use of media.
°   differences from direct contact between lecturers and students.

2.   O. Mackenzie, E. Christensen and P. Rigby
     (1968)   In   1968   an   analysis   of   dis-
     tance education in the United States of America
     was undertaken by three American scholars,
     Mackenzie, Christensen and Rigby. In their
     book Correspondence instruction in the United
     States they provide the following:

> Correspondence instruction is a method
> of instruction in which correspondence
> is the means of communication between
> student and teacher and which requires
> interaction between the student and the
> instruction. (1968: 2-4)

Programmes that would otherwise qualify but
are rejected because they do not provide for
appropriate interaction they term 'self-study
programs'.

Two elements characterise this definition:

° student and teacher united by correspondence.
° necessity of interaction between student and
  institution.

3.   French law (1971)   On 12 July 1971 the French
     Government passed a law regulating the conduct
     of distance education in its territories.
     The law contained this definition:

> Distance education is education which
> either does not imply the physical pres-
> ence of the teacher appointed to dispense
> it in the place where it is received
> or in which the teacher is present only
> on occasion or for selected tasks. (Loi
> 71.556 du 12 juillet 1971)

Again two elements are basic to this definition:

° the separation of teacher and learner.
° the possibility of occasional seminars or
  meetings between student and teacher.

The wording of the law can be challenged in that
it is so broad that it could include certain forms
of conventional education.

4.   O. Peters (1973)

> Distance    teaching/education   (Fernun-
> terricht) is a method of imparting knowl-
> edge,    skills    and    attitudes    which
> is rationalised by the application of
> division of labour and organisational
> principles as well as by the extensive
> use of technical media, especially for
> the purpose of reproducing high quality
> teaching material which makes it possible
> to instruct great numbers of students
> at the same time wherever they live.
> It is an industrialised form of teaching
> and learning. (Peters, 1973:206)

Characteristic of Peters' position are:

o   the use of technical media.
o   the mass education of students at a distance.
o   the industrialisation of the teaching process.

5.   M. Moore (1973)   This definition is presented
     in 1973 and repeated without modifications
     in 1977:

> Distance teaching may be defined as the
> family of instructional methods in which
> the teaching behaviours are executed
> apart from the learning behaviours, in-
> cluding those that in a contiguous situ-
> ation would be performed in the learner's
> presence, so that communication between
> the teacher and the learner must
> be facilitated by print, electronic,
> mechanical or other devices.(Moore, 1973:
> 664; 1977:8)

Central to Moore's position are:

o   the separation of teacher and learner.
o   the use of technical media.

6.   B. Holmberg (1977)

> The term 'distance education' covers
> the various forms of study at all levels
> which are not under the continuous,
> immediate supervision of tutors present
> with their students in lecture rooms
> or on the same premises, but which,

41

nevertheless, benefit from the planning, guidance and tuition of a tutorial organisation. (Holmberg, 1977:9).

Basic to Holmberg's definition are two elements both of which can be considered essential:

&#9702;   the separation of teacher and learner.
&#9702;   the planning of an educational organisation.

The separation of teacher and learner is fundamental to all forms of distance education whether they be print-based, audio/radio-based, video/television-based or computer-based. This separation differentiates distance education from all forms of conventional, face-to-face, direct teaching and learning.
The structuring of learning materials and the linking of these learning materials to effective learning by students through an educational organisation differentiates distance education from private study, learning from interesting books or cultural television programmes.

## Towards a synthesis

In an article published in 1980 'On defining distance education' a number of similar definitions were brought together and analysed. Six basic defining elements of distance education were proposed:

&#9702;   the separation of teacher and learner which distinguishes it from face-to-face lecturing.
&#9702;   the influence of an educational organisation which distinguishes it from private study.
&#9702;   the use of technical media, usually print, to unite teacher and learner and carry the educational content.
&#9702;   the provision of two-way communication so that the student may benefit from or even initiate dialogue.
&#9702;   the possibility of occasional meetings for both didactic and socialisation purposes.
&#9702;   the participation in an industrialised form of education which, if accepted, contains the genus of radical separation of distance education from other forms within the educational spectrum.

The publication of this definition in 1980 led

to extensive citation and feedback. In some cases (Peruniak 1983:66, Store 1982:61) it seemed that the definition was accepted as the basis for further research; in others commentary was provided which might lead to further precision. Further analysis and case studies of existing institutions led to the considerations which follow:

1.  The separation of teacher and learner. An analysis of the definitions given in this chapter shows that the separation of teacher and learner is central to nearly all of them. This characteristic distinguishes distance education from conventional, oral, group-based education. Both the general public and educational writers appear to coincide in their acceptance of the separation of teacher and learner as a central characteristic of this form of education. An examination of institutions revealed various levels of separation, in which contact could range from nil, to voluntary, to compulsory. 'Quasi-permanent separation throughout the length of the learning process' was finally chosen as a suitable overall summing up of the mean of practice.

2.  The role of the educational organisation. It is important to delineate distance education not only from what happens in lecture theatres and classrooms but also from private study at home. Distance education is an institution-alised offering through public or private providers. This may be represented sche-matically:

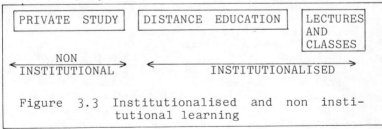

Figure 3.3 Institutionalised and non insti-tutional learning

It is clear that people learn a lot through-out their lives, generally away from teachers and educational institutions. This may be from private reading, from TV, from attending a talk, from a friend or in a thousand different ways. Distance education in an institutionalised form of provision. It shares with private study the individualised and private nature of study outside the structures of the learning group and at the same time has much of the administrative characteristics of institutionalised education on-campus. Fieldwork in distance institutions shows that the entry of an educational bureaucracy into what appears to be a private form of education is not always without trauma.

3. The place of the technological medium (media)
In conventional systems the content of the course, especially that part that is not contained in recommended textbooks, is communicated by the teacher mainly by word of mouth – though it is clear that from primary school through to university the amount of self-study in project work and from textbooks may gradually increase. Distance education shatters this interpersonal communication and replaces it with some form of mechanical or electronic communication: print, telephone, audio, video, broadcasting, computer. All of the communication has to take place by the use of one of a number of technological media. Many years ago Delling (1966:173) called this element in a distance system the 'signal-carrier' and because of the diversity of procedures involved, careful formulation is needed of the role of the technological media in a definition of distance education.

4. Two-way communication. A definition of distance education needs to distinguish it from educational technology with which it is often confused. This can be accomplished neatly by defining as essential two-way communication in distance education and showing its absence in educational technology. It is important that the student in a distance system can profit from dialogue with the institution that provides the learning materials; the student should be able to initiate this dialogue and not be just the recipient of it.
    Two-way communication is not provided by the publishers of textbooks nor even of Do-it-yourself books. Two-way communication is not possible with educational television or radio programmes like Sesame Street or

'Learn French at home by radio' nor even by video- or audio-cassettes produced as resource materials for lecture or classroom use.

5. The separation of learner and the learning group. In the 1980 definition the 'possibility of occasional seminars' was listed as one of the constituents of a definition of distance education. In the light of feedback and further research it has been found necessary to restructure this formulation. Some definitions of distance education and an earlier form of the one being developed in this chapter tended to emphasise 'the teaching of students as individuals' and the importance of individualisation in this form of education.

Comparative research carried on after the publication of the 1980 definition, however, showed the survival in certain Scandinavian countries of group-based distance education (Edström, 1970). The presentation of individualisation in the formulation of the definitions had, therefore, to be modified, as a prerequisite for the methodology adopted was that all the evidence should be reflected. It became clearer, moreover, that a focus on the study situation of the student was central to the concept of distance education. Some formula had to be found to reflect both the individualisation/learning group situation of the distance student and the practice of institutions of providing either no, or voluntary or compulsory face-to-face sessions. The reason for this is that in most conventional educational institutions one has to join a learning group or class if one wants to enrol in a course. The presence of the learning group is as fundamental a characteristic of conventional education as the timetabling of classes so that the teacher and student can be present in the same place and at the same time.

Distance education is different in that it does not compel the student to join the learning group in order to study. Most distance systems treat the student basically as an individual; group work may be compulsory, optional or may never occur, depending on the structure of the distance system in which one enrols.

45

The advantages and disadvantages of the absence of the learning group in distance education is a practically untouched area for future research, though two recent articles by Sewart (1981:160) and Cropley and Kahl (1983:30) have alluded to this feature. Together with the separation of the learner from the teacher, the separation of the learner from the learning group throughout the length of the learning process is a characteristic feature of this form of education which distinguishes it from conventional, oral, group-based education.

6. <u>Industrialisation</u>. The 1980 definition incorporated as an inherent characteristic an evaluation of Peters' industrialisation theory. This decision was made after an analysis of the hundreds of institutional case studies presented by Peters in his study of distance education at technological and further education levels (Peters, 1965) and at higher education level (Peters, 1968) in all countries of the world plus the analysis undertaken by the author of the same or new institutions.

Reaction has been mixed. Administrators like Rumble are very much on the side of Peters and believe that he has provided an essential insight. Others have hesitated especially as they are uncomfortable with the harshness of Peters' terminology and because they come in the main from mixed institutions (e.g. Australia and Sweden) in which the institutional aspects of industrialised processes can be softened. Two of the commentaries from Willén and Bääth are:

(i) Willén argues:

If we return to Keegan's definition, we can conclude that five of the six elements mentioned can be found even in our definition. On the other hand, we have never questioned or even discussed, whether distance education should be considered basically different from other forms of education, and therefore the last point taken up by Keegan does not fit into our definition. Keegan himself, acknowledges that this point can be excluded, if one does not accept that distance education rests on its own theoretical basis. (1981:244-245)

Willén chooses thus to bypass the industrial-isation concept and focus on the five other elements of the definition and comments that in Australia and Sweden 'distance education is to be seen as a supplement to other existing forms of university education e.g. regular teaching, evening classes, de-centralised education'. (1981:245)

(ii) Bääth claims that Peters' industrialisation concept cannot be applied to:

°      very small correspondence schools (Irish Correspondence School, Dublin).
°      distance teaching without preproduced materials (some National Extension College courses).
°      short stencilled study guides (Swedish university departments).
°      Australian integrated mode (1981:213).

There are many real points of value in Bääth's position: he claims these are handi-craft rather than industrialised operations. Some of the Australian universities and col-leges of advanced education deal with small numbers of students, pride themselves on chang-ing the learning materials annually, and strive to maintain the same tutorial relationship between under-graduate and post-graduate students and their lecturers as obtains on-campus, by allocating the same number of dis-tance students per lecturer as in the face-to-face situation.

These are important features and it would be pedantic to try to force interesting and innovative didactic structures into a pattern. Nevertheless there are industrial features of these small scale operations that do not negate the overall value of Peters' position: in the main they deal with the packaging of materials; with the replacing of oral communi-cation with printing or recording machinery; with extensive use of postal and telecommuni-cations facilities.

As a result of these considerations, the definition had by 1983 evolved to the following formulation:

> Distance education is that field of educational endeavour in which the learner is quasi-permanently separated from the teacher throughout the length of the learning process; the learner is quasi-permanently separated from the learning group throughout the length of the learning process; a technological medium replaces the interpersonal communication of conventional, oral, group-based education; the teaching/learning process is institutionalised (thus distinguishing it from Teach-yourself programmes); two-way communication is possible for both student and teacher (thus distinguishing it from other forms of educational technology). It represents an industrialisation of the educational process. (1983: 503)

It can be seen that the support for industrialisation as a component of distance education remains unchanged; it has, however, been moved outside the definition proper.

## Privatisation

Early definitions of distance education, especially those of Wedemeyer and Moore tended to emphasise the independence, autonomy and freedom of the distance learner. A recent definition by Gough of Deakin University reflects this tradition:

> Distance education is a means of providing learning experiences for students through the use of self-instructional materials and access to educational resources, the use of which is largely determined by the student and which allow the student, for the most part, to choose the time, place and circumstances of learning. (1981:10).

There are excellent elements in this definition but when it is compared with the reality of existing systems, it can be shown to have elements of Sheffler's programmatic type of definition in it. It proposes a programme, an ideal - many systems in fact do not promote learner autonomy in the way this definition would wish. Sharp cut off dates for TMAS and CMAS, rigidity of content of learning materials, inflexible learning structures are all too common in distance systems.

Independence therefore is not the element that the definition should reflect. The term 'privatisation' is much closer to the reality. A distance system takes the student from the learning group and places him/her in a more private situation. Learning is often private when it is not institutionalised. Distance education is characterised by the privatisation of institutional learning.

Conclusion

In the light of these considerations the following definition of distance education is proposed:

Distance education is a form of education characterised by

° the quasi-permanent separation of teacher and learner throughout the length of the learning process; this distinguishes it from conventional face-to-face education.

° the influence of an educational organisation both in the planning and preparation of learning materials and in the provision of student support services; this distinguishes it from private study and teach-yourself programmes.

° the use of technical media; print, audio, video or computer, to unite teacher and learner and carry the content of the course.

° the provision of two-way communication so that the student may benefit from or even initiate dialogue; this distinguishes it from other uses of technology in education.

° the quasi-permanent absence of the learning group throughout the length of the learning process so that people are usually taught as individuals and not in groups, with the possibility of occasional meetings for both didactic and socialisation purposes.

Distance education is to be regarded as being constituted of these five interdependent elements, which remain constant essential components even if their content is different in separate institutional situations. In addition there are two socio-cultural determinants which are both necessary pre-conditions and necessary consequences of distance education. These are:

° the presence of more industrialised features than in conventional oral education.
° the privatisation of institutional learning.

In the preparation of this study Peters' concept of the industrialisation of education has been subjected to lengthy scrutiny. The scrutiny has focused on components of distance education that were not central to Peters' own research: institutional structures, physical plant, the administration of course development. The validity of Peters' insight remains unchallenged and the reasons for the change of presentation here are definitional in character. It is felt that the heuristic value of the concept of industrialisation is better emphasised by placing it, together with the privatisation of institutional learning, as a concomitant characteristic rather than a constituting element.

Excursus

The definition presented in the previous section seeks to take up the middle ground between the extremes of defining distance education so narrowly that it becomes an abstraction which does not correspond to existing reality, or defining distance education so broadly that it becomes meaningless.
An example of a definition that is so narrow that it is not helpful in practice is that provided in the UNESCO study:

> Distance education: 'Education conducted through the postal services, radio, television, telephone or newspaper, without face-to-face contact between teacher and learner. Teaching is done by specially prepared material transmitted to individuals or learning groups. Learners' progress is monitored through written or taped exercises, sent to the teacher, who corrects them and returns them to learners with criticism and advice.'(1975:21)

Comparative studies of distance systems show that the element of face-to-face contact may be either non-existent, compulsory or voluntary. The volume of face-to-face contact that would be consistent with the definition adopted for this study is indicated by the phrase 'the quasi-permanent

separation of the learner from the teacher and
from the learning group throughout the length of
the learning process'.
Too vague a definition would be equally faulty.
The range of 'education at a distance' is vast
and comprises both distance education as defined
here and a range of other resource-based teaching
and learning strategies. If the confusion of
the past is to be avoided and if the goal of this
study is to be achieved (the identification of
a discrete area of educational activity in such
a way that it can provide a basis for other scholars
to build a valid theoretical structure and guides
to good practice), then to be excluded from the
concept of distance education are:

○    the use of printed, audio-based, video-based
     computer-based learning materials in classroom,
     lecture theatres, seminars, tutorial and lab-
     oratory sessions for on-campus programmes.
○    the use of printed, audio-based, video-based/
     learning material and computer in private
     study.

Thus the use of broadcasting in schools does not
fall within distance education as defined in this
study. There have been many interesting and important achievements in this area: Radio Math-
ematics project in Nicaragua; Radio Santa Maria
in the Dominican Republic; Mauritius College of
the Air are three of the best known. These do
not fall within the definition of distance education adopted in this study. They are the subject
of other studies. They form a specific area of
educational research - the use of educational technology as a support to the classroom - and have
been well served by an excellent group of researchers: Patrick Suppes, Emile McAnany, Dean Jamison,
Hilary Perraton, François Orivel and Jean-Claude
Eicher.
Jamison and Orivel provide a precise analysis
of the point in question:

          Distance teaching systems can be use-
          fully classified according to the fre-
          quency with which learners assemble for
          supervised group study. With in-school
          systems the learner spends a substantial
          proportion of his learning time in a
          classroom, usually attending daily, though
          most teaching in the classroom is mediated

rather than face-to-face. With <u>out-of-school systems</u> the learner does most of his studying alone with only occasional meetings with other learners and a tutor or monitor. (1980:376-377)

What are here termed 'out-of-school systems' are the equivalent of 'distance education' as defined in this chapter; 'in-school systems' are the work of other studies.

Neither do flexi-study, multi-mode or mixed mode programmes form part of distance education as defined in this book. They represent the use of distance education materials for conventional students, with a reduced attendance rate at classes. The reason for this is purely heuristic and does not imply any judgment for or against the mixing of distance education with conventional forms.

Distance education, as defined, remains an extremely complex grouping of educational activities. It is a tenet of this study that it represents a coherent and identifiable cluster of educational processes, even though these cross the normal sectoral boundaries within which education is administered and studied: primary and secondary schooling; technical and further education; college and university higher and postgraduate education. The consequences of the position taken up in this chapter on the nature of distance education will not have escaped readers who have followed closely the debate on the industrialisation of education. Many authorities would see educational provision as represented in Fig. 2.2 at the end of the previous chapter as a continuum and one might place institutional structures along the continuum in accordance with their provision of forms of conventional or distance education. Alternatively one could rank institutional structures in accordance with the percentage of face-to-face provision which they provide and whether this is compulsory or voluntary. The position of Peters and to a certain extent of this study is quite different. It is that the continuum is broken once one enters the area defined as 'distance education' and that new situations, some of them advantageous and others disadvantageous, are set up automatically and pose problems of a different nature from those of conventional education.

## References

Aristotle, Nichomachaean Ethics, 1.1.

Bääth, J. (1981) On the nature of distance education. Distance Education, 2,2, 212-213.

Cropley, A. and Kahl, T. (1983) Distance education and distance learning: some psychological considerations. Distance Education, 4,1,27-39.

Delling, R.M. (1966) Versuch der Grundlegung zu einer systematischen Theorie des Fernunterricht, In Sroka, L. (ed.) Fernunterricht 1966, Festschrift zum 50 Geburtstag von Walter Schultz-Rahe. Hamburg: Hamburger Fernlehrinstitut.

Dohmen, G. (1967) Das Fernstudium, Ein neues pädagogisches Forschungs-und Arbeitsfeld. Tübingen: DIFF.

Edstrom, L. et. al (1970) Mass education: studies in adult education and teaching by correspondence in some developing countries. Stockholm: Almquist and Wiksell.

Gough, E. (1981) Distance education at Deaking University and University Sains Malaysia. Open Campus, 3,1,10-15.

Holmberg, B. (1977) Distance education: a survey and bibliography. London Kogan Page.

Jamison, D. and Orivel, F. (1981) The cost-effectiveness of distance teaching for school equivalency. In Perraton, H. (ed.) Alternative routes to formal education. Washington: World Bank.

Keegan, D. (1980) On defining distance education. Distance Education, 1,1, 13-36.

Keegan, D. (1983) Review of Daniel et. al Learning at a distance. A world perspective. International Review of Education, 29, 4, 501-503.

Mackenzie, O., Christensen, E. and Rigby, P. (1968) Correspondence institution in the United States. New York: McGraw-Hill.

Markowitz, H. (1983) Independent study by correspondence in American universities. Distance Education, 4, 2, 149-170.

Moore, M.G. (1973) Toward a theory of independent learning and teaching. Journal of Higher Education, 44, 66-679.

Moore, M.G. (1977) On a theory of independent study. Hagen: Fernuniversität (DIFF).

Peruniak, G. (1983) Interactive perspectives in

distance education: a case study. Distance Education, 4, 1, 63-89.

Peters, O. (1965) Der Fernunterricht. Weinheim: Beltz.

Peters, O. (1968) Das Hochschulfernstudium.Weinheim: Beltz.

Peters, O. (1973) Die didaktische Struktur der Fernunterrichts. Weinheim and Basel: Beltz.

Rawson-Jones, K. (1974) Some trends in distance education. Epistolodidaktika. 1, 67-68.

Sheffler, I. (1968) The philosophy of education. New York: Wiley.

Sewart, D. (1980) Creating an information base for an individualized support system in distance education. Distance Education, 1, 2, 171-187.

Store, R. (1981) An analysis of student responses in distance education systems. British Journal of Educational Technology, 171-196.

UNESCO (1979) Terminology of adult education/ Terminologie de la educación de adultos/ Terminologie de l'education des adultes. Paris: Ibedata.

Wedemeyer, C.A. (1977) Independent study. In Knowles, A.S. (ed.) The international encyclopedia of higher education. Boston: Northeastern University.

Willén, B. (1981) Distance education at Swedish universities. Stockholm: Almquist and Wiksell.

PART TWO: THEORIES OF DISTANCE EDUCATION

CHAPTER FOUR

INDEPENDENCE AND AUTONOMY

It is unfortunately true that the failure of correspondence study to develop a theory related to
the mainstream of educational thought and practice
has seriously handicapped the development and recognition of this field. Charles A. Wedemeyer, 1974

## Introduction

Early pioneers of correspondence education, William
Rainey Harper of Chicago, William H. Lightly of
Wisconsin, Hans Hermod of Malmö, wrote with verve
and enthusiasm about the advantages and disadvan-
tages of this form of education.
But the historian of distance education, Rudolf
Manfred Delling from Tübingen wrote in 1966:

> Institutionalised distance teaching has
> existed for about 100 years. Only during
> the last few years, however, has the
> practice of distance teaching commenced
> to rely on theory. Nevertheless there
> is no systematic theory of distance teach-
> ing which might make it possible
> to classify practitioners' individual
> experiences in relation to their essence.
> (1966:183)

Delling shows that the first theoretical work was
developed in the 1950s by the East German scholar
Joannes Riechert, at the Bergakademie in Freiberg
and the Hochschule für Okonomie, Berlin-Karlshort.
This was published in 1959 as Schreiben, Lehren
und Verstehen (Write, teach and learn). Shortly
afterwards from Sweden came an international description of the field On the methods of teaching
by correspondence by Börje Holberg (1960). This
was translated into German in 1962.
When theoretical approaches began to emerge
in the last decade, their development was fitful.
The first major theoretical structure, and to date
the most comprehensive, categorised distance education as an industrialisation of the education

process and suggested that the closest parallel to distance teaching is the industrialised production of goods. A mail order firm would have a structure similar to an institution for this form of education.

The claim of Wedemeyer that distance education has failed 'to develop a theory related to the mainstream of educational thought and practice' remains true today. The following chapters present a detailed analysis of the theoretical approaches that have been attempted to date. They are presented here because they are among the best available in the literature and because it is correct to present a detailed expose of the work of previous writers before attempting to suggest a new basis for theoretical structure. Nascent, if fragile, theoretical proposals have been found in the writings of Moore, O. Peters and Holmberg; ideas of value have been contributed by Delling, Wedemeyer, Bääth, Daniel, Smith and Sewart.

For the purposes of this book the more important positions formulated to date are classified into three groupings:

° Theories of autonomy and independence. These contributions come mainly from the late 1960s and early 1970s and the major representatives are Rudolf Manfred Delling (Federal Republic of Germany), Charles A. Wedemeyer (U.S.A.) and Michael G. Moore (U.K.). (Chapter 4).

° Theory of industrialisation. Otto Peters' work in the Federal Republic of Germany comprised comparative studies throughout the 1960s and theoretical formulation in the early 1970s. (Chapter 5).

° Theories of interaction and communication. More contemporary views from Börje Holmberg (Sweden/Federal Republic of Germany), John A. Bääth (Sweden), David Sewart (U.K), Kevin C. Smith (Australia) and John S. Daniel (Canada). (Chapter 6).

## A helping organisation

Rudolf Manfred Delling of the Deutsches Institut für Fernstudien an der Universität Tübingen is a historian and bibliographer. In 1966 he provided this definition:

> Distance education (Fernunterricht) is a planned and systematic activity which

> comprises the choice, didactic preparation and presentation of teaching materials as well as the supervision and support of student learning and which is achieved by bridging the physical distance between student and teacher by means of at least one appropriate technical medium. (1966: 186).

Delling sees distance education as a multi-dimensional system of learning and communication processes, with the aid of an artificial signal-carrier. In many of his writings (1968, 1978) he lists eight dimensions:

º a learner.
º society (including legislation, administration, family etc.).
º a helping organisation (distance teaching institutions).
º a learning objective.
º the content to be learned.
º the result of learning.
º distance.
º a signal-carrier.

Remarkable in his approach are his hesitation to label distance education a teaching process (distance colleges or departments are organisations which 'help' learning) and the absence of the teacher from the eight dimensions of the system.

A distance education course is an artificial, dialogic opportunity for learning in which the distance between the learner and the helping organisation is bridged by an artificial signal-carrier. From the start the concepts of feedback and two-way communication are central to Delling's position. He sees an essential difference between learning opportunities that are <u>monologues</u> (books, newspapers, journals, documentary films, lectures without discussion, broadcasts, self-teaching courses and other self-instructional material) and those that are <u>dialogic</u> (normal classroom or school teaching, conversations, letters with answers and distance education courses). Monologues are based on one-way communication, whereas dialogues are characterised by two-way communication.

The world of distance education, he claims, has little of the characteristics of 'teaching' because there is, in general, no teacher in the system and the functions relating to student

learning within the helping organisation are performed by a variety of machines, people and materials. Delling tends to reduce the role of the
teacher and of the educational organisation to
a minimum and throw the whole emphasis on the autonomy and independence of the learner. This is
especially important because adults are normally
the learners in distance programmes. Adults do
not, he suggests, accept the conventional educator-
pupil relationship. The function of the 'helping
organisation' is to take over, upon the wish of
learners, everything that they cannot yet do for
themselves, with the tendency that the learners
eventually become autonomous. When this occurs
the only function left for the helping organisation
is to provide information, documentation and library
facilities. Delling seems to want to place distance
education outside the field of educational theory.
He sees it falling within the range of communication
processes and to be characterised by industrialised
mechanisms which carry on its artificial dialogic
and two-way communication processes. He reduces
to a minimum the role of the teacher and throws
the whole weight of his analysis on the learning
of the student studying at a distance.

## Independent study

The term 'independent study' was used by Charles
A. Wedemeyer to describe distance education at
university level. For much of his professional
life he was professor of education at the University
of Wisconsin, Madison and closely associated with
the Independent Study Division of the National
University Extension Association of the United
States of America.
       He uses the term 'independent study' to de-
scribe distance education at university level and
gives this definition of independent learning:

> 'Independent learning' is that learning,
> that changed behaviour, that results
> from activities carried on by learners
> in space and time, learners whose en-
> vironment is different from that of the
> school, learners who may be guided by
> teachers but who are not dependent upon
> them, learners who accept degrees of
> freedom and responsibility in initiating
> and carrying out the activities that
> lead to learning. (1973:73)

Wedemeyer's thought is generous and liberal. A major influence is the philosophy of Carl Rogers. There are two bases for his views on independent study: a democratic social ideal and a liberal educational philosophy. He considers that nobody should be denied the opportunity to learn because he is poor, geographically isolated, socially disadvantaged, in poor health, institutionalised or otherwise unable to place himself within the institution's special environment for learning. Thus he claims that independent study should be self-pacing, individualised and offer freedom in goal selection.

Wedemeyer sees the independent learner as the original or 'proto'-learner whose success in learning enables him to survive and he claims that each individual commences with a period of pre-school individual learning. Group instruction which evolved in schools was first intended, he tells us, for the elite, and the long history of formal education is characterised by a persistent pattern of the learner in the group - a <u>dependent</u> learner whose goals, activities, rewards and punishments are decided by the policies and practices of an everpresent group of teachers.

The pattern of the learner in the group underwent a gradual breakdown process in which he sees the space and time barriers to independent study being dissipated in six successive stages:

1. The invention of writing.
2. The invention of printing.
3. The invention of correspondence education: the first formally structured format for the independent learner, which made use of new technology in the form of a reliable mail service in the mid 1800s.
4. Development of democratic and egalitarian philosophies.
5. Application of telecommunications media to teaching.
6. Development of programmed-learning theory. (1973:75).

These series of developments led in his own day to the possibility for people, cut off from the regular schools, to continue learning in ever larger numbers. Wedemeyer uses three terms for such programmes: 'independent study', 'open learning' and 'distance education'. He saw in the 1960s the re-emergence of the independent learner, with a new elan for independent programmes in areas where conventional group-based formal learning was less able to succeed.

Wedemeyer writes well on the difference between open learning, distance education and independent study. On 'open learning':

> It is difficult to find a common defi-
> nition for the many experimental pro-
> grammes that call themselves open. How-
> ever, all open schools have one principle
> in common; they are to a greater or lesser
> extent efforts to expand the freedoms
> of learners. Some are open only in a
> spatial sense... while others provide
> freedoms in more significant dimensions
> - in admissions, selection of courses,
> individual adaptation of the curriculum
> and time, goal selection and evaluation.
> (1977:2117)

and on 'distance education':

> The term distance education has a usage
> somewhat comparable to that of independent
> study in the United States. It is in-
> creasingly used in Europe as an omnibus
> term to include correspondence study,
> open learning, instruction by radio and
> television - in short, all learning-
> teaching arrangements that are not face-
> to-face. (1977:2121)

He made a determined effort to establish the term 'independent study' as the umbrella term for this field of education both in the U.S. and through-out the world. Today the term is used extensively in the U.S. for correspondence and distance edu-cation programmes at university level. His defi-nition is:

> Independent study consists of various
> forms of teaching-learning arrangements
> in which teachers and learners carry
> out their essential tasks and responsi-
> bilities apart from one another, com-
> municating in a variety of ways. Its
> purposes are to free on-campus or internal
> learners from inappropriate class placings
> or patterns, to provide off-campus or
> external learners with the opportunity

> to continue learning in their own en-
> vironments, and developing in all learners
> the capacity to carry on self-directed
> learning, the ultimate maturity required
> of the educated person. (1977:2114)

It will be noticed at once that Wedemeyer's
concept of 'independent study' comprises two different forms of education: 'independent study for
the internal student' and 'independent study for
the external student'. Independent study for the
internal student makes freedom from lecture attendance possible for exceptional university students
by the allocation of series of readings and individual study programmes. One can see elements
in his thought of ideas similar to the contract
programmes and educational brokerage ideas favoured
in some experimental American programmes of the
mid 1970s. The linking of external and internal
programmes in the one definition, however, tends
to diffuse Wedemeyer's ideas and the emphasis on
internal independent study disappears in his later
articles.

Wedemeyer's liberal educational theory and
egalitarian social philosophy were ill-at-ease
with the conventional educational system and many
of his writings are marked by comments on the short-
comings of the contemporary scene both at school
and university level:

> Conventional teaching and learning, makes
> use of concepts of learning and teaching
> that have preserved the old mystiques,
> that have maintained space-time barriers
> to learning. The invention of modern
> television, the computer, laser beams,
> holography, and the tele-communications
> satellite have significance for education
> that (except for writing and printing)
> has been largely unperceived, unaccepted,
> and unrealized. (Childs and Wedemeyer
> 1961:71)

Within this context he set out a conceptual
structure for an educational system that would
be more akin to his views. Most of his writings
list ten characteristics of the proposed system:

1. The system should be capable of operation
   any place where there are students - or even
   only one student - whether or not there are

teachers at the same place at the same time.

2. The system should place greater responsibility for learning on the student.

3. The system should free faculty members from custodial type duties so that more time can be given to truly educational tasks.

4. The system should offer students and adults wider choices (more opportunities) in courses, formats, methodologies.

5. The system should use, as appropriate, all the teaching media and methods that have been proved effective.

6. The system should mix and combine media and methods so that each subject or unit within a subject is taught in the best way known.

7. The system should cause the redesign and development of courses to fit into an 'articulated media programme'.

8. The system should preserve and enhance opportunities for adaptation to individual differences.

9. The system should evaluate student achievement simply, not by raising barriers concerned with the place the student studies, the rate at which he studies, the method by which he studies or the sequence within which he studies.

10. The system should permit students to start, stop and learn at their own pace. (1968:328, 1981:36)

Wedemeyer saw instinctively that the only way to break what he called the 'space-time barriers' of education was by separating teaching from learning. This involved planning each as a separate activity. Planning teaching and learning as separate activities leads him to postulate six characteristics of distance or independent systems that are capable of operation any place there are students - or even only one student - whether or not there are teachers at the same place at the same time:

1. The student and teacher are separated.

2. The normal processes of teaching and learning are carried on in writing or through some other medium.

3. Teaching is individualised.

4. Learning takes place through the student's activity.

5. Learning is made convenient for the student

in his own environment.

6.  The learner takes responsibility for his pro-
    gress, with freedom to start and stop at any
    time and to pace himself. (1973:76)

In many of his writings Wedemeyer presents
these thoughts diagramatically. He claims, that
every teaching-learning situation comprises four
elements:

°   a teacher;
°   a learner or learners;
°   a communications system or mode;
°   something to be taught/learned.

He then claims that a traditional classroom could
be represented as a box which encompassed
the four elements:

> If the communications system is a given,
> either because it is the only system
> available (think of Plato meeting learners
> in the Grove of Akademos) or is a cultural
> artifact acting as an imperative, then
> there are no options, and the communi-
> cation must be face-to-face, eyeball-
> to-eyeball, earpan-to-earpan speech.
> Then, if a box is put around the four
> essential elements, we have a classroom:

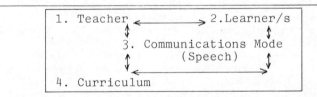

Figure 4.1 A teaching-learning situation. The class-
          room. (Wedemeyer)

> A teaching-learning system that must
> work any place, any time, for one learner
> or many, directly confronts the space-
> time-elite barriers of the classroom
> model. In fact, however, distance has
> long been a problem in the classroom
> model. As classes became larger, and
> lectures replaced the dialogue that Plato
> conducted, the integrity of the model
> was breached. Only the illusion of being

effectively face-to-face remains, as
distance within the box lengthens between
teacher and learners and speech is ampli-
fied for ever more distant reception.
The concept of 'distance' involves more
than physical distance. There is social
distance, cultural distance, and what
I have been calling 'physical' distance
for want of a better term. All of these
are present wherever teaching and learning
are carried on. (1981:38-40, 1978:13-
14)

However if we are to achieve a 'teaching-learning
system that can work any place, any time, for one
learner or many', Wedemeyer tells us that the 'class-
room-box' must be re-structured thus:

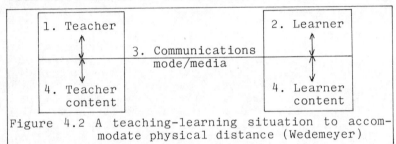

Figure 4.2 A teaching-learning situation to accommodate physical distance (Wedemeyer)

The four elements of the previous structure
remáin but have been reorganised to accommodate
physical space. This representation of the teaching-learning process to accommodate the 'any time,
any place, single or multiple learner's requirement' has as its aim the concern to organise instruction so that greater freedom in learning is
possible for learners. As an outcome of this he
proposes three conceptualisations of freedom for
learners in all independent or distance programmes:

(i) learning should be self-pacing: the
learner should be able to pace his studies
in accordance with his circumstances
and needs.
(ii) learning should be individualised and
the learners should be free to follow
any of several courses of learning.
(iii) the learner should have freedom in selection of goals and activities. (1973:101)

Wedemeyer ran into some criticism when he tried

to suggest that these theoretical propositions about the freedom of the distance learner should be implemented in practice. These criticisms came both from those looking for a workable system and from those who feared that public monies spent on distance systems would be transferred back to conventional education if the learning in the distance system could not be accurately evaluated or if the evaluation was that the learning in the independent system was inferior.

Despite the idealistic nature of much of Wedemeyer's writing he had a very extensive knowledge of the day-to-day workings of correspondence systems. 'Not every student', he warns, 'will be able to succeed by correspondence instruction. This is not an easy method of learning'. (1963:30) And he details five serious obstacles to success as a distance learner:

- developing interest in the task and motivation.
- readiness for study is a problem in correspondence study witnessed by 'the non-start, the early drop-out, the under achiever'.
- grasping the structure of the subject to be learned at a distance.
- learning both analytic and instructive thinking.
- evaluating progress in learning. (1962:14)

The secret of success in Wedemeyer's thought is placed squarely on the shoulders of the instructor who is in a continuous tutorial relationship with the correspondence student. The teacher is the daily monitor and motivator of the distance student. The chief value of the correspondence method lies in the tutorial relationship developed between the teacher and the student, and to minimize or destroy this relationship (by check-off type lessons, multiple-choice answers) actually changes the character of the work offered. Schools that depend solely on the use of objective or machine-type scoring have abandoned distance education. Such programmes are in fact programmes of 'self study'. (1963:29) In a similar vein he dismisses close-circuit television, radio, telephone, teaching machines, computer and satellite from consideration as forms of independent study or distance education except under strict conditions:

> If media (CCTV, for example) are employed
> merely to replicate a regular class

> without broadening opportunity and shift-
> ing responsibility and freedom to the
> learner, the system cannot be defined
> as independent study. (1971:552)

He undertook the uphill struggle of trying
to promote non-traditional education programmes
in the highly structured United States university
scene. The rather bleak title he chose for the
edited collection of his writings published on
his retirement, Learning at the back-door shows
his own assessment of the Sisyphan task of gaining
status for non-traditional, open and distance programmes for credit in the United States.

Wedemeyer's earlier writings are more incisive
than his later articles which tend to reproduce
with precision ideas presented earlier. All the
important ideas are there in the 1960s and there
is little deepening, evaluation or reformulation
in the 1970s. Although the writings of the 1960s
show familiarity with the day-to-day problems of
the organisation of independent programmes and
the difficulties of both teaching and learning
at a distance, there is little formulation at a
later date of planning mechanisms or management
analyses that would allow others to build on his
ideas. Ellis claimed that Wedemeyer's criteria
for conducting a distance education system 'lacked
specific context, purposes, constraints and cost-
consciousness' (1978:16-17). The criticism of
conventional schooling and university education
in his writings is frequent. Progress for distance
education does not lie down this cul-de-
sac. Criticism of on-campus programmes, calls
for the improvement of on-campus programmes - not
for the development of distance systems.

The failure of distance education to make
much progress in the U.S. in the 1970s and early
1980s shows the necessity for more thinkers like
Wedemeyer to focus on the specific context of university education in the U.S. His personal dedication, generosity and liberal vision contributed
much to the growth of a consensus among distance
educators throughout the world and influenced many
of the writers treated in the next chapters.

## Autonomy and distance

Writing in 1973 Michael G. Moore, formerly of the
University of Wisconsin at Madison and today at
the Open University of the United Kingdom,

complained that progress in distance education was being hindered by lack of attention to what he called the 'macro-factors':

- description
- definition
- discrimination
- identification
- building a theoretical framework.

His own contribution was the development of a theory of distance education based on the variables 'autonomy' and 'distance'.

Moore's main contributions to a theory of distance education came in the early 1970s but they read with surprising freshness today. A number of themes are immediately apparent in his writing: he states clearly that he wishes to develop a theory of education at a distance, defines which aspects of educational endeavour he is dealing with and which are excluded, speaks of those students who <u>will</u> not attend groupings but choose to learn apart from teachers, uses confidently terms like 'distance teaching' and 'distance education' as 'a field of education' at a time when most were classifying it merely as a method or a mode.(1975)

Moore's focus is on all forms of deliberate, planned, structured learning and teaching that are carried on outside the school environment. He defines the school environment as 'the classroom, lecture or seminar, the setting in which the events of teaching are contemporaneous and co-terminous with the events of learning'. Distance education (he uses the term 'independent learning and teaching') is an educational system in which the learner is autonomous and separated from the teacher by space and time so that communication is by a non-human medium. The distance system has three sub-systems: a learner, a teacher and a method of communication. These sub-systems have critical characteristics distinguishing them from learning, teaching and communication in other forms of education.

His research began with the belief that instruction can be considered as comprising two families of teaching activities: face-to-face or 'contiguous' teaching and 'distance teaching':

> Teaching consists of two families of activity with many characteristics in common, but different in one aspect so important that a theory explaining one

> cannot satisfactorily explain the other.
> The first of these families, the older,
> better understood, more fully researched,
> includes all educational situations where
> the teacher is physically contiguous
> with the students, so that the primary
> means of communication is his voice,
> and in which teaching is a 'service'
> that is 'consumed' simultaneously with
> its production. The second family of
> teaching methods, and the subject of
> our concern, includes educational situ-
> ations distinguished by the separation
> of the teacher from his learners, so
> that communication has to be facilitated
> by a mechanical or electronic medium.
> Teaching in this environment is 'consumed'
> at a time or place different from that
> at which it is 'produced' and to reach
> the learner it must be contained, trans-
> ported, stored and delivered. (1977b:6)

From an exhaustive search of the literature,
Moore lists the forms of educational provision
that fall within his concept of 'distance teaching':
an open university, a university without walls,
an independent study programme on-campus, an external degree programme and even a teach-yourself
book. This is a much wider classification than
that accepted for distance education in this book.
The reason for it is, as with Wedemeyer, the inclusion of on-campus independent study programmes
within the definition, and an opening up of the
concept 'independence' to include programmes without
two-way communication.

Within this theoretical structure Moore identifies two clusters of educational offerings
as essential components of independent study:

° programmes designed for learners in environ-
  ments apart from their instructors - distance
  teaching.
° programmes designing for the encouragement
  of independent/self-directed learning - learner
  autonomy.

Here he brings together two traditions - distance
teaching which he traces back (with Noffsinger)
to the 1840s and self-directed study which he traces
back through a range of practices in American higher
education to the tutor system in Oxford University

in the 19th century.

Distance teaching is defined as the family of instructional methods:

> In which the teaching behaviours are executed apart from the learning behaviours, including those that in a contiguous situation would be performed in the learner's presence, so that communication between the teacher and the learner must be facilitated by print, electronic, mechanical or other devices. (1977a:68)

Moore accepted that teaching consists of two phases 'the preactive' and the 'interactive':

> In the preactive phase, the teacher selects objectives and plans the curriculum and instructional strategies, while in the 'interactive', face-to-face with the learners, he provides verbal stimulation, makes explanations, asks questions and provides guidance.(1977b:15)

He is clearly concerned that most educational research treats teaching as 'the activity which takes place during school and within the classroom setting' where communication is by the human voice and there is 'immediate, spontaneous, often emotionally-motivated interaction between the learner and the teacher, and usually between the learner and other learners: there is a social interactional relationship which assumes no delay in communication, no distance in space or time'. Since the introduction of compulsory education for children, Moore points out, face-to-face teaching has been accepted as the norm. But distance teaching situations do exist, particularly with adult learners. Moore correctly identifies the concept of separation of learner and teacher as the origin of the concept 'distance' in education, and as crucial for determining the selection of research data from which theoretical frameworks in this field may be constructed.

Basic to Moore's position is that distance teaching programmes can be classified according to the distance between learner and teacher. He wants programmes to be classified by the provision for two-way communication (dialogue or D) and by the extent to which a programme can be responsive to a learner's individual needs (structure or S).

He believes that the element of two-way communication in all distance teaching programmes can
be measured and suggests that an educational telephone network is an example of high two-way communication or dialogue (+D) and an educational radio
broadcast is an example of a distance teaching
methodology in which two-way communication is not
possible (-D) and hence would not be counted as
an example of distance education as defined in
this book. (He is classifying educational uses
of media, not communications media).

Moore also measures programmes in so far as
they are responsive to students' needs as individuals, and labels this 'structure'. In a highly
structured programme (+S) no variation of the programme is possible (as in a Linear Programmed Instruction Text), but when there is a minimum of
structure teachers and learners can respond easily
to stimuli. Thus Moore feels it is important
to measure the extent of the responsiveness of
a teaching programme to a learner's individual
needs, goals, progress or achievements (is it highly
structured or not?) whether the communications
medium on which it is based permits two-way communication or not. He presents this diagrammatically
in Figure 4.3 (with S representing structure and
D dialogue).

The more tentative section of Moore's theory
is when he tries to establish learner autonomy
as the second dimension of independent learning
(1972). In his various publications Moore writes
well on the autonomy of the independent learner.
There is a strong humanistic tendency in his writing. He is influenced by Charles Wedemeyer, Carl
Rogers, Allan Tough and Malcolm Knowles, but the
synthesis is his own. Starting from a general obser-
vation that learners both in schools and universities are very dependent on teachers for explanations, guidance, questions and stimulation, Moore
shows that such an approach places more decision-
making powers in the hands of the teacher than
is acceptable to some adult education theorists.
Like Wedemeyer he seeks for learner autonomy in:

(i)   the setting of objectives.
(ii)  methods of study and
(iii) evaluation.

There are possible programmes he tells us
that achieve these goals but most do not. Both
in conventional education and in most programmes

| | Type | Programme Types | Examples |
|---|---|---|---|
| Most Distance | -D-S | 1. Programme with no dialogue and no structure. | Independent reading study programmes of the 'self directed' kind. |
| | -D+S | 2. Programmes with no dialogue but with structure. | Programmes in which the communication method is radio or television. |
| | +D+S | 3. Programmes with dialogue and structured. | Typically programmes using the correspondence method. |
| Least Distance | +D-S | 4. Programmes with dialogue and no structure. | e.g. a Rogerian type of tutorial programme. |

Figure 4.3. Types of distance teaching programmes (Moore)

of distance teaching and learning, Maslow's analysis is only too true:

> The teacher is the active one who teaches a passive person who is shaped and taught and who is given something which he then accummulates and which he may then lose or retain. This kind of learning too easily reflects the goals of the teacher, and ignores the values and ends of the learner. (1977b:21)

The basis for learner autonomy as a necessary theoretical component of distance education is justified by Moore from his analysis of the separation between teacher and learner in education at a distance. He asks whether the concept of 'distance' or 'separation' or 'apartness' is adequate to explain the gap between teacher and learner. His own answer is no. The existence of this gap means that the activities of teachers and learner will be influenced by it. Because the learner is alone, he is compelled to accept a comparatively high degree of responsibility for the conduct of the learning programme. He also exercises a greater degree of control over his/her learning.

The autonomous learner proceeds without need for admonition and little need for direction. If highly autonomous he may have no personal relationship with a teacher but if he has a personal teacher he will be able to control the effect and significance of teacher input in a realistic and unemotional way. To the highly autonomous, the teacher's role is that of respondent rather than director and the institution becomes a helping organisation. There are some adult learners, however, who need help in formulating their learning objectives and in identifying sources of information and in measuring achievements, whereas there are many others who are autonomous learners, with the abilities of self stimulation, knowledge of ways to achieve their objectives and ways of measuring achievement. It is necessary therefore to be able to measure the 'autonomy' dimension of educational programmes.

Moore sets out to do this in terms of his statement that all teaching-learning processes have these characteristic components:

(i) establishment or preparatory activities in which problems are identified, goals

set and strategies planned.
(ii) <u>executive activities</u> in which data, information and ideas are patterned, experiments and tests take place in order to arrive at instructional solutions.
(iii)<u>evaluatory activities</u> in which the instructional processes make judgments about the appropriateness of the information and ideas for solving the problems and meeting the goals. (1977b:21)

Moore claims that in conventional education the establishment activities are entirely in the purview of the teacher, whereas at a distance the teacher merely prepares instructional materials to be used and drawn upon to the extent that the learner desires. The teacher hopes that his material will meet the goals established by learners and will be used in their executive activities. In distance education, whether or not the material is used remains outside the distant teacher's control, and is dependent almost entirely on the worth of the material, as distant learners accept only executive material that meets their goals.

Similarly in evaluation, the conventional teacher invariably establishes both the criteria of successful learning and passes judgment on whether the criteria are satisfied; where the teachers' and learners' goals do not coincide the latter invariably compromise through fear, apathy or courtesy. This learner autonomy is heightened by distance and the learner is compelled by distance to assume a degree of autonomy that might be uncomfortable in other circumstances.

Programmes are classified according to the extent to which the learner can exercise autonomy in learning by asking three questions:

° <u>Autonomy in setting of objectives</u>? Is the selection of learning objectives in the programme that of the learner or the teacher?
° <u>Autonomy in methods of study</u>? Is the selection and use of resource persons, of bodies and other media, the decision of the teacher or the learner?
° <u>Autonomy in evaluation</u>? Are the decisions about the method of evaluation and criteria to be used made by the learner or teacher?

By applying these questions to teaching programmes Moore arrives at the following classification in which A = learner determined (autonomous) and N = teacher determined (non-autonomous). An indication of the type of programme Moore might be considering is given for each of his eight categories.

Since learner autonomy is the extent to which in an independent study programme the learner determines the objectives, implementation strategies and evaluation and since distance means a combination of the availability of two-way communication plus the extent to which a programme is adaptable to the individuality of students, it follows that Moore can classify all educational programmes by his own variables 'distance' and 'autonomy'.

This he proposes to do by super-imposing Figure 4.3. on Figure 4.4 in such a way that he can categorise all educational programmes so that they range from having most independent study to the least independent study.

In diagram 4.5 type AAA-D-S represents the most independent form of education: totally private study with no two-way-communication and completely unstructured with the learner completely autonomous in goals, methods and evaluation. Type NNN+D-S is the least independent where autonomy and distance are very low and the learner is extremely controlled by the teacher.

Thus for Moore independent study is any educational programme in which the learning programme occurs separate in time and place from the teaching programme, and in which the learner has an influence at least equal to the teacher in determining learning goals, resources and evaluation decisions.

But learners vary in the extent to which they are able to exercise autonomy and hence there is no value judgment in the use of the terms 'autonomy' and 'distance'. There are programmes with much autonomy and dialogue and programmes with less, and they vary in distance. A programme of high autonomy may be as damaging to a person as one of low autonomy. The problem is to match programmes to learners so that each learner exercises the maximum autonomy and grows.

The first pole of his theoretical position 'distance' is well established, but further contribution is required from Moore to justify 'autonomy' (1972, 1983) as a second pole.

| A/N | Example | Objective Setting | Implementation | Evaluation |
|---|---|---|---|---|
| A = Learner Determined ('Autonomous') | 1. Private study | A | A | A |
| | 2. University of London External Degree | A | A | N |
| | 3. Learning sports skills | A | N | A |
| | 4. Learning car driving | A | N | N |
| | 5. Learner controls course and evaluation | N | A | A |
| | 6. Learner controls evaluation | N | N | A |
| | 7. Many independent study courses | N | A | N |
| N = Teacher Determined "Non-autonomous" | 8. Independent study for credit | N | N | N |

Figure 4.4. Types of independent study programmes by variable learner autonomy (Moore)

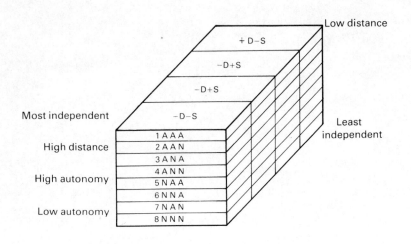

Figure 4.5 Typology of educational programmes
(Moore)

References

Childs, G. and Wedemeyer, C.A. (1961) New perspective in university correspondence study. Chicago: Centre for Study of Education of Adults.
Delling, R.M. (1966) Versuch der Grundlegung zu einer systematischen Theorie des Fernunterrichts, In Sroka, L. (ed.) Fernunterricht 1966, Festschrift zum 50 Geburtstag von Walter Schultz-Rahe. Hamburg: Hamburger Fernlehrinstitut.
Delling, R.M. (1968) Protokoll des I Brief-Sympositions über Fernunterrich und Fernstudium. Epistoldidaktika, 1 (Sonderheft) 6-10.
Delling, R.M. (1978) Briefwechsel als Bestandteil und Vorlaufer des Fernstudiums (Ziff Papiere 19). Hagen: FeU (ZIFF).
Ellis, J. (1978) A response to Charles A. Wedemeyer. Canadian Journal of University Continuing Education, 6,1,16-17.
Holmberg, B. (1960) On the methods of teaching by correspondence. Lund: Gleerup.
Moore, M. (1972) Learner autonomy: the second dimension of independent learning. Convergence,

5,2,76-78.
Moore, M. (1973) Toward a theory of independent learning and teaching. Journal of Higher Education, 44,661-679.
Moore, M. (1975) Cognitive style and telemathic (distance) teaching. ICCE Newsletter, 4,3-10.
Moore, M. (1977a) A model of independent study. Epistolodidaktika, 1,6-40.
Moore, M. (1977b) On a theory of independent study. Hagen: FernUniversität.
Moore, M. (1983) The individual adult learner. In Tight, M. (ed.) Adult learning and education. London: Croom Helm.
Riechert, J. (1959) Schreiben, Lehren und Verstehen, Freiberg: Bergakademie.
Wedemeyer, C. (1962) Report of the conference on newer media in correspondence study. Austin, Texas: University Texas, 10-14.
Wedemeyer, C. (1963) Going to college at home. Home Study Review, 4,3,24-32.
Wedemeyer, C. (1968) With whom will you dance? The new educational technology Journal of the American Dietetic Association, 53,325-328.
Wedemeyer, C. (1971) Independent study. In Deighton, L. (ed.) The encyclopaedia of education. New York: Macmillan, 4,548-557.
Wedemeyer, C. (1973) The use of correspondence education for post-secondary education. In Kabwasa, A. and Kaunda, M. (eds.) Correspondence education in Africa. London: Routledge and Kegan Paul.
Wedemeyer, C. (1974) Characteristics of open learning systems. In Open learning systems. Washington: National Association of Educational Broadcasters.
Wedemeyer, C. (1977) Independent study. In Knowles, A.S. (ed.) The international encyclopaedia of higher education. Boston: CIHED, 2114-2132.
Wedemeyer, C. (1978) Criteria for constructing and distance education system, 6,1,9-15. Canadian Journal of University Continuing Education, 6,1,9-15.
Wedemeyer, C. (1981) Learning at the back-door. Madison: University of Wisconsin.

CHAPTER FIVE

THE INDUSTRIALISATION OF TEACHING

Anyone professionally involved in education is
obliged to presume the existence of two forms of
instruction which are strictly separable: traditional face-to-face teaching based on interpersonal communication and industrialised teaching
which is based on an objectivised, rationalised,
technologically - produced interaction.   O. Peters,
1973.

## Introduction

Much of the early research work in distance education was accomplished by Otto Peters in the early
1960s. Peters worked at the German Institute for
Distance Education (D.I.F.F.) at Tübingen in the
Federal Republic of Germany, then at the Berlin
College of Education before becoming in 1975 the
foundation Vice-Chancellor (Gründungsrektor) of
the Fernuniversität in Hagen.  In 1965 he published
an authoritative analytical and comparative survey
of distance institutions at further education level
throughout the world.  This was followed in 1968
by a survey of distance teaching at higher education
level.
     Peters states that, when his analytical and
comparative analysis of distance teaching systems
was complete, he proceeded to develop a theoretical
structure for the field.  He claims that the traditional categories of educational research proved
inadequate for a didactical analysis of distance
systems and he was forced to abandon them. Building
up systems for teaching at a distance, he tells
us, is structured so differently from conventional,
oral education that the didactical analyst must
look elsewhere for his models. For Peters the most
fruitful model was the similarities between the
industrial production process and the teaching/
learning process in distance education. He analysed
the industrial production process and found that
not only did this provide a satisfactory basis
for an analysis of distance teaching but that a
fruitful explanatory and forecasting theory of
teaching at a distance was possible when one considered it as the most industrialised form of teaching and learning.

Peters justified his search for a new theoretical basis for distance teaching on the grounds that it is a new form of industrialised and technological education. He states that from many points of view conventional, oral, group-based education is a pre-industrial form of education.

In the universities of the middle ages, the ancient rhetorical form of education was replaced by the lecture, the seminar and the lesson and these have remained permanent characteristics of traditional education ever since. The humanistic influence added the tutorial. These can all be regarded as pre-industrialised forms of education in which the individual lecturer remains in close contact with the whole teaching process just as an artisan does with his craft. Attempts to adapt the lecture, seminar and tutorial to industrialised techniques by the use of educational technology will not prove successful because of the pre-industrial characteristics of the didactic structures.

Distance teaching however is recent. It could not have existed before the Industrial Era. It began, at most, 130 years ago, he says, writing in 1980. It was no historical accident that correspondence education and the industrialisation of society began about the same time because they are intrinsically linked. Distance education is impossible without a relatively fast and regular postal service and transport system: 'the first railway lines and the first correspondence schools were established around the same time'.

Traditional educational concepts are only of partial use in analysing and describing this industrialised form of education so new categories for analysis must be found and they can best be found from the sciences which analyse industrial processes. All forms of human life have been heavily influenced by the industrial revolution. Only traditional forms of education in schools, colleges and universities have remained outside it - except for the phenomenon of education at a distance. Then Peters justifies his decision to compare distance education with the industrial production of goods as the most satisfactory way of explaining it. It should be realised that Peters does this only for what he calls heuristic reasons, that is for explanatory purposes. He finds some justifications for this in the fact that the production of learning materials for distance students is, in itself, an industrialised process and one that is quite different in its teaching procedures from book production.

## Didactical analysis

Peters' theoretical presentation of distance teaching commences with a didactical analysis. In this presentation distance teaching is analysed as a distinct field of educational endeavour and not as a teaching 'mode'. The analysis of the didactic structure of distance teaching (1967:3-17) follows exactly the structures proposed by Paul Heimann and Wolfgang Schultz, two German educational technologists who founded the Berlin School of didactics - now also referred to as the Hamburg model, as Schultz is now a professor at the University of Hamburg (Heidt, 1978:48, Holmberg, 1982:139).

Heimann and Schultz claim that all teaching-learning processes can be analysed in terms of six intrinsic structural elements: aims, content, methods, choice of medium, human pre-requisites and socio-cultural pre-requisites. Peters analyses distance education, as Heimann and Schultz had analysed education in general, in terms of the six essential structures of the educational process in this model and has little difficulty in demonstrating profound structural differences between distance education and conventional education for all six of the constituent characteristics (1967: 4-16).

Aim The aim of distance teaching is determined by structural considerations as in all forms of teaching. Specific structural differences in the cognitive, emotional and practical domains are indicated for distance teaching.

Contents The teaching of knowledge, skills and practical 'hand-on' learning are examined and the difficulties and/or possibility of teaching certain content at a distance is considered.

Methods The drastic reduction or complete suppression of interpersonal communication is treated and its substitution by written information carriers and motivators.

Choice of medium It is claimed that communication suffers an essential loss of substance in its transfer from human speech to the written word and the possible compensating role of other media is considered.

Human pre-requisites Employment conditions, age, diagnostic counselling for entry to courses are contrasted with the condition of conventional students.

Socio-cultural pre-requisites Ideological, political, academic status and tradition aspects of distance education in different cultures (U.S.A., U.S.S.R., South Africa, England, Sweden) are considered.

The conclusion for Peters is inescapable. Distance education and conventional education have been shown to be essentially diverse on each of the six constituent components of an educational process as defined by the most 'adequate theoretical basis for dealing with instructional media' (Heidt, 1978:47) known to German educational theorists. This analysis leads to a fundamental separation between direct and indirect teaching and the claim that educational theorists have focused on direct teaching, especially in its conventional oral, group-based form to the virtual exclusion of that other component of the educational scene: indirect teaching, of which distance teaching is one of the elements. He lists the other components of teaching which are not direct, but which are not however, to be identified as distance education: education by letter; printed learning materials; audio-visual teaching; educational radio and television; programmed learning; computer-based instruction; independent study; private study and learning from teaching materials.

Industrial comparison

At this point in his treatment of the subject (1967, 1971, 1973, 1981) Peters presents a comparison of distance teaching and the industrial production of goods under the following headings: rationalisation; division of labour; mechanisation; assembly line; mass production; preparatory work; formalisation; standarisation; functional change; objectification; concentration and centralisation.

Rationalisation is seen as a characteristic of distance teaching when the knowledge and skills of a teacher are transmitted to a theoretically unlimited number of students by the detached objectivity of a distance education course of constant quality.

<u>Division of labour</u> is the main pre-requisite for the advantages of distance teaching to become effective and is thus a constituent element of it. If the number of students enrolled in a distance course is high, regular assessment of performance is not carried out by those academics who developed the course and other elements of the teaching/learning process are assigned to others.

<u>Mechanisation</u> Conventional education proceeds at a pre-industrial level with the teacher using the tools of the trade (pictures, objects, books) without these changing the structure of teaching; in distance teaching mechanisation eventually changes the nature of the teaching process.

<u>Assembly line</u> In distance teaching the staff remain at their posts but the teaching (manuscript for example) is passed from one area of responsibility to another and specific changes are made at each stage.

<u>Mass production</u> Traditional forms of teaching envisage small groups and can only be applied to mass education artificially (e.g. a loudspeaker from one lecture hall to an adjoining one). Distance teaching copes confidently with mass production which is essential to it.

<u>Planning and preparation</u> As in industry distance teaching is characterised by extensive planning by senior specialist staff in special departments and prior financial investment. Success is linked to the preparatory phase in a way that is different from conventional teaching.

<u>Standardisation</u> A greater degree of standarisation is required than in conventional teaching and the educational advantages of the interesting deviation at a particular time with a particular group of students is not possible: the objective requirements of the total course profile dominate the particular interests of the teacher.

<u>Functional change and objectification</u> are further essential elements of the most industrialised form of education especially when the functional role of teacher is split at least three ways: provider of knowledge (distance unit author), evaluator of knowledge and progress (course maker or tutor) and counsellor (subject programme adviser).

Monopolisation. Concentration and centralisation are characteristics of the management of distance systems and of industrial enterprise; distance teaching institutions have a tendency to monopolisation within a state or national educational provision.

## Educational technology

The completion of this comparative study of distance education and the industrial production of goods leads Peters to an analysis of distance teaching in the light of current ideas (mid 1960s) about educational technology. He follows distance education through five groupings of educational technologists which he takes over from the German didactician Flechsig:

    (i)   simulation models,
    (ii)  planning models (Zweckrationalität),
    (iii)materials development strategies,
    (iv)  systems approach,
    (v)   curriculum development.

Peters studies the affinities between distance education and educational technology, especially programmed learning. He shares with Flechsig and the eduational technologists of the period the belief that planning and technology will achieve educational success. It was felt that the application of technical categories to educational processes would achieve beneficial results and that systematic planning and rationalisation of educational means to reach defined goals (Zweckrationalität) could achieve both educational and economic efficiency.

## Conclusions

The final dimension of Peter's analysis of distance education is what he calls the historical, sociological and anthropological perspective. Humanistic attacks on the industrialisation of society and its contribution to mass culture lead Peters to expect criticism from humanists of his theory of distance education as the most industrialised form of education.

    Tracing the historical evolution of educational structures back to Indo-European origins Peters finds them characterised by six elements: elitism; sacral aspects; hierarchical aspects; family-small group structures; personal communication and time-place-person ties. Distance education is the final phase of evolution of education from these socio-cultural structures, presenting a new, strange and foreign educational pattern that has six characteristics: it is egalitarian, profane, demo-cratic, aimed at a mass audience, technologically-based and free from the dimensions of educational time, places and persons.

A sociological analysis based on the German philosophical Gemeinschaft/Gesellschaft positions taken from Weber, Tönnies and Habermas shows that traditional, oral, group-based education follows the 'Gemeinschaft' categorisation with distance education falling into the 'Gesellschaft' grouping. In general terms 'Gemeinschaft' structures are friendly and community-based; Gesellschaft implies a wider, society-based structure that may be un-friendly. The communication processes within these two sociological groupings show that the inter-subjectivity and reciprocity of inter-personal communication in conventional education is radically to be contrasted with the 'context-free', mechanical communication of education at a distance. The possibility of alienation is not overlooked.

Peters sees as practical consequences of his theory that there is something unnatural about education at a distance. The process of communi-cation is broken up and artificial substitutes for it are provided. Then the whole communication process is changed and this changes the teaching acts and the learning acts which take place in the education system. He feels that it is a slow process for a teacher to adapt to a distance edu-cation system because there will always be clashes between traditional teaching and the carefully structured procedures of a distance teaching uni-versity, in which the unity of the teaching/learning process is split into many units performed by dif-ferent persons and elements of the education system. The process of adaptation however can be furthered by reflection on the characteristics of distance education. The student in an industrialised edu-cation system finds that instruction is available in such ways that he can choose his own way. In-struction is not linked to fixed times, to fixed places, to fixed persons. This throws new responsi-bilities on the learner that are not characteristic of pre-industrialised education systems.

Peters has no desire to criticise conventional education. His view, however, is that in-

dustrialised society of today has developed so
many needs for education that it is absurd to im-
agine that conventional systems can satisfy them.
New techniques are needed and these must be industrial. He recognises that traditionalists will
say: What happens to the highly valued traditions
of face-to-face education? What happens to the
spirit of the learning community? These are all,
he admits, of value but you cannot have 40,000-
50,000 students in a system like an open university
and try to provide face-to-face tuition with finite
means. Almost alone among distance educators writing about distance education, Peters finds much
to query in the industralisation of education.
He finds distance education unnatural; it breaks
up the process of communication; artificial mechanical substitutes for interpersonal communication
are provided; this changes the teaching behaviours
and the learning behaviours; there is a definite
propensity to alienation. If you are going to
teach in the most industrialised form of education,
he tells us, you have to be ready to live with
the problems that the industrialisation of education
brings.

Evaluation

Reactions and objections to Peters' thesis have
been many and there are those who deplore the introduction of industrial concepts into an educational
field. Four of these reactions are considered
here: Christof Ehmann, Karl-Heinz Rebel, Manfred
Hamann and integrationist responses.

Ehmann (1981:231) criticises Peters' position
because of its dependence on faith in the value
of planning in education and faith in technical
progress. He claims that these faiths, strong
in the 1960s, have been shown to be wrong in the
1980s and that 'the application of technical categories to social processes is just as questionable
as the use of biological analogies:' Planning
euphoria, programmed learning, faith in the cal-
culability of processes - all central features
of Peters' industrialised models - have all been
dissipated before the 1980s started.
   Ehmann's evaluation of Peters' contribution
is negative. He feels that as an academic position
it is largely dated because of its reliance on
theories of planning and technical progress, that
its influence on Peters' own institution - the

Fernuniversität - has been nil, as has been its influence on the world of commercial correspondence schools.

Karl-Heinz Rebel complains (1983:200) that 'the basis of Otto Peters' assumption - the six inter-dependent elements that constitute each teaching - learning process (the so called Berlin Didactic School of Paul Heimann and Wolfgang Schulz) - could never be expressed in such a way that research data capable of falsifying this theory could be collected'. This statement is probably true. But is it helpful?
    The data provided by Peters in the 650 pages of his (1965) Der Fernunterricht. Materialien zur Diskussion einer neunen Unterrichtsform, followed by the closely researched 620 pages of his (1968) Das Hochschulfernstudium. Materialien zur Diskussion einer neuen Studienform provide an impeccable data-base for the grounding of a theoretical position.

Hamann argues that all forms of Zweckrationalität whether they be called media didactics, learning psychology, systems theory or information theory, have been without success: there have been oc-casional glimpses of didactic possibilities but no progress towards increased cost-efficiency in education. He accuses Peters of simply applying the structure of Heimann-Schultz to distance edu-cation and nothing more. This reproach is jus-tifiable for only the didactical analysis part of Peters' presentation. The theory of indus-trialisation is certainly original and owes nothing to Heimann-Schultz either in its presentation or in its origin.

Integrationist criticisms. There are critics of Peters' position who claim that he exaggerates the difference between conventional education and distance education. Many professors at the Fern-universität would argue that learning at university level consists of extensive readings plus occasional meetings with one's professor and distance edu-cation is composed of extensive reading plus oc-casional meetings with a tutor. The long tradition of German university teaching is based on learning from textual materials so that Peters' position tends to over-emphasise the difference in the com-munication process in distance education.
    Australian systems in which numbers of students are taught on-campus and off-campus by the same

lecturer reflect a similar position. In the external studies division of the University
of Queensland, for instance, each lecturer has
responsibility for a defined group of students.
For these students the lecturer devises the course,
develops the learning materials, sees them through
the production process, checks the proofs, marks
the assignments for the students when enrolled,
provides correspondence and telephone tuition as
required, may visit the students either at study
centres or in their homes, conducts the examinations. Where, representatives of this system
ask, is the division of labour, the industrialisation, the mass production in this system? Where
is the great role differentiation between the lecturer in a conventional and a distance system?

Peters has not replied to these critics. His
most recent contribution to distance education
theory (1981:47-63) merely restates his position.
It implies that if he were to restate his theory
today for the mid-1980s he would change only the
references to economic theory and industrial analysis but would maintain the didactical structure
of his position. He claims that by substituting
more modern economic and industrial references
he could produce a theory of the industrialisation
of education even more convincing than what he
has achieved so far.

It is disappointing to find that the 1981
presentation repeats word-for-word the formulation
of the theoretical position as it was in 1967.
The positions of scholars like Ehmann, Rebel and
Hamann have not been answered.

Peters' strength is his knowledge of distance
systems as they were throughout the world in the
period 1960-1965 and the fact that his theoretical
positions are clearly grounded in the data he
accumulated at that time. The theory has also
a certain heuristic value, in that it offers some
explanation of the nature of educational institutions in which the warehouse and the production
process dominate and in which there are few educational installations and that such systems have
a propensity to alienation and monopolisation.

## References

Ehmann, C. (1981) Fernstudium/Fernunterricht. Re-
    flections on Otto Peters' research. Distance
    Education, 2,2,228-233.
Hamann, M. (1978) Fernstudienkonzeptionen für

den tertiären Bildungsbereich. Analyse des Scheiterns bildungspolitischer Reformversuche in einem Teilbereich. Hamburg: Arbeitsgemeinschaft für Hochschuldidaktik.

Heidt, E. (1978) Instructional media and the individual learner. London: Kogan Page.

Holmberg, B. (1982) Scholarship and ideology: a study of present-day West German educational thinking. Compare, 12,2,133-142.

Peters, O. (1965) Der Fernunterricht. Materialien zur Diskussion einer neuen Unterrichtsform. Weinheim: Beltz.

Peters, O. (1967) Das Fernstudium an Universitäten und Hochschulen. Didaktische Struktur und vergleichende Interpretation: ein Beitrag zur Theorie der Fernlehne. Weinheim: Beltz.

Peters, O. (1968) Das Hochschulfernstudium. Materialien zur Diskussion einer neuen Studienform. Weinheim: Beltz.

Peters, O. (1971) Theoretical aspects of correspondence instruction. In Mackenzie, O. and Christensen, E.L. (eds) The changing world of correspondence study. University Park and London: Penn. State.

Peters, O. (1973) Die didaktische Struktur des Fernunterrichts. Untersuchungen zu einer industrialisierten Form des Lehrens und Lernens. Weinheim: Beltz.

Peters, O. (1981) Fernstudium and industrielle Produktion. Skizze einer vergleichenden Interpretation. In Clever, P. et al (eds) Okonomische Theorie und wirtschaftliche Praxis. Herne/Berlin: Neue Wirtschaftsbriefe.

Rebel, K.H. (1983) Distance study in West Germany: the D.I.F.F.'s conceptional contribution. Distance Education 4,2,171-178.

CHAPTER SIX

INTERACTION AND COMMUNICATION

Whatever a dead teacher may accomplish in the classroom, he can do nothing by correspondence.   William
Rainey Harper, 1880


Introduction

This chapter presents writers who have emphasized
interaction and communication as central to any
concept of distance education.   In very general
terms Moore, Wedemeyer and Delling tended to concentrate on the autonomy and isolation of
the student as the basis for their views, while
Peters' focus is the functions of the institution
developing learning materials.   The authors in
this chapter take as their starting point the role
of the institution in providing a satisfactory
learning experience for students, once the materials
have been developed and dispatched.
        Five authors have been selected: Bääth,
Holmberg, Daniel, Sewart and K.C. Smith.   Bääth
is particularly associated with an emphasis on
two-way communication and Holmberg with a theory
of guided didactic conversation.   Daniel, Sewart
and Smith are, or have been, managers of distance
systems.   They would probably blush to be called
theorists.   Their writings are developed from the
day-to-day pressure of managing distance systems.
Their inclusion is justified by the wide-ranging
and influential character of their contributions.

Two-way communication

John A. Bääth (pronounced 'boat') is Swedish and
worked for many years for Hermods at Malmö.   His
work benefits from a knowledge of the literature
of distance education in the Scandinavian languages,
English, German and French.   During the 1970s he
was associated with the concept two-way communication in correspondence education.   He would not
claim to be the originator of the concept but made

91

an important theoretical and empirical contribution to establishing this idea as a major defining feature of distance systems today.

One part of his research aimed to relate modern education research to distance education. He examined the applicability of the teaching models of Skinner, Rothkopf, Ausubel, Egan, Bruner, Rogers and Gagné to correspondence education which he regards as a subset of distance education (1980:12). He was able to show the functions of two-way communication in correspondence education in the light of each of the teaching models:

| MODEL | TWO-WAY COMMUNICATION |
|---|---|
| B.K.Skinner's behaviour control model | Checking students' achievements; individualizing functions: assess students' starting-level, consider special abilities, previous reinforcement patterns. |
| E.Z.Rothkopf's model for written instruction | Helping students get started. |
| D.P. Ausubel's advance organizers model | Determine each students' previous knowledge and cognitive structure. Promote positive transfer to subsequent parts of course. |
| K. Egan's model for structural communication | Individually devised discussion comments and "reverse" assignments. |
| J. Bruner's discovery learning model | Provide individually adapted help. Stimulate students' discovery of knowledge. |
| C. Rogers' model for facilitation of learning | Check 'open' assignments for submission; dialogue with each individual student. |
| R.M. Gagné's general teaching model | Activating motivation Stimulating recall Providing learner guidance Providing feedback |

Figure 6.1. Analysis of teaching models (Bääth)

His conclusions are:

° Models with stricter control of learning towards fixed goals tend to imply, in distance
education, a greater emphasis on the teaching
material than on the two-way communication
between student and tutor/institution.

° Models with less control of learning towards
fixed goals tend to make simultaneous communication between student and tutor/institution
more desirable; this communication taking
the form of either face-to-face or telephone
contacts. (1979:21).

Holmberg (1981:27) summarises Bääth's analysis:

° All the models investigated are applicable
to distance study.

° Some of them (Skinner, Gagné, Rothkopf,
Ausubel, Structural communication) seem particularly adaptable to distance study in its
fairly strictly structured form.

° Bruner's more open model and even Rogers'
model can be applied to distance study, though
not without special measures, e.g. concerning
simultaneous non-contiguous communication
(telephone, etc.).

° Demands on distance study systems which would
inspire new developments can be inferred from
the models studied.

In Postal two-way communication in correspondence Bääth adds empirical analysis of two-way
communication to the theoretical analysis of his
previous book. In particular he studied:

(i)   the relationship of submission density
      (frequency of assignment submission during
      a course) to two-way communication.
(ii)  the replacement of tutor marked assign-
      ments by self assessment questions and
(iii) the introduction of computer marked
      assignments as a form of two-way communi-
      cation.

Bääth's theoretical and conceptual contributions
stem from his experience in Sweden. He tells us
how his own situation led to his involvement:

> From its beginnings... correspondence
> education often grew into big enterprises,
> where the teaching became more indus-
> trialised - if you allow the expression
> of Otto Peters - with considerable divi-
> sion of labour, specialisation of teaching
> functions, mass production of the ma-
> terial, application of the assembly line
> principle for certain functions, piece-
> wages to the correspondence tutors, and
> so on.  As we know, this mass education
> form of teaching is nowadays the prevalent
> type of correspondence education.
>
> What about the role of two-way com-
> munication by mail in this kind of corre-
> spondence teaching?  Is it still an im-
> portant element?
>
> This question became real to me
> during the sixties when I worked as a
> correspondence course writer, editor
> and senior tutor.  From personal experi-
> ence I found that a correspondence tutor
> could stimulate his students to most
> remarkable improvements, by means of
> constructive criticism, encouragement
> and personal involvement in the individual
> student's learning problems.
>
> When writing correspondence course
> materials I was struck by the idea that
> it was possible to provide some kind
> of two-way communication within the ma-
> terial, by means of exercises, questions
> or self-check tests with detailed model
> or specimen answers.  Could such two-
> way communication, to any considerable
> extent, replace the postal two-way com-
> munication induced by assignments for
> submission? (1980:11-12)

This combination of personal experience and theoretical and empirical investigation led Bääth to
place two-way communication as central to the distance education process and the distant tutor
as central to his concept.

Bääth writes well of the importance of the
tutor in a distance system.  He indicates that
there is evidence to show that distance learners
need special help with the start of their studies
and that they need help in particular to promote
their study motivation. (1982:22)

Bääth sees the role of the tutor going well

beyond that of correcting errors and assessing
students' progress:

> This is the role of the distant tutor:
> he can have important pedagogical func-
> tions, not only that of correcting errors
> and assessing students' papers. He may
> play a principal part in the linking
> of learning materials to learning - by
> trying to relate the learning material
> to each student's previous reinforcement
> patterns (Skinner), or to his mathemagenic
> activities (Rothkopf), or to his previous
> knowledge and cognitive structure
> (Ausubel), or to his previous compre-
> hension of the basic concepts and prin-
> ciples of the curriculum (Bruner), or
> by concentrating on the task of estab-
> lishing a good personal relationship
> with the learner (Rogers) - as I have
> tried to demonstrate (Bääth, 1980:121).

and he quotes with approval the hundred year-old
statement on tutors in correspondence studies:

> The correspondence teacher must be pains-
> taking, patient, sympathetic and alive;
> whatever a dead teacher may accomplish
> in the classroom, he can do nothing by
> correspondence. (William Rainey Harper,
> 1880)

A query about Bääth's work is that he does
not seem to attempt a theoretical framework for
two-way communication in correspondence education.
He has greatly furthered our understanding of two-
way communication but has not explained how it
would fit in an overview of this field.

## Guided didactic conversation

Börje Holmberg (pronounced Burr-ye Holm-bery) is
also from Sweden and today is Professor of the
Methodology of Distance Education at the Fern-
Universitat in Hagen in the Federal Republic of
Germany. He has written profusely on distance
education in Swedish, German and English.
A number of characteristic traits link together
the publications of Holmberg across a twenty-five
year span. Among these are a generous, humanistic
philosophy that values highly student independence

and autonomy, an early concentration on two-way communication in distance education, an emerging concept of distance education as guided didactic conversation, an unhappiness with non-print media and the provision of face-to-face sessions as components of a system, a concentration on assignment marking and its importance in a system, a difficulty to move from further education to university level education (Hermods is cited, even in 1981, as an example for a university teaching at a distance - 1981:45).

Like the dedicated humanist he is, Holmberg bases his view of distance education on his conviction that the only important thing in education is learning by individual students. Administration, counselling, teaching, group work, enrolment and evaluation are of importance only in so far as they support individual learning. He would like to see systems with completely free pacing, a free choice of examination periods and plenty of two-way communication for tutorial and feedback purposes.

Distance education is considered to be particularly suitable for individual learning because it is usually based on personal work by individual students more or less independent from the direct guidance of tutors. The distance student is in a situation where the chances of individually selecting what educational offerings he/she is to partake of can be much greater than that of conventional students. The student studying at a distance can, and frequently does, ignore elements of the teaching package that has been prepared for the course being studied. TV programmes or comments on assignments or face-to-face sessions or visits to study centres may all be ignored.

Holmberg characterises study in a distance system as self-study but it is not, he insists, private reading, for the student is not alone. The student benefits from having a course developed for him and also from interaction with his tutors and other representatives of a supporting organisation. The relationship between the supporting organisation and the student is described as a guided didactic conversation. The general approach agrees closely with Wedemeyer's. Holmberg insists on allowing students a maximum freedom of choice in matters of both content and study procedures, individual pacing of the study and far-reaching autonomy generally. Two-way communication in writing and on the telephone between students and tutors has been one of his chief concerns. Students' assignments are regarded as facilitators of this communication rather than as instruments of assessment.

Distance education is seen as a guided didactic conversation that aims at learning and it is felt that the presence of the typical traits of successful conversation will facilitate learning. The continuous interaction between the student on the one hand and the tutors and counsellors and other representatives of the institution administering the study programme is seen as a kind of conversation. There is a kind of two-way conversational traffic through the written and telephone interaction between student and institution. More dubiously Holmberg also argues for what he calls simulated conversation from the students' study of the learning materials that have been prepared in a didactic style.

Holmberg's view of distance education as guided didactic conversation might be presented schematically thus:

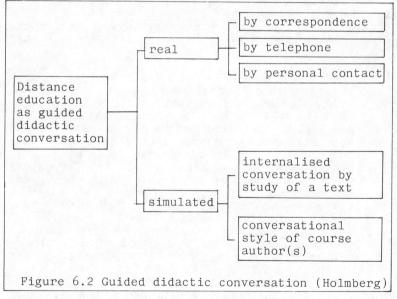

Figure 6.2 Guided didactic conversation (Holmberg)

There are traces of these ideas in Holmberg's early writings but it is only in recent years that he has developed them into the basis for a general theory of distance education.

In <u>On the methods of teaching by correspondence</u>

in 1960 he wrote:

> A considerable portion of all oral tuition
> can rightly be described as didactive
> conversation. In a great number of suc-
> cessful correspondence courses the at-
> mosphere and style of such conversation
> is found. It is typical of the style
> of didactive conversation that advice
> is given on how to tackle problems, what
> to learn more or less carefully, how
> to connect items of knowledge discussed
> in different lessons and this also
> characterises many good correspondence
> courses. It seems to me that advice
> and suggestions should preferably be
> expressed in phrases of personal address,
> such as "When you have read these para-
> graphs, make sure that...". (1960:15-
> 16)

The same paragraph appears with 'didactive' changed
to 'didactic' in Holmberg 1967:26-27 and is repeated
in Distance education: a short handbook 1974:27-
28 and in 1982 in the revised edition of that book.
Elsewhere Holmberg gives seven bases for his position:

1. that feelings of personal relation between
   the teaching and learning parties promote
   study pleasure and motivation;
2. that such feelings can be fostered by well
   developed self-instructional material and
   suitable two-way communication at a distance;
3. that intellectual pleasure and study motivation
   are favourable to the attainment of study
   goals and the use of proper study processes
   and methods;
4. that the atmosphere, language and conventions
   of friendly conversation favour feelings of
   personal relation according to postulate 1;
5. that messages given and received in conversational forms are comparatively easily understood and remembered;
6. that the conversation concept can be success-
   fully translated for use by the media available
   to distance education;
7. that planning and guiding the work, whether
   provided by the teacher organisation or the
   student are necessary for organised study,
   which is characterised by explicit or implicit

goal concepts. (1978:20 repeated 1983:115-116).

Distance learning materials developed in the light of Holmberg's theory of guided didactic conversation would present the following characteristics:

° Easily accessible presentations of study matter: clear, somewhat colloquial language, in writing that is easily readable; moderate density of information.

° Explicit advice and suggestions to the student as to what to do and what to avoid, what to pay particular attention to and consider, with reasons provided.

° Invitations to an exchange of views, to questions, to judgements of what is to be accepted and what is to be rejected.

° Attempts to involve the student emotionally so that he or she takes a personal interest in the subject and its problems.

° Personal style including the use of the personal and possessive pronouns.

° Demarcation of changes of themes through explicit statements, typographical means or, in recorded, spoken communications, through a change of speakers, e.g. male followed by female, or through pauses. (This is a characteristic of the guidance rather than of the conversation.) (1983:117)

If a course is prepared following these principles Holmberg (1977) forecasts that it will be attractive to students, will motivate students to study and will facilitate learning. In two interesting experiments Holmberg recently re-wrote a Fernuniversitat post-graduate course on educational planning and a basic Hermods course on English grammar in accordance with his theoretical position and replaced the rather analytical textbook-like approaches of the originals with a more conversational style designed to promote empathy with the student.

By any estimation Holmberg's contribution to the field of distance education is extensive (1979, 1980). His early pre-occupation with two-way communication in correspondence education provided an impetus for the research of Bääth, Flinck and Wängdahl in the 1970s. Although he is not the only scholar to recommend a conversational

style for distance learning materials he has been
the only one who has developed a coherent theory
from his early (1960:8) statement:

> 'A correspondence course must by defi-
> nition be something different from a
> textbook with questions. A correspondence
> course provides actual teaching by itself
> and is thus a substitute for both a text-
> book and the exposition of a teacher,'

and then submitted it to empirical testing. In
general this position has been beneficial
to practicioners in the field and has contributed
to making distance learning materials now a recog-
nisably different genre from text books.

## Interaction and independence

From 1973 to 1977 John Daniel was director
of studies at the Télé-université, Université du
Québec, and then Vice-President, Learning Services
at Athabasca University in Edmonton, Alberta,
Canada. In 1980 he took up the post of Vice-Rector
(Academic) of Concordia University, a conventional
university in Montreal and moved to Laurentian
University, a conventional university with a small
distance department in the summer of 1984.

Daniel has thus had experience of academic
management in both French and English distance
systems and his theorising about distance education
is frequently from a management perspective. He
sees the emergence of distance education systems
as coming from three sources: a long tradition
of independent study; modern developments in the
technology of education; new theoretical interest
in open learning. The fusion of these elements
has produced new educational enterprises which
teach at a distance and fulfil important economic
and political needs of societies.

When Holmberg and Bääth write extensively
of two-way communication in education at a distance
they envisage constantly a situation in which the
major part of the communication will be by postal
correspondence; Daniel (writing from the start
from a university perspective) sees distance systems
as comprising activities in which the student works
alone and those which bring him into contact with
other people. The first grouping of activities
he labels 'independent activities' and the latter
'interactive'. He provides a listing of possible

activities in the two groups:

| Independent | Interactive |
|---|---|
| - reading a text<br>- watching television at home<br>- conducting a home experiment<br>- writing an assignment | - discussion on telephone<br>- marking and commenting on assignments<br>- group discussions<br>- residential summer schools |

Figure 6.3. Interaction and independence (Daniel)

A major function of distance systems is to achieve the difficult synthesis between the two: interaction and independence - getting the mixture right. All learning in a distance system is achieved by a balance between the learning activities the student carries out independently and those which involve interaction with other people. The balance between the two is the crucial issue facing distance study systems.

The balance chosen between the interactive and independent activities in a distance system has extensive repercussions on the administration and economics of the system:

> Independent activities have great possibilities of economies of scale since the marginal costs of printing extra copies of texts or broadcasting to more students are low. However, the cost of interactive activities tends to increase in direct proportion to the number of students. (Daniel and Marquis, 1979:32)

Increasing the proportion of interactive activities improves student performance but it does so at a price. The cost of interactive activities is broadly proportional to the number of students involved. There is little opportunity for the economies of scale which characterise independent activities, and are responsible for the overall cost advantage of distance education. Daniel states that distance systems should be dearer: things done at a distance usually are. He then parts company from much of the writing on the economics of distance education by stating that there are two economic structures for distance systems: one for the independent activities in which economies of scale are possible; and one for the interactive activities in which they may not be. (Snowden and Daniel, 1980).

He believes that courses should not be designed that are entirely independent. Socialisation and feedback are the main functions of the interactive activities and whereas the importance of social-isation in education is less vital for adults study-ing part-time than for children and those involved in compulsory and full-time education, the feedback role of interaction is of crucial importance. Students want to know how they are doing in relation both to their peers and to the criteria of mastery set by the course authors. Distance students are only weakly integrated into the social system of the teaching institution and feel low involvement with it. Therefore they are at risk and the import-ance of interactive activities is enhanced.

The thrust of Daniel's thinking on distance education comes through clearly in his attitude to pacing. (Daniel and Shale, 1979) He suggests that the more freedom a learner has the less likely he is to complete the course. He is of the opinion that distance systems can either give students the dignity of succeeding by pacing them or the freedom to proceed towards failure without pacing. Holmberg, on the other hand, claims that students should be free to pursue distance courses without the pressure of pacing. Where Moore and Wedemeyer emphasize autonomy and independence of the learner studying at a distance, Daniel looks for a balance between interaction and independence in the struc-turing of the system and shows how this affects the pacing of students and the cost structures.

## Continuity of concern

David Sewart joined the Open University of the United Kingdom in 1973. After a period in the Manchester regional office he moved to the uni-versity's central site at Walton Hall near Milton Keynes where he had managerial responsibilities for the provision of support services to students. In 1980 he returned to Manchester as regional di-rector.

Sewart sometimes tries to trace distance edu-cation back as far as the epistles of St. Paul but sees a rapid development in the last two dec-ades. This he attributes to the new communications techniques which have been perfected in the twentieth century, the increasing costs of conventional education and the rapidly expanding range of knowledge.

His theoretical approach to teaching at a distance can be summed up as a continuity of concern for students learning at a distance (1978).

Teaching, he tells us, is a complex matter. It is an amalgam of the provision of knowledge and information plus all the advisory and supportive processes with which this provision is normally surrounded in conventional education. He is unhappy with the notion that the package of materials in a distance system can perform all the functions of the teacher in face-to-face education. He shows that, if it could, it would become an infinitely expensive package as it would have to reflect the complex interactive process of the teacher and each individual student.

In many of his writings he discusses the efforts of course developers in distance systems to produce the 'hypothetically perfect teaching package'. He finds this unrealisable and seeks to prove this with his view of the role of the intermediary in complex civilisations. He argues that just as in most complex bureaucracies an intermediary is necessary (a social worker, a hospital orderly) to bridge the gap between the individual and the institution, so in distance systems an intermediary is necessary between the individual student and the teaching package. The intermediary is employed by the institution but works for the individuals· in the system and individualises their problems when confronted with the bureaucracy.

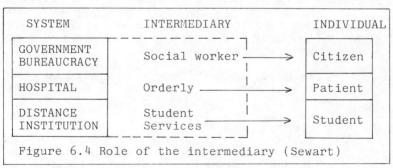

| SYSTEM | INTERMEDIARY | INDIVIDUAL |
|---|---|---|
| GOVERNMENT BUREAUCRACY | Social worker ⟶ | Citizen |
| HOSPITAL | Orderly ⟶ | Patient |
| DISTANCE INSTITUTION | Student Services ⟶ | Student |

Figure 6.4 Role of the intermediary (Sewart)

Sewart's clear emphasis not only on teaching at a distance but on the needs of students learning at a distance, demands an interactive mode in distance systems which can hardly be supplied by the

learning materials however well they are developed.
Failure to recognise this has, he considers, led
to the almost universal lack of esteem for distance
systems which he judges to have been the norm until
quite recently.  He considers that advice and support for students in a system of learning at a
distance poses almost infinitely variable problems
and this creates the need for an advisory and supportive role of a distance institution in addition
to the provision of a teaching package.

Sewart writes clearly of the differences between conventional and distance education and presents both the advantages and disadvantages of
education at a distance.  As advantages he lists:

- Freedom from the 'strait-jacket of the lecture hall'
- ability to study whenever and wherever desired.
- freedom inherent in the individuality of the distance students' situation
- student not bound by the learning pattern of a learning group
- distance students needs are not subservient to the needs of a learning group.

The debits are also well presented in Sewart's
writings:

- no measure of progress available
- no framework of study for the distance student
- no peer group clarification or pressure
- no benchmarks on progress or failure. (1981)

He considers the situation of the student
learning at a distance to be quite different from
that of conventional students because of the absence
of swift feedback and because the learner's peer
group does not act as a benchmark:

> Perhaps this failure to recognise and
> concentrate on individual needs arises
> out of a failure adequately to appreciate
> the difference between the conventional
> student and the student learning at a
> distance.  Conventional students in
> digesting the academic pabulum of their
> chosen study, exist within a highly arti-
> ficial and wholly supportive framework.
> For most of them their study is merely
> a further stage in an unbroken linear
> development which began when they were

infants. Whereas the infant school class and the university lecture have easily discernable differences, they are generically similar in offering a group learning situation with a face-to-face teacher/student contact, and the subsequent possibility for instant feedback of an oral and visual nature. The group learning situation is itself supportive of the learning process, not only because of the potential interaction between students in relation to the academic content of the course - learning through discussion with one's peers - but also because the group learning offers a benchmark to the individual members of the group. The students might naturally expect to fall short of the comprehension of a particular subject which is demonstrated by their teacher. The benchmark of 'how far short or how much of this are we expected to understand?' is provided by the group and through the group a common denominator of success or achievement is established for all its members. The situation of students learning at a distance is wholly different. Often they are returning to learning after a number of years. For such people the concept and practice of their previous learning is somewhat clouded. They have an experience of life and work and hence a framework into which their new learning has to be set. Often the students learning at a distance are part-time. Their work and families are of prime importance. It is not open to them, as it is open to the conventional students, to devote themselves entirely and with singular purpose to learning. Moreover, the process of learning at a distance is generically different from the conventional mode. The swift feedback available from the face-to-face learning model is almost entirely absent. (1980:177).

The differing study patterns of distance students, the need for intermediaries in complex processes, the absence of the learning group against which the distance learner can measure himself and the infinite variety of individual problems

all lead him to the conclusion that the introduction
of the human element is the only way to adapt a
distance system to individual needs. This provision
should ideally be available whenever and as often
as the student needs it and is part of the richness
and variety of a system that can adapt to the needs
of individualised, independent study. Unlike Peters,
however, he clearly sees all education provision
as a continuum with forms of distance education
fusing into conventional provision.

Sewart's views provide an effective counter-
balance to those who see distance education merely
as a materials production process. He claims that
it is the continuity of the institution's concern
for the quality of support in a distance system
that has been the Open University of the United
Kingdom's success in solving the age old problem
of distance systems - the avoidance of avoidable
drop-out.

## An integrated mode

When the University of New England, Armidale, New
South Wales, Australia began teaching externally
in 1955 it adopted a system of integrating external
and internal teaching by the full-time faculty
of the university. External enrolments were limited
on the basis of a staff-student ratio similar to
that already existing in the traditional lecture
situation so that staff bore responsibility for
teaching both student groups as part of their normal
duties.

This system (which came to be known as the
'Australian integrated mode') has had two able
proponents, Howard C. Sheath (1956-1972) and Kevin
C. Smith (1973-). It would be too much to say
that the writings of Sheath (1965,1973) and Smith
(1979) contain a theory of distance education;
rather they present a series of heartfelt beliefs
on how external studies should be administered.

Smith feels that institutions planning external
studies must come to terms with an educational
dilemma. The dilemma lies in the fact that external
studies depend essentially on an independent learning situation and must be designed so that motivated
mature-age students can plot their own path through
a particular course with a minimum of outside
assistance. On the other hand, systems which rely
solely upon the stamina, perseverance and intellectual capabilities of students to survive the
rigors of external studies without assistance do

not fulfil their academic responsibilities. The
compromise is to provide a core of independent
learning material but add compulsory provision
for staff/student contacts and regular student
group activity.

In contrast to Peters' theory of industrialisation, Smith advocates dividing the work of the
university faculty equally between on-campus and
off-campus students. For the distance education
students the lecturer performs all those functions,
and more, that are performed for normal students:
the design and presentation of courses, the marking
of assignments, the conduct of residential and
weekend schools, final assessment and examination
of students. The external students enrol in the
same courses, follow the same syllabus, are tutored
by the same lecturers, sit for the same examinations
and are awarded the same degrees as the conventional
ones.

Smith bases this structure on the following
principles:

° external teaching should not be done by part-
time tutors but by the full-time university
faculty
° by being part of a normal university a distance
system remains in the educational mainstream
° a university has only a small pool of outstanding staff; external students should be
in contact with them, not with what he calls
'part-time recruits' (1979:57)
° a university is a community of scholars and
all distance students must become part of
this community by attending compulsory residential schools
° concentration on the 'learning package' can
lead to a dehumanising of the learning process,
as this is a social experience
° distance education must not depend solely
on correspondence methods. Some degree of
interaction not only with materials but also
with other students and the teachers is essential. (1979:31)

The system of the University of New England
which embodies the principles listed above is contrasted by Smith with other systems in the following
passage:

Compared with most distance education systems overseas, the New England model has a certain cohesiveness and underlying strength that appears to be lacking elsewhere. These qualities are derived mainly from the fact that academic staff are responsible for the total teaching/learning process of writing courses, teaching them through a combination of independent study materials and face-to-face tuition and assessing the students by way of assignments and normal examinations. In almost all other contexts, in Britain, North America and Europe, teaching at a distance is a shared responsibility. Courses are generally written by authors on a contractual basis, teaching in tutorial sessions and grading of assignments is delegated to part-time or adjunct staff recruited for the purpose and assessment often falls between these part time recruits and the full-time staff of the institution concerned. Consequently there is a distinct tendency for the quality of the product to be regarded with suspicion. In other cases where open learning institutions have been set up to cater exclusively for off-campus students, there seems to be a certain self-consciousness about operating on the periphery of the educational mainstream. (1979:33)

In conclusion Smith lists his eight beliefs about how a distance education system should be justified (1979:54):

1. Legitimacy: continuing education and external studies are legitimate functions of universities.
2. Mainstream activity: distance teaching should be undertaken by full-time academic staff as part of their normal teaching responsibilities so that it will receive the scholarship, resource allocation and status it deserves.
3. Commitment: commitment is likely if the whole process remains the responsibilities of the academic staff and is not divided; personal contact between academic staff and students is required; quotas are imposed to reduce

external numbers to the same ratio as on-campus allocations.

4. Parity: parity of esteem for degrees can best be achieved if the same staff of the university teach and assess both categories of students.

5. Interaction: group discussions between staff and students and between students themselves are beneficial.

6. Variety: variety of teaching methods is rec-ommended because of the diversity of students.

7. Independence/pacing: pacing of students is a characteristic of successful systems.

8. Communication: a distance system requires an adequate administration.

A critique of Smith's position is that he frequently puts forward the particular solutions of his own institution as normative for other in-stitutions. The Australian integrated mode as it evolved at New England is certainly of interest as a model for a small system of less than 5,000 students, but even in other Australian universities which teach both at a distance (Deakin University, Murdoch University for example) and on-campus it has by no means been followed in all its details. Far from being in the mainstream of university studies as Smith (1979:33) claims, the distance departments of many integrated systems appear to be well on the periphery with little influence on university budgets or planning.

There is the constant problem that when a lecturer's time is divided between the demands of conventional and distance education, both func-tions are done less than perfectly. (Shott, 1983)

If an institution is offering full degrees or diplomas in a non-traditional way it does not seem appropriate that such provision should be located amongst the continuing education and extra-mural departments which do not normally offer full university degrees (Townsend-Coles 1982:29-37), yet this is where one normally finds integrated distance departments.

Nevertheless, Smith's contribution is a re-freshing one. It is of value to find a thoughtful basis for rejecting concepts of mass production, cost effectiveness and industrialisation in distance education especially when one finds emphasis placed on bringing the distance student into continuous contact with the best brains of the university and, secondly, the admission that the education of a distance student should be just as costly as a conventional one.

## References

Bääth, J., Flinck, R. and Wängdahl, A. (1975-1977) Pedagogical reports, Lund: University of Lund (Department of Education).

Bääth, J. (1979) Correspondence education in the light of a number of contemporary teaching models. Malmö: Liber. Hermods.

Bääth, J. (1980) Postal two-way communication in correspondence education. Lund: Gleerup.

Bääth, J. (1982) Distance students' learning - empirical findings and theoretical deliberations. Distance Education, 3,1,6-27.

Daniel, J. and Marquis, C. (1979) Interaction and independence: getting the mixture right. Teaching at a Distance, 15,25-44.

Daniel, J. and Snowden, B. (1980) The economics and management of small post-secondary distance education systems. Distance Education, 1,1, 68-91.

Daniel, J. and Shale, D. (1979) The role of pacing in distance systems. The Open University Conference on the Education of Adults at a Distance. Paper No.9.

Harper, W.R. (1880) Cited in Mackenzie, O. and Christensen, B. (eds). (1971) The changing world of correspondence study. University Park, Penn.: Penn State University.

Holmberg, B. (1960) On the methods of teaching by correspondence. Lund: Gleerup.

Holmberg, B. (1967) Correspondence education. Malmö: Hermods.

Holmberg, B. (1974) Distance education - a short handbook. Malmö: Hermods.

Holmberg, B. (1977) Distance education - a survey and bibliography. London: Kogan Page.

Holmberg, B. (1978) Practice in distance education - a conceptual framework. Canadian Journal of University Continuing Education, 6,1,18-30.

Holmberg, B. (1979) Fernstudiendidaktik als wissenschaftliches Fach. Hagen: FeU (ZIFF).

Holmberg, B. (1980) Aspects of distance education. Comparative Education, 16,2,107-119.

Holmberg, B. (1981) Status and trends of distance education. London: Kogan Page.

Holmberg, B. (1983) Guided didactic conversation in distance education. In Sewart, D., Keegan, D., and Holmberg, B. (eds) Distance education:

international perspectives, 114-122.

Sewart, D. (1978) Continuity of concern for students in a system of learning at a distance. Hagen: FeU (ZIFF).

Sewart, D. (1980) Providing an information base for students studying at a distance. Distance Education, 1,2,171-187.

Sewart, D. (1981) Distance Education - a contradiction in terms. Teaching at a distance, 19,8-18.

Sheath, H. (1965) External studies at New England: the first ten years. Armidale: UNE.

Sheath, H. (1973) Report on external studies. Armidale: UNE.

Shott, M. (1983) External studies in Australia at the crossroads? ASPESA Newsletter, 5,2,2-9.

Smith, K.C. (1979) External studies at New England: a silver jubilee review. Armidale: UNE.

Townsend-Coles, E. (1983) Maverick of the education family. Oxford: Pergamon.

PART THREE: SYNTHESIS

CHAPTER SEVEN

A THEORETICAL FRAMEWORK

Distance teaching: a contradition in terms? David
Sewart, 1981

A theoretical framework

In this study distance education is an activity
which has the following characteristics:

° quasi-permanent separation of a teacher and
a learner throughout the length of the teaching
process.
° quasi-permanent separation of a learner from
a learning group throughout the length of
the learning process.
° participation in a bureaucratised form of
educational provision.
° utilisation of mechanical or electronic means
of communication to carry the content of the
course.
° provision of means for two-way communication
so that the learner can benefit from or initiate dialogue.

Institutions which organise activities of
this kind are labelled 'distance education institutions' or 'distance education departments' of
other institutions. It is claimed that the characteristics outlined above render these institutions
distinct from and recognisable from other institutions.
The theoretician confronted with a cluster
of activities of this kind needs to address three
questions:

1.   Is distance education an educational activity?
2.   Is distance education a conventional educational activity?
3.   Is distance education possible? Is it a contradiction in terms?

# A THEORETICAL FRAMEWORK

## 1. Is distance education an educational activity?

There have been occasional suggestions that distance education does not contain any teaching function and therefore should not be classed as an educational activity. Some would wish to classify some distance education institutions with mail-order firms as a subset of business, rather than educational institutions. The data from a number of the institutions studied showed that they were characterised by:

- °　input-process-output functions of an industrial rather than educational nature.
- °　warehousing, publishing and dispatch as characteristic functions.
- °　administration by manager and clerical staff.
- °　'teaching' done by accountants, bank officials, lawyers as well as school teachers.
- °　institution oriented largely to production of financial profit.

In spite of these characteristics this study takes up the position that the theoretical underpinnings of distance education are to be found within general education theory. Distance education, the study claims, is a more industrialised form of education but the practice of distance education as evidenced in the second half of this book shows that the educational activities are dominant.

## 2. Is distance education a form of conventional education?

Most organised formal education is carried out in classroom or lecture halls with an individualised teacher in person imparting knowledge and skills to a group of students. It is oral and group-based. The education imparted by such means depends on the availability of teachers at appropriate pupil/teacher ratios in appropriate buildings.

This study proposes that the basis for a theory of distance education is to be found within general educational theory but not within the theoretical structures of oral, group-based education. This is because distance education is not based on interpersonal communication and is characterised by a privatisation of institutionalised learning. Thus the conclusion of O. Peters, already referred to above, is accepted:

> Anyone professionally involved in edu-
> cation must presume the existence of
> two forms of instruction which are
> strictly separable: traditional face-
> to-face teaching based on interpersonal
> communication and institutionalised teach-
> ing which is based on rationalised, tech-
> nologically produced reaction. (1973:303)

## 3. Is distance education possible? Is it a contra-diction in terms?

Distance education is now examined in the light
of a generally acceptable theory of education to
see whether it is possible or contradictory to
speak of teaching at a distance or learning at
a distance. For this purpose the neo-classical
positions of R.S. Peters, P.H. Hirst and M.
Oakeshott have been chosen as suitable because
of their insistence on trying to identify the nature
of teaching and learning.
Teaching is described by Oakeshott as:

> The deliberate and intentional initiation
> of a pupil into the world of human
> achievement, or into some part of it.
> A pupil is a learner known to the teacher,
> and teaching, properly speaking, is im-
> possible in his absence. (1967:159-160)

Teaching then, for this group of theorists, is
a reciprocal act that is impossible in the absence
of a learner. One cannot teach without someone
being taught. In conventional, oral education
the essential reciprocity is clear: if the students
do not arrive one can speak to the empty room but
that is not teaching.
It is clear also that all learning is not
dependent on teaching. People learn from the day
of their birth to their death. People learn from
books, from television, from gazing at the sky.
Much of this learning has little to do with educational institutions whether on-campus or at a
distance. Nevertheless, in educational analysis
one is concerned only with learning that is the
result of communication from a teacher.
R.S. Peters summarised his views on learning
and teaching by the concept 'intersubjectivity'
between teacher and learner in which learning is
experienced as a conversation or a group experience.
The intersubjectivity becomes a shared enterprise

in which teacher and learner are united by a common zeal:

> At the culminating stages of education there is little distinction between teacher and taught; they are both participating in the shared experience of exploring a common world. The teacher is simply more familiar with its contours and more skilled in handling the tools for laying bare its mysteries and appraising its nuances. Occasionally in a tutorial this exploration takes the form of a dialogue. But more usually it is a group experience. The great teachers are those who can conduct such a shared exploration in accordance with rigorous canons, and convey, at the same time, the contagion of a shared enterprise in which all are united by a common zeal. (1972:104)

Oakeshott goes further by claiming that many of the important aspects of teaching cannot be taught directly and can only be learned in the presence of persons who have the qualities to be learned:

> How does a person learn disinterested zeal?
> How does he learn style, a personal idiom? It is implanted unobtrusively in the manner in which information is conveyed, in a tone of voice, in the gesture which accompanies instruction, in asides and oblique utterences, and by example. (1967:174)

If the position of this group of theorists has validity, is distance education a contradiction in terms? If the teaching-learning relationship is one of intersubjectivity, is basically a group experience in which much is learned by association with those who have the qualities to be learned - can this take place at a distance? Analysists of distance education (Carnoy and Levin, 1975; Mace, 1976; Escotet, 1981) come to similar conclusions. Carnoy and Levin, and Mace conclude that the quality of the graduate from a distance system will be different from that of a normal system; Escotet that distance instruction (the imparting of information at a distance) is possible but that distance education (the imparting of information plus the social and community aspects of normal education) is not.

## The nature of distance education

An essential feature of distance education is that the teaching acts are separated in time and place from the learning acts. The learning materials may be offered to students one, five or ten years after they were developed and to students spread throughout a nation or overseas. In distance education a teacher prepares learning materials from which he or she may never teach. Another teacher may use the materials and evaluate students' work. The pedagogical structuring of the learning materials, instructional design and execution may be assigned to persons other than the author. Teaching becomes institutionalised: the course may continue in use after the lecturer responsible for producing it has left the institution. Materials may be developed by a course team or group. Institutions which use only part-time staff may contract out the development of the teaching to writers who are employed only for the period of writing; tutoring and counselling is contracted out to other staff employed only for the period of the presentation of the course.

Moore's analysis is particularly pertinent here. Using 'telemathic' teaching for 'distance' teaching he concludes that teaching at a distance comprises:

> All those teaching methods in which because of physical separatedness of learners and teachers, the interactive, as well as the proactive phase of teaching, is conducted through print, mechanical, or electronic devices. Whereas in non-telemathic teaching, only the proactive phase of teaching is conducted apart in space and time from the learners, in telemathic teaching both the proactive and interactive phases are conducted separately from the learners. (1977:15)

By the 'proactive' phase he means the teacher selecting objectives, planning the curriculum and instructional strategies; this is contrasted with the 'interactive' phase in which the teacher provides verbal stimulation, makes explanations, asks questions and provides guidance face-to-face with the students. Moore's position is supported by the institutional data collected for this study. In all institutions both public and private from all sectors of the educational spectrum that fall within the definition of distance education adopted, one can identify organisational task boundaries that centre around the development of learning materials and another grouping of tasks that focuses around the teaching of the students who eventually enrol in the courses for which the materials were developed.

## Reintegration of teaching acts

A theoretical justification for distance education can be found in the attempt to reintegrate the teaching acts which are divided by the nature of distance education. The intersubjectivity of teacher and learner, in which learning from teaching occurs, has to be artificially recreated. Over space and time a distance system seeks to reconstruct the moment in which the teaching-learning interaction occurs. The linking of learning materials to learning is central to this process. It may be represented schematically thus:

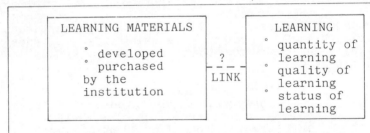

Figure 7.1. Relationship of learning materials to learning in a distance education system

In conventional education this link is automatically set up. It may, of course, fail if students sleep or lack motivation but the learner is placed in a privileged situation totally geared to learning. In distance systems the position is quite different as the link between materials and potential learning has to be artificially maintained. Carefully developed distance teaching materials often fail because they are developed for and dispatched to students who do not open them, or who open them but do not study them or who study them but do not reciprocate in any way. In a similar way distance education television or radio programmes may go unwatched or unheard, at least by the students enrolled in the course for which they were designed. The link has not been achieved; the essential reciprocity of the teaching act - shattered by the nature of distance education - has not been recreated.

The concept of interpersonal communication is central to the reintegration of the teaching acts in distance education. In conventional education teacher and learner are linked by interpersonal communication which consists of language and non-verbal communication or cues. Clearly, conventional education uses textbooks and other materials in addition to interpersonal communication and as the student proceeds from primary schooling to post-graduate study the proportion of printed materials used in the learning process tends to increase. Interpersonal communication, nevertheless, remains central to the teaching-learning process and its functions may be analysed:

| | | |
|---|---|---|
| ° | to provide information | (information function) |
| ° | to express feelings | (expression function) |
| ° | to get someone to behave | (control function) |
| ° | to relieve privacy | (social contact function) |
| ° | to stimulate | (stimulation function) |
| ° | to seek contact for basic needs | (alleviation of anxiety function) |
| ° | to justify roles | (role related function). |

Distance education presents a cluster of educational efforts to replace these functions of interpersonal communication by printed, electronic or computer-based interaction because the interpersonal communication of conventional education is, by definition, excluded except for occasional sessions or meetings. Thus distance education has to attempt to compensate for the following characteristics:

° no heard language
° absence of non-language communication (environmental factors, proxemics, kinesis, touching behaviour, paralanguage, physical characteristics)
° absence of feed-back processes student-to-

121

° teacher
° absence of feed-back processes teacher-to-student
° delayed reinforcement
° absence of student-to-student communication
° change in role of non-cognitive learning processes (peer contact, anxiety, peer support and criticism).

Two German studies have analysed the differences between the interpersonal communication of conventional education and the artificial communication processes of distance education. Peters (1973:295) labels his analysis 'the industrialisation of teaching' and Cropley and Kahl's (1983: 37) study is called 'the psychodynamics of teaching at a distance' (see figures 7.2 and 7.3.).

<u>What can be achieved?</u>

Distance systems attempt the re-integration of the act of teaching in two ways. Learning materials, both print and non-print, are designed to achieve as many of the characteristics of interpersonal communication as possible. Various writers suggest the incorporation of:

° easily readable style
° anticipation of students' problems
° careful structuring of content
° self-testing questions
° instructional objectives
° inserted questions
° model answers
° typographical considerations etc.

in print, audio-visual, video and computer packages and laboratory kits. Holmberg (see chapter 6) has suggested that a guided didactic conversation can be simulated by such means and it is generally acknowledged that in the 1970s much progress was achieved in the pedagogical structuring of learning materials for distance education (Daniel and Stroud, 1981).
Subsequently, when the courses are being presented, the re-integration of the teaching act is attempted by:

° communication by correspondence
° telephone tutorials
° on-line computer communication

| FACE-TO-FACE TEACHING | DISTANCE TEACHING |
|---|---|
| Institution where communicative action takes place | System of educational action determined by rational means-ends thinking |
| Students' and teachers' actions are predominantly determined by social norms | Teachers' and students' actions are predominantly determined by technical rules |
| The medium of interaction between students and teachers is "the inter-subjectively shared everyday language" | The medium of interaction between students and teachers is "context-free language" |
| Teaching is determined by "reciprocal behaviour expectations" | Teaching follows "conditional prognoses" and "conditional imperatives" |
| The focus is on the "internalisation of roles" | The focus is on the learning of "skills and qualifications" |
| Teaching aims at preserving the institution | Teaching aims at "problem solving, attainment of objectives by applying means-to-and-end principles" |
| Students are punished on the basis of conventional sanctions. They fail because of decisions made by the authority of teacher, headmaster, director of education | Students fail because of their inability to cope with the reality of learning at a distance. They drop out of their courses, for instance |
| Dimensions of "rationality" emancipation, individuation, extension of dominance-free communication | Increase of the effectiveness of the teaching system. Extension of the teaching system. |

Figure 7.2. O. Peters (1973:295) Differences between
face-to-face teaching and distance teaching.

| FACE-TO-FACE EDUCATION | DISTANCE EDUCATION |
|---|---|
| Immediate, personal contact between learner and teacher | Contact through communications media |
| Teacher can readily adapt to learner's immediate behaviour | Adaptation delayed |
| Learner's environment is primarily designed to support learning activities | Learner's environment is designed to serve other purposes (distractors) |
| Metacommunication between teacher and learner is possible | Metacommunication is difficult |
| Personal relationships can moderate learning | Personal relationship is of little importance |
| Direct control of learner by teacher is possible | Teacher's influence is indirect |
| Learning materials can be of low didactic standard | Learning materials must be of high didactic standard (well organised, clear, etc.) |
| Learners experience limited degree of freedom | Learners experience a high degree of freedom |
| Wide opportunities exist for imitation/identification learning | Few opportunities exist for imitation/ identification learning |
| Communication need not be planned to last detail | Communication is usually highly planned |
| Information is provided by a mixture of cues (Personal, content-related, organisation-related) | Information is mainly provided by content and organisation |
| A high degree of evaluation and feed-back from the teacher is possible | A comparatively low degree of evaluation and feed-back from the teacher is possible |
| Internal motivation, self-direction, self-evaluation, planning, etc. can be low | Internal motivation, self-direction, self-evaluation, planning ability, etc. must be high |
| Willingness and ability of learner to work without direct supervision may be low | Willingness and ability of learner to work without direct supervision must be high |

Figure 7.3. Cropley and Kahl (1983:37)
Differences between face-to-face education
and distance education

　° 　　　comments on assignments by tutors or computers
　° 　　　teleconferences etc.

Many institutions feel that personal contact
must be available too and provide for optional
or compulsory seminars, weekend meetings or residential summer schools. Thus distance institutions
are not institutions for developing learning materials. They seek to re-integrate the structures
of teaching by providing a complete learning package
that parallels the provision of conventional education from pre-enrolment counselling to examination
and accreditation.

## Consequences

The process of the re-integration of the act of
teaching in distance education brings with it a
series of changes to the normal structures of oral,
group-based education. Five of the most important
are considered briefly.

1. The industrialisation of teaching. The interpersonal communication of conventional education
is replaced by what are basically industrialised
processes; the design of mechanical and electronic
means of communication, the physical production
of printed, audio, video and computer-based materials, and the distribution of these materials
throughout the territory served by the institution
or throughout the world.

2. The privatisation of institutional learning.
The learning group is splintered and students study,
basically at home, throughout the territory served
by the institution. Teaching is focused on the
individual student who does not, however, study
as a private learner but as a member of an often
complex educational bureaucracy.

3. Change of administrative structure. Distance
institutions are characterised by two characteristic
operating sub-systems which have specific task
and psychological boundaries: course development
sub-system and student support services sub-system.

4. Different plant and buildings. The warehouse
is central, together with postal or other distribution services. Greatly reduced or spread throughout the territory are student facilities ranging
from seminar rooms to library and laboratory

facilities.

5. Change of costing structures. Distance systems
are characterised by high, initial start-up costs,
lower variable costs per student and give the potential for significantly lower average costs per
student provided the student population is large
enough. This represents a move away from
the labour-intensive costs of education towards
the capital investment structures of industrial
enterprises.

## Three hypotheses

The separation of the teaching acts and the learning
acts that is characteristic of distance education
brings about a weak integration of the student
into the life of the institution and this has been
linked to drop-out (Tinto, 1975). It is hypothesised therefore that distance students have a
tendancy to drop-out in those institutions in which
structures for the re-integration of the teaching
acts are not satisfactorily achieved.
    The separation of the teaching acts and the
learning acts that is characteristic of distance
education brings about difficulties in the achievement of interpersonal communication between teacher
and student and this has been linked to the eventual
quality of the learning achieved (Carnoy and Levin,
1975, Mace, 1978; Escotet, 1981). It is hypothesised therefore that distance students have difficulty in achieving quality of learning in those
institutions in which structures for the re-integration of the teaching acts are not satisfactorily
achieved.
    The separation of the teaching acts and the
learning acts that is characteristic of distance
education places distance education among the non-
traditional forms of education (Moore, 1973) in
which degrees, diplomas and qualifications achieved
may not receive full academic acceptance. It is
hypothesised therefore that the status of learning
at a distance may be questioned in those institutions in which the re-integration of the teaching
acts is not satisfactorily achieved.

## Rationale

A citizen in a country is normally linked to a
defined work place and unless this is a major urban
centre it is impossible for the State to provide

educational facilities at all levels near the citizen's home or workplace. The provision of distance systems is therefore the only means of educational access for most citizens who work, for many who have families and for all who live at a distance. Children, too, are linked to their parents' workplace - the parents may be itinerant, live in outlying districts or overseas. Distance education represents a further democratisation of educational provision and enables the State to provide access to a far wider range of citizens.

The official provision of distance education is particularly pressing in a period in which the rapidity of technological change is making obsolete qualifications achieved even in the recent past. Citizens today seek re-qualification not only for promotion possibilities but even to remain in present employment and avoid redundancy. Few can leave employment for study on-campus.

Furthermore, most Western countries are now experiencing a decline in the duration of the working week, increase in vacations and changes in the length of the working life. People enter the labour force later, usually due to a longer study period, retirement policies are changing and life expectancy has increased significantly. The result of all these tendencies is that the early 1980s witnessed a significant change in the distribution of 'work' and 'non-work' in people's lives. 'Non-work' is comprised by unemployment, leisure or education. There seems little doubt that the time available for it will increase for many in the period 1985-2000. Citizens will choose to spend much of this time on non-educational activities. A careful analysis by educational institutions of the changes that are taking place will show the need for a new flexibility in dealing with them: not all of the clientele will be willing to travel to educational institutions and to join a learning group to study. Distance education institutions are one of the groupings of educational structures that have some possibility of grappling with the problems of a changing working and social scenario.

Distance programmes are also indicated for an ageing society. Demographers speak of the movement of a population bulge through a period of time 'the way of python swallows a pig'. Recent population statistics, however, show that between 1971 and 1981 the number of pensioners in Britain increased by 10% when the population increase was

only one half of one per cent. Over the same period
the number of those under 16 declined by
12%. Roughly one in six of Britain's population
is of pensionable age today. (OPCS, 1982). Similar
statistics can be cited for the United States,
the Federal Republic of Germany and many developed
societies. The bulge in the python has disappeared.
One gets a diamond and a gradually ageing society.
The social and educational philosophy with which
most Western societies are entering a period of
ageing of their societies seems out of step with
the demographical data and distance programmes
may be one way to redress the balance.

Apart from the necessity of increasing educational access to the working adult and the adult
with family responsibilities, distance programmes
seem well placed to make a valid contribution to
educational provision in the period 1985-2000,
as this provision may have the following characteristics:

° capable of responding to the greater proportion
   of 'non-work' time available to many
° characterised as 'not-for-children' to
   a greater extent than today
° flexible and adapted to the needs of
   the public.

## References

Cropley, A. and Kahl, T. (1983) Distance education:
   a psychological analysis. Distance Education,
   4,1,30-42.
Carnoy, M. and Levin, H. (1975) Evaluation of educational media: some issues. Instructional
   Science, 4,385-406.
Daniel, J. and Stroud, M. (1981) Distance education
   - a re-appraisal for the 1980s. Distance Education, 2,1,35-51.
Escotet, M. (no date) La educación superior a distancia frente al paradigma de Instrucción
   y Formación. In Penalver, L. and Escotet,
   M. (eds) Teoria y praxis de la Universidad
   a Distancia. Caracas: FEDES.
Mace, J. (1978) Mythology in the making: is the
   OU really cost effective? Higher Education,
   7,295-309.
Moore, M. (1973) Toward a theory of independent
   learning and teaching. Journal of Higher Education, 44,661-679.
Moore, M. (1977) On a theory of independent study.

Hagen: FeU.
Oakeshott, M. (1967) Learning and teaching. In Peters, R.S. (ed.) The concept of education. London: Routledge and Kegan Paul.
Office for Population Census Statistics (U.K) (1982) 1981 Census Monitor. London: OPCS.
Peter, O. (1973) Die didaktische Struktur des Fernunterrichts. Weinheim: Beltz.
Peters, R.S. (1972) Education as initiation. In Achambault, R. (ed) Philosophical analysis and education. London: Routledge and Kegan Paul.
Sewart, D. (1981) Distance teaching: a contradiction in terms? Teaching at a Distance, 19,8-18.
Tinto, V. (1975) Drop-out from higher education: a theoretical synthesis of recent research. Review of Educational Research, 45, 89-125.

CHAPTER EIGHT

A TYPOLOGY OF DISTANCE TEACHING SYSTEMS

There are distance teaching universities only in
South Africa and the U.S.S.R.  Otto Peters, 1965

## Background

It used to be accepted that distance teaching
started in 1840. Holmberg (1960,3) gives that
as the date when Isaac Pitman offered tuition by
post in shorthand to students in England. In 1856
Charles Toussaint and Gustave Langensheidt commenced
language teaching by correspondence in Germany.
Delling (1979,13), however, has argued convincingly
that institutions which exhibit all the characteristics suggested in chapter three are little more
than a century old.
Today a listing of distance institutions would
embrace most countries of the world and all levels
of education. In previous chapters an attempt
has been made to delineate and characterise what
has been called 'the farrago that is distance education: open universities and schools of the air;
TV and radio projects; government sponsored institutions prohibited by statute from charging fees
alongside profit-making colleges; literacy and
rural improvement projects; computer-based instruction and instruction based on roneod-notes'. A
stringent listing of systemic characteristics has
been proposed whereby only those institutions ex-
hibiting certain academic and administrative
peculiarities, which are reflected · in decisions
about physical plant, are considered to be distance
education institutions for the purpose of this
study.
    Even then the field remaining is vast (Harry,
1984) and there is great variety of provision.
Global statements about distance education as a
whole are rarely valid and most general statements
must be hedged with qualifications. The need to
provide the reader with groupings or classifications

130

about which at least some general statements may with confidence be made is pressing. In this chapter some existing classifications which contain elements that contribute to an understanding of the field of distance education are discussed, then a new classification specially prepared for this study is suggested.

## Existing typologies

1. O. Peters (1971). The first systematic classification of distance institutions at higher education level is provided by Peters' Texte zum Hochschulfernstudium. This proposes two major groupings: a Western model based on printed materials and correspondence feedback and an Eastern model based on printed materials and regular face-to-face sessions.

Peters (1971: 8-12) gives four bases for his classification which might be represented as in Figure 8.1.

Peters' view that there are two basic forms of distance provision: an Eastern one based on printed materials plus consultations and a Western one based on printed materials plus correspondence feedback was not followed by the two other major comparative studies of distance education published in the 1970s. Both the UNESCO Open learning (1975) study and the Swedish TRU report (1975) saw broadcast radio and television as central.

2. J. El Bushra (1973). El Bushra, of the International Extension College in Cambridge, developed a classification of correspondence teaching at universities, comprising six categories as in Figure 8.2.

This presentation contains elements of value for an understanding of university distance provision, though a number of the groupings chosen are too small for valid use.

3. M. Neil (1981). Neil of the OUUK presents a classification of distance institutions based on (i) the degree of authority and (ii) the degree of control exerted in key operational areas by the various types of institution (1981: 138-141). The relationships of autonomous distance education institutions with other institutions in the nation or state can be characterised as contractual or commercial and the relationships are not reciprocal. By contrast, other distance institutions - those

| | Western models (pp 29 - 139) | Eastern models (pp 143-229) |
|---|---|---|
| Political considerations | ° tries to help the individual<br>° is a fringe form of educational provision<br>° characterised by proprietary influences | ° a planned component of socio-cultural development<br>° an integral part of national provision<br>° enrols 20%-50% of all under-graduates |
| Curriculum | fragmented provision from individual insti-tutions | centralised national provision |
| Organisational structure | loosely integrated into the main-stream of university life | more influential role in university structures |
| Didactic structure | based on proprietary precedents: - mono media system of printed materials plus regular correspondence correction of assignments | based on imitation of direct education - correspondence correction of assignments is reduced or replaced by regular voluntary or com-pulsory seminars |
| Examples in 1971 | Wisconsin and Nebraska (USA)<br>New England (Australia)<br>UNISA (South Africa)<br>Chuo, Hosei, Kaio (Japan)<br>Open University (UK) | Karl-Marx Leipzig (DDR)<br>Karls Prague (Czechoslovakia)<br>North Western Polytechnic Léningrad (USSR)<br>° Poland and Peoples Republic of China |

Figure 8.1  Typology of O. Peters (1971)

| TYPE | EXAMPLES |
|---|---|
| 1. Universities dealing exclusively with external students. | UNISA, OUUK |
| 2. Universities offering external examination facilities only. | External degrees of the University of London. |
| 3. Universities offering correspondence teaching in one department only. | College of Estate Management (University of Reading) and School of Education, University of the South Pacific. |
| 4. Universities in which teaching departments are required to accept both internal and external students. | University of New England. |
| 5. Universities in which external teaching is provided in a separate department. | University of Queensland External Studies Department. University of Wisconsin Extension. |
| 6. Universities collaborating to provide instruction on a cooperative basis. | Massey University, New Zealand. Texas Association for Graduate Engineering and Research (TAGER). |

Figure 8.2. Typology of J. El Bushra (1983)

called 'mixed' in this book - are embedded in other systems so that mutual benefit between institutions is an important bond.

Neil (1981:130) sums up by claiming that an autonomous distance teaching university is a 'whole system control model', whereas distance institutions which are not autonomous are 'embedded into communities of educational agencies' for the purpose of mutual benefits. These 'mixed' models have to share control or authority in four areas:

> finance
> examination and accreditation
> curriculum and materials
> delivery and student support systems.

Neil proposes a classification in five groupings as in Figure 8.3.

4. Chester Zelaya Goodman. The two volume Peñalver - Escotet analysis of distance education Teoria y praxis de la universidad a distancia contains a typology of distance systems by Chester Zelaya Goodman in his chapter 'La administración de los sistemas de educación a distancia y sus costos' (no date: 141:157) as in Figure 8.4. This is a well-informed and carefully presented typology of distance systems at university level. The reader will notice how Zelaya accommodates within his structure both the correspondence schools which teach at a distance towards University of London degrees and the co-operative ventures in Eastern France and from Tübingen - to these might easily be added the Norwegian fjernundervisnung. Zelaya's category 'conventional universities which offer distance courses which they also accredit' can easily accommodate the 64 independent study departments of United States universities, the 20 similar structures in Canada and external studies provision from Swedish and Australian universities. The decision to separate out the CNEC in France as a major provider in an autonomous multi-level distance system is quite justified.

He calls his final grouping the SEAD (Sistemas de Educación a Distancia) and claims that these institutions are totally dedicated to external students. Their characteristics are absence of conflicts of loyalty on the part of academic staff between on-campus and off-campus students, greater motivation for methodological experiment; freedom from conventional academic traditions, and - in

| Title | Description | Example |
|---|---|---|
| 1. Classical centre-periphery model | Whole system control model | OUUK, Milton Keynes |
| 2. Associated centre | An autonomous university with centralized control diminished in area of financing and support services | Universidad Nacional de Educación a Distancia, Madrid |
| 3. Dispersed centre model | An autonomous institution which cooperates with a wide variety of institutions | Coastline Community College, California |
| 4. Switchboard organization model | A facilitating centre for distance education projects with much control exercised by other educational and public bodies | Norsk fjernundervis-nung, Norway |
| 5. Service institutions model | A service institution based on cooperation with other institutions | DIFF, Tübingen |

Figure 8.3. Typology of M. Neil (1981)

| Title and description | Example |
|---|---|
| 1. Private institutions providing distance teaching for a public institution | Wolsley Hall, Oxford. National Extension College, Cambridge |
| 2. Conventional universities which offer distance course which they also accredit | Universidad Nacional Autonoma de Mexico. Universidad Xavariana, Bogotà |
| 3. Groupings of conventional universities which unite to offer distance courses | Entente de l'est, France. DIFF, Tübingen |
| 4. Autonomous multi-level distance institutions which teach at university level | Centre National d'Enseignement par Correspondance, France |
| 5. Universities specially created to offer and accredit degrees at a distance. | OUUK, UNED Spain, UNA Venezuala, UNED Costa Rica. |

Figure 8.4. Typology of Chester Zelaya G.

general - ability to develop new educational initiatives for new target groups.

5. D. Keegan and G. Rumble (1982). In the preparation of the book The distance teaching universities Keegan and Rumble wrestled with the problem of the classification of distance systems at university level and came up with seven basic organisational structures illustrated in Figure 8.5.

Typology for this study (see Figure 8.6)

The classification in this study is based on the following premises for the construction of a usable typology:

- ° it should be helpful to the readers enabling them to focus on a range of institutions within the field 'distance teaching institutions' about which statements can be made that identify what this grouping of institutions has in common, and what it is that distinguishes it from the other groupings.
- ° to be helpful it should not be artificial - each grouping should contain dozens, preferably hundreds, of institutions.
- ° it should not be artificial with regard to students - each grouping should enrol thousands, preferably millions, of students.
- ° it should not be artificial with regard to time - each grouping should have been identifiable for at least a decade, preferably longer.
- ° it should try to encompass all distance teaching institutions, public and private, at all levels from primary schooling to post-graduate levels - and not just concentrate on distance education at university level.
- ° it should only include those distance teaching institutions or departments of existing institutions which exhibit both the major characteristic subsystems of distance institutions (course development and student support services) - for without this limitation the variants are legion. Institutions or departments which are considered not to exhibit both these operational subsystems are excluded (though some of them have made excellent contributions to distance education).

Fundamental to the classification proposed

| Name | Description | Examples |
|---|---|---|
| 1. Autonomous, centrally controlled distance teaching universities | Open universities with centralised, autonomous structures | OUUK EU, AU UNED Costa Rica |
| 2. Autonomous, decentralized distance teaching universities | Open universities with some devolution of powers | UNED Spain |
| 3. Essentially autonomous distance teaching universities operating within a federated university structure | Federal university with both conventional universities and a distance teaching unit | Télé-université of the federal University of Québec |
| 4. Autonomous centralized distance teaching system with a high degree of control using facilities based in and run by conventional universities | Ministry control of distance education departments within conventional universities | Central Office for Distance Education, Dresden, DDR |
| 5. Mixed mode, uni-departmental model | Special academic distance teaching department in conventional university | External Studies Department, University of Queensland |
| 6. Mixed mode, multi-departmental model | Academic staff responsible for both internal and external students | Australian integrated mode; New England model |
| 7. Mixed mode, multi-institutional model | Mixed mode with responsibility for students at other universities | Massey University, New Zealand |
| Figure 8.5 Typology of Keegan and Rumble (1982) | | |

here is the acceptance (with Neil; Keegan and Rumble) that the basic distinction is between <u>autonomous distance teaching institutions</u> and <u>distance subsections of conventional institutions</u>. As an explanation of 'autonomous' Neil's (1981:140) listing of autonomy in (i) finance, (ii) in examination and accreditation, (iii) in curriculum and materials, and (iv) in delivery and student support systems, is accepted as accurate. Clearly it is a question of autonomy at the institutional level because autonomous distance institutions like the Open University of the United Kingdom, the Centre National de Télé-enseignement in France and the New South Wales College of External Studies in Australia are components of state or national education systems. Neil explains:

> Although the OUUK is enmeshed in, and utterly dependent upon, the United Kingdom infrastructure, its relationships with other organisations are basically contractual and commercial in nature (1981: 139).

What is important is that autonomous institutions are totally committed to external students; their staff and administrators can regard as peripheral or unimportant what happens in conventional institutions and they can focus on the needs of students for whom the provision of conventional institutions is unsuitable, unwanted or unavailable.
Within these two groupings the division is by didactic structure, that is the linking that the institution provides between learning materials and learning. It is quickly evident that when groupings of institutions are classified in this way distinct characteristics emerge for each grouping and universal statements about distance education of the type 'all distance institution do this' or 'distance teaching institutions don't have classes for students' must usually be qualified or nuanced.

## Autonomous distance teaching institutions

The autonomous distance teaching institutions have been divided into two major types for the purpose of this study: Type 1 is called 'Public and private correspondence schools and colleges', and Type 2 - 'Distance teaching universities'. The division is based on complexity of didactic structure and

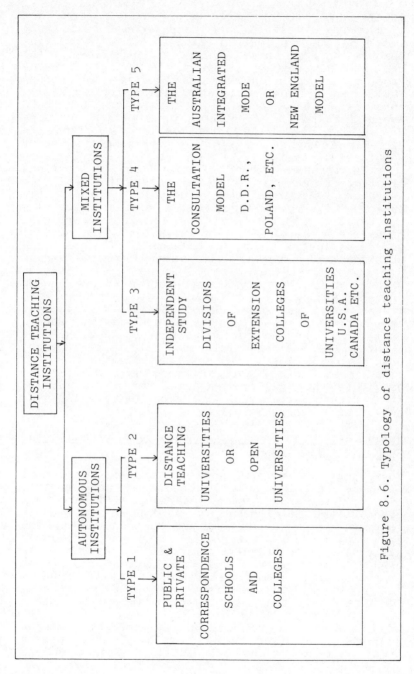

Figure 8.6. Typology of distance teaching institutions

level of provision. In very general terms the link between learning and learning materials provided by institutions of Type 1 tends to be less complex than by those of Type 2 especially in the use of 'Big Media' (Schramm, 1977) and face-to-face meetings. Institutions of Type 1, whether public or private, sometimes state that students enrol with them precisely because they wish to avoid face-to-face contact; institutions of Type 2 sometimes have the intention of supporting the distance learner by as rich a provision of support services as possible.

In terms of level of provision institutions of Type 1 normally provide courses for children and adults at lower than university level. Institutions of Type 2 are called distance teaching universities. The division is not watertight, however, as many Type 1 institutions (i.e. Leidse Onderweijsinstellingen in Leiden) offer some university level courses, while most distance teaching universities (except the Russian institutions, UNISA and the Fernuniversität) offer courses below university level. Of particular importance are those autonomous distance teaching institutions that provide a full range of courses for adults from basic adult education to university programmes (Centre National de Téléenseignement in France, Open Learning Institute, British Columbia). Rather than create a new category for these multi-level providers they will be regarded here as a mixture of elements from the two groupings delineated, and referred to as Type 1/2.

## Public and private correspondence schools and colleges (Type 1)

Correspondence schools and colleges are autonomous distance teaching institutions: they have control of or authority over staffing, finance, accreditation, development of materials and student services without reference to other parts of the same institution, even when they are part of a state-wide or nation-wide system. The model is used widely throughout the world both by government sponsored and by proprietary institutions. Schools and colleges of this type have existed for over 100 years and today there are examples in nearly every country of the western world.

Examples are to be found particularly amongst publicly sponsored schools at primary and secondary level together with both publicly sponsored and

privately supported colleges at technical, vocational and further education levels.

At technical, vocational and further education
levels correspondence colleges or colleges of external studies are of a similar structure. They
are both government-sponsored and privately-sup-
ported and offer a wide range of subjects at a
distance teaching to middle-level qualifications
in:

| | | |
|---|---|---|
| Accounting | Real Estate | Adult Matriculation |
| Business | Rural Studies | Adult 'second |
| Banking | Horticulture | chance' |
| Management | Health | Automotive |
| English as a | Studies | Building |
| Second | Art and | Refrigeration |
| Language | Craft | Electronics |
| Modern Lan- | Journalism | Technology |
| guages | | |

Some well known examples are the National Extension
College, Cambridge; Leidse Onderweijsinstellingen,
Leiden; New South Wales College of External Studies,
Sydney. Karov (1979) listed 144 of them (all pro-
prietary) in the Federal Republic of Germany and
there must be at least as many in France.

Type 1 is an institutional structure which
emphasises the correspondence element in distance
education. It might be represented diagrammatically
thus: (Figure 8.7)

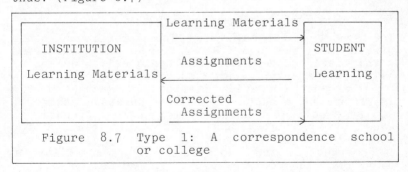

Figure 8.7   Type 1:  A  correspondence  school
or college

The  didactic  structure  is  frequently  patterned
thus:  the  correspondence  schools  and  colleges  develop  or  purchase  learning  materials  and  send  them
by  post  to  the  student.   The  student  studies  the
materials  and  posts  assignments  back  to  the  institution  which  marks  and  comments  on  them  and  posts
them  back  to  the  student.   The  student  studies

141

the comments, completes the next assignment and
the process is repeated. Print tends to be the
didactic medium with some use of audio cassettes.
From this description and the diagrammatic representation above it can be indicated that the
environment for student learning provided by this
model can be fragile. The student's main contact
with the representatives of the institution is
by post so that isolation can become a problem.
As many correspondence schools and colleges have
a philosophy that suggests that students enrol
with them because 'they want to be left alone',
it can be maintained that student support services
and face-to-face sessions can infringe learner
autonomy or the independence of the adult learner.
Gone are peer group support and the presence of
the teacher. Drop-out can be enormous.

There are, nevertheless, institutions which
have turned these disadvantages into factors to
benefit student learning. There is evidence to
claim (Bääth (1979), Bääth and Wängdahl (1976),
Rekkedal (1981) and Holmberg (1981, 83-94)) that
the dedication of the correspondence tutor can
forge with the distant student by letter and by
telephone such a creative link that a correspondence
course can become a form of privileged one-to-
one study. A type of one-on-one bonding has often
been created that is difficult to achieve in the
lecture or tutorial.

## Distance teaching universities (Type 2)

In 1965 Otto Peters wrote 'The Republic of South
Africa and the U.S.S.R. are the only countries
with distance teaching universities'. The scene
is quite different twenty years later.

Distance education started the decade of the
1970s as the cinderella of the education spectrum:
it was practically unknown as a segment of national
education provision and at times criticized for
the malpractice of some of its representatives.
It emerged in the 1980s with the possibility of
a radical change of image. The foundation of the
open universities was a major element in this fairy-
tale like transformation, together with the growing
privatisation of urban society which characterized
the decade and the benefits of industrialisation
in a period of growing financial stringency.

At the head of the list of distance teaching
universities stands the Open University of the
United Kingdom at Milton Keynes which received

its Royal Charter in 1969 and taught its first students in 1971. Each commentator will have a personal list of the constituents of the OUUK's immediate success, but amongst them were brilliant political and educational leadership, an unswerving concentration on the needs of students studying at a distance and a national backlog of intelligent adults for whom the provisions of face-to-face universities were no longer relevant. These factors and others quickly brought this non-traditional university structure the status of a permanent provider of university education in the United Kingdom with an annual enrolment of 100,000. The OUUK was followed by a series of foundations in both developed and developing countries of similar institutions called 'Fernuniversitäten', 'open universities' or 'universidades de educación a distancia'. Not only does the foundation of these universities mark a watershed in distance education, it provides the most advanced stage yet in the evolution of the concept of a university. These universities do not have students in residence, neither do they have full-time day-time students, nor even part-time night-time students. They place their students at home. One looks in vain for a student as one walks around the campus at Milton Keynes. Many of the other universities are off-putting, factory-like buildings and there is little or nothing for students to do at them. Gone too is the concept of the university library with places for undergraduate and post-graduate research, gone are the lecture rooms, tutorial rooms, seminar rooms, laboratories for student research and fa-cilities for the student community. These are uni-versities of a nation or a state, not of a city like Oxford or Bologna. Frequently they are uni-versities on tens or hundreds of sites spread throughout the nation.

These universities present the most radical challenge yet to the idea of a university enunciated by John H. Newman and developed in the western world. They represent the final democratisation of the concept of a university by opening up the possibility of university studies to many who were formerly barred from enrolling by the time-tabling of lectures and the necessity of set periods of research at the universities' facilities. Full-time workers, the disabled, imprisoned and hospital-ised together with those tied to the home can now enrol at a university if it teaches at a distance.

In didactic structure, institutions of Type

2 (Distance teaching universities) differ from Type 1 in three ways:

(i)   the level of provision
(ii)  the use of media
(iii) the more comprehensive link between learning materials and potential learning.

The level of provision. The previous grouping, concentrates on education for school children and adult further education - the vast panorama of non-university adult programmes that defy organisation in many national systems. This grouping focuses on the provision of university degrees, though many of the group offer further education courses as well.

The use of media. Type 2 institutions profess a more comprehensive use of non-print educational media than does the previous one. It is true that print remains the dominant medium but a recent analysis by Keegan and Rumble (1982:213) shows a movement towards more extensive employment of media.

The didactic link. Type 2 institutions profess to provide a more coherent link between learning materials and learning so that the student is supported by a wide range of activities, many of them optional, designed to provide a satisfactory university level educational experience and prevent avoidable drop-out.
   This attempt at providing a more comprehensive linkage between learning materials and student learning might be represented as in Figure 8.8.

Multi-level autonomous distance teaching institutions (Type 1/Type 2)

It can be admitted frankly that the lines of demarcation between the two autonomous groupings proposed - correspondence schools or colleges (Type 1) and distance teaching universities (Type 2) - is frequently fragile. Some correspondence colleges use more non-print media than do some distance teaching universities; most distance teaching universities teach at levels other than university degrees and one, the Télé-université at Québec, emerged from a recent reorganisation with its power to offer degrees reduced. The Russian institutions and UNISA are the main offerers of doctoral

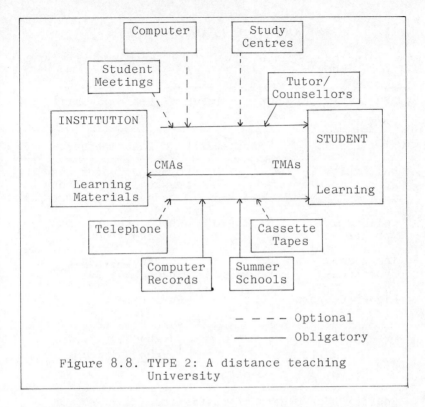

Figure 8.8. TYPE 2: A distance teaching
University

degrees at a distance; only these institutions and the Fernuniversität maintain that they are university institutions and do not teach further and continuing education courses.

Carr points out that most of the distance teaching universities are in fact multi-level autonomous distance teaching institutions offering adult distance programmes at university, college and technical/vocational levels:

> Several of the DTUs offer a very wide range of types of courses, such as Allama Iqbal Open University in Pakistan (teacher education, general education and functional education), Everyman's University (pre-academic, degree programmes, adult education and vocational courses) and the Open University (undergraduate, postgraduate and associate student programmes, the latter including an increasing number of non-degree continuing education courses

and packs). (1983:80)

In these terms the 1983 enrolment figures for the OUUK would be:

| Table 8.1. OUUK enrolment by level of study (1983) | | |
|---|---|---|
| Level | Enrolment | Description |
| University level programmes | 73770 | Undergraduates and associate students on diploma courses |
| College level programmes | 16420 | Associate students on short courses |
| Technical/ vocational | 13344 | Continuing education pack purchases |
| Higher degrees | 760 | Full-time higher degrees, Part-time higher degrees, Taught - M.Sc. |
| Total | 104405 | |
| Source: OUUK Digest of Statistics | | |

The basic example of multi-level autonomous distance teaching institutions (Type 1/Type 2) is the Centre National d'Enseignement par Correspondance, founded in Paris in 1939 as Hitler approached. By 1983 the CNEC had 220,000 enrolments per year - 15% of them representing its original mandate for primary and secondary schooling. The enrolments came from 107 countries as it is a French tradition that French government or business officials working overseas enrol their children for their full French school programme at the CNEC for the years when the family is outside France. 85% are adults enrolled in programmes at every possible level from post-literacy and numeracy to post-graduate university level work (CAPES, agrégation), though as an organ of the Ministry of Education CNEC students do not show in university statistics.

The CNEC represents a massive, governmental, multi-level provision of distance education on a national basis and the Type 1/Type 2 model deserves careful study by national education planners in both developed and developing countries. This model has had much less influence in the design of distance systems than it deserves but has had at least one important parallel in recent years: the Open Learning Institute at Richmond, British Columbia - a suburb of Vancouver. The government of British Columbia set up in 1979 an autonomous three-level distance teaching institution to complement a range of small providers of university study by correspondence through departments in conventional universities (Type 3). It has the following structure:

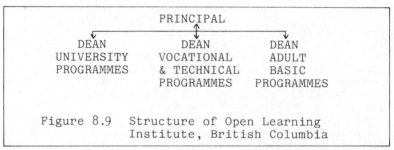

Figure 8.9   Structure of Open Learning
            Institute, British Columbia

This structure provides a full range of distance programmes for adults within the one institution ranging from literacy/numeracy, through a wide range of technical/vocational community college programmes, to the availability of university degrees. All three levels share the same production facilities, the same course development and instructional design expertise and the same student support services.

Conventional institutions with a distance education department

For the purpose of this study three types of a distance education section or department within the structures of a conventional institution have been distinguished. These are:

>    independent study divisions of a conventional college or university

>    distance education (Fernstudium) departments of institutions in the socialist republics of Central and Eastern Europe (the consultation model)

the Australian integrated mode (New England model).

It is felt that these three groupings can be satis-factorily distinguished one from the other both administratively and didactically, though it is clear that they share many common characteristics. Institutions within each of the groupings have been in existence for many decades and have enrolled many tens of thousands of students studying entirely at a distance. Each grouping contains many dozens of institutions teaching, normally, at higher edu-cation level.

## Independent study divisions of a conventional college or university (Type 3)

Examples of independent study divisions are very numerous and they have been in existence for almost a century. Noteworthy amongst them are the Inde-pendent Study Divisions of Extension Colleges of American and Canadian universities. At the time of writing 64 American universities had independent study departments which were members of the Inde-pendent Study Division of the National University Continuing Education Association of the U.S.A. and there were 20 similar structures in Canada. In France the Centres de Télé-enseignement Uni-versitaire (CTUs) fall within this category. In Sweden distance education is organized in this way from a number of Swedish universities following the decision to reject the TRU report and not found an open university. A large number of universities throughout Latin America and many universities in India have correspondence or distance education departments within this category.

Recent studies have been published of a number of these institutional arrangements, notably by Markowitz (1983) on the independent study depart-ments of United States universities, by Willén (1983) on distance education in Swedish univer-sities, by Escotet (1980) on the Latin American provision and by Singh (1980) and Carr (1983) on India. These studies are complemented here by a brief analysis of a typical independent study division and presentation of the French Centres de Télé-enseignement Universitaire on which the literature in English is particularly sparse.

## Independent study divisions (Type 3)

In his 1971 text Peters provided comprehensive case studies of two of these institutions: the University of Wisconsin by Wedemeyer and Bern (1971: 29-56) and the University of Nebraska by Childs (1975:57-70). Wedemeyer and Bern traced the origins of distance education at the University of Wisconsin back to 1891 and showed that by 1896 there were already 63 distance courses in 20 faculties ranging from Astronomy to New Testament Greek. This tradition is exemplified today by the Department of Independent study of the University of Minnesota at Minneapolis.

## University of Minnesota

The University of Minnesota at Minneapolis is a large midwestern United States university, with a student body of over 50,000 full-time students plus an additional 50,000 part-time degree students together with 30,000 students auditing courses. One of the many administrative structures of the University of Minnesota is the Continuing Education and Extension College. (C.E.E.) Its purpose is, within the structures of the University of Minnesota, to create a collegiate unit to help students pursue educational interests at home, on campus and in the community, while they are actively working and meeting personal and family obligations. Continuing Education and Extension serves its community by opening up the resources of the university to as many people as possible.
It contains the following subsections which are listed here so that the reader can place the Department of Independent Study within the total university structure: Department of C.E.E. Counselling Services, Department of Conferences, Department of Extension Classes, Department of Independent Study, Department of Continuing Education for Women and twenty other similar departments.
It is the fourth component of the Continuing Education and Extension College, the Department of Independent Study which concerns us here. The Department of Independent Study offers courses in ten major delivery modes within the field of distance education:

- ° Correspondence lessons
- ° Credit by examination
- ° Contract alternative

- Directed individual study
- Special programmes for groups
- Television courses
- Video cassette courses
- Radio courses
- Audio cassette courses
- University Without Walls

The department is staffed by a director, two assist-
ant directors and fourteen other staff including
editorial assistants and secretaries. Course development is usually by university faculty paid
overload to produce the courses, though a smaller
number of faculty (called adjunct faculty) come
from other universities, and occasionally from
other sectors of the academic community. Tuition
is also provided by the university faculty and
the students study for degrees or certificates
awarded by the university. However, there are limitations on the use of independent study credits
and degree programmes in certain departments or
schools of the university, and in many cases, one
is not permitted to complete a full degree by independent study.

The status of distance education in the United
States is fragile. Independent study departments
tend to be peripheral to the mainstream of university budget and planning decisions and it is
rare that a degree can be completed at a distance
especially at Masters' level.

## The CTUs

In France 18 of the 75 universities have university
distance education centres (Centre de Télé-enseignement Universitaire).

The CTUs are small administrative offices
in the universities concerned, and are staffed
by a Director and a few administrative officers.
The main subjects offered are in the Arts area
for both the D.E.U.G. (two-year University Qualification), and Licence (four-year Degree), and
at D.E.U.G. level in Law. The method of teaching
is a combination of radio and correspondence, with
monthly seminars.

The Directors of the CTUs receive a small
subvention from the Ministry of Education and Research in Paris, and this is used mainly for the
payment of part-time markers: they depend almost
totally on the university faculties for their course
material, a fair proportion of which is on audio-

cassette or radio. Television is no longer used. Although slight concessions are made to the distance students in the amount of time available for the study of each unit, the general aim of the CTUs is for their students to study at the same rate as their on-campus counterparts and to sit for the same examination. Over 75% of the students enrolled in these courses are in full-time employment. Distance students form between 5% and 20% of the total enrolment of the universities in which the CTU is located. The CTUs are organized and administered in a manner which bears resemblance to the independent study departments of North American universities.

## Distance education (Fernstudium) departments in the socialist republics of Central and Eastern Europe (the consultation model) (Type 4)

Peters' 1971 classification of two basic structures for distance education, print-based with correspondence feedback in the West and print-based with consultations in the East, was a valid presentation of distance education in the 1960s and still has its uses today. This study, however, differs from Peters in taking the autonomy of the distance teaching structure as fundamental for classification. For this reason the USSR's autonomous distance teaching universities are placed in Type 2 with the distance teaching universities and a special category (Type 4) is created for the consultation model when 'it is a subset of a mixed institution which teaches both on-campus and at a distance. This model has recently been documented for the German Democratic Republic by Möhle (1978), Dietze (1979) and Schwarz (1978), for the USSR by Gorochov (1979) and Ilyin (1983), for Bulgaria by Christow and Mutojischiew (1979) and for Hungary by Fekete and Nahlik (1979).

The didactic model of Type 4 is quite different from Western systems and 'correspondence' usually plays little role in it. Learning materials for use throughout the nation are developed by course teams of professors brought together in some countries by a Centre for Distance Education established by the Ministry. The materials are distributed to the institutions which are going to enrol and teach students in that particular discipline. On enrolment students are allocated both to the institution from which they will get their degree (which may be far away) and to a consultation centre at an institution near to their home and work. Study commences with a residential seminar on campus after which students study at home from the learning materials provided. This home study is interspersed at regular intervals (often once a fortnight) by consultations which are frequently compulsory. A consultation consists of a day's work on-campus in which the student receives face-to-face guidance in each of the subjects being studied.

The consultation model highlights character- istics of distance education that are not found, or are not found so clearly, in Types 1, 2, 3 and 5. Among these are:

° distance education is seen as an explicit democratization of educational provision by opening up to all adults, irrespective of their place of work, access to qualifications at all levels.

° distance education provides for the nation a means of training the work-force without withdrawing students from contributing to GNP throughout the length of their studies.

° distance education is essentially linked to the students' work and there is constant inter- action between work and study.

° of all the major types of distance education provision it is the one which is closest to conventional face-to-face provision.

Ilyin (1983) gives a presentation of the consul- tation model in the USSR. Apart from the 14 DTUs dealt with in Type 2 above, he refers to no-fewer than '800 distance subsidiaries and branches of full-time universities and institutes'. These have four goals:

° better training of experienced specialists for the national economy and state management since students studying at a distance combine studies and practical work.

° more economic training since the expenditure for a distance student is 2 - 3 times less than that for a full-time student.

° lesser fluctuation in the work force reducing great losses for the national economy due to the fact that some specialists (15 - 20%) upon graduation from full-time institutions engage in a profession different from the one they were trained for.

° return for the state from the distance student

already in the process of education when after full-time education 2 - 3 years are needed for adapting and mastering professional skills.

Ilyin describes distance education thus:

> students study individually and period-ically attend classes and take examin-ations. For this they must come to the nearest branch of their institute. Dis-tance students are to cover not less than 30% of the learning matter in class. (1983:73)

The proportion of face-to-face clàsses in a pro-gramme labelled 'distance education' is high and represents the maximum that could be included within a normal definition.

In the German Democratic Republic the ratio of face-to-face consultations to individual study at home is 20% as the 1:1 rhythm of equal attendance on-campus and private study expected of conventional students is replaced by a 5:1 rhythm in <u>Fernstudium</u>. A typical study programme for the first semester of the first year of an engineering degree at a distance shows this ratio:

Table 8.2 Structure of DDR Distance Degree in Transport Engineering

| Distance Engineering (Transport) Degree: Semester 1 | | |
|---|---|---|
| Subject | Selfstudy time in hours | Consultations in hours | Lectures in hours |
| Marxism-Leninism | 50 | 10 | 2 |
| Russian | 80 | 15 | 14 |
| Mathematics | 135 | 30 | 4 |
| Physics | 85 | 14 | 2 |
| Materials Technology | 50 | 10 | 2 |
| Total | 400 | 80 | 36 |

In the system of the German Democratic Republic learning materials are developed by course teams set up under the direction of the Ministry of Further and Higher Education; the institute is at Dresden (Zentralstelle für Hochschulfernstudium) for university-level distance courses and a similar institute at Karl-Marx Stadt organizes the technological courses. Besides the learning materials there are three other major components of the didactic structure: private study, the students' workplace and regular seminars (consultations).

The students' workplace plays an important role in the study programme. Students are usually sponsored by their firm, they receive by law 48 days paid study leave per year, their thesis is usually on some aspect of the company's product or management. They are in effect practically guaranteed a promotion position upon graduation. It is claimed that this interaction of work and study provides a unique blending of theoretical and practical learning that is not paralleled in ordinary education. In the GDR attendance at consultations is obligatory once every two weeks during the first two years of study, with a slight decrease thereafter. In this way a four-year on-campus degree programme is achieved externally in five and a half years.

Schwarz (1978) and Möhle (1979) present the didactic structure schematically shown in Figure 8.10.

There are evident tensions in such a didactic structure between the problems of self-study and the regular consultations and between the lecturing strategies of professors with their conventional students on-campus and the distance students in the consultation. These tensions are brought out well by Dietze:

> The following rhythm seems to have established itself as the pattern of the study process: two weeks private study, one day consultation, two weeks private study and so on. A number of disciplines are covered in both the private study periods and the consultation days. We consider the distance education consultation to be a didactic element of fundamental significance: it guides, consolidates, controls and supplements private study. It is an essential didactic,

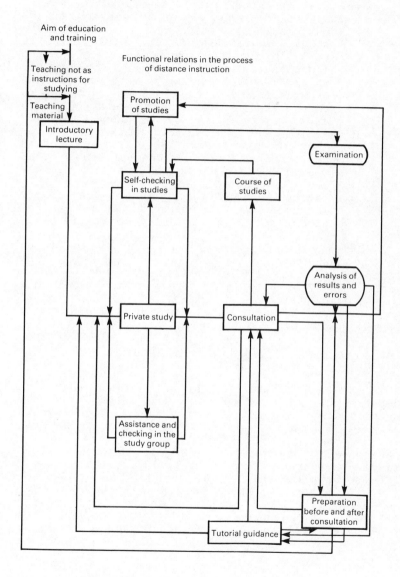

Figure 8.10   TYPE 4: A consultation model

methodological and organisational element in the distance education. Its importance can, however, only be fully recognised when it is considered the didactic element by means of which university lecturers systematically guide and support private study, especially in the first decisive years. The lecturer's approach to the consultation must, however, be correct in terms of content, methodology and organisation if he is to do justice to this task. Experience shows that an attempt to replace the guidance, consolidation and control of private study by lecturing has a negative effect on student performance. It is understandable that the specific pedagogical approach necessary for the distance education consultation is difficult for a university lecturer who is used to the methods of direct study in his daily work. (1979:33)

Common elements and problems are to be found in the consultation model (Type 4) and both the independent study divisions (Type 3) and the integrated mode (Type 5). The consultation model suggests, nevertheless, a range of methodological and didactic elements that are of value for all forms of distance education.

## The Australian integrated mode (New England model) (Type 5) (See Figure 8.11)

A specifically distinct form of distance education department within a conventional college or university has evolved in Australia. It is known as the 'New England Model' (New England is an area in New South Wales, 300 km NW of Sydney) or the 'Australian integrated mode'. It has been extensively presented: Sheath (1965, 1973), Smith (1979, 1984), Ortmeier (1981), Laverty (1980), Dahllöf (1978), Guiton (1981), White (1982), Shott (1983a, 1983b). It is found, with variations, in Australian colleges of advanced education and universities that teach at a distance. Systems in Zambia, Fiji, Papua - New Guinea and Jamaica have been modelled on it.

There had been a long history of distance education in Australia prior to the founding of the University of New England at Armidale in 1955. At technical and further education level the state

colleges of external studies date back to 1910
and at primary and secondary level the correspondence schools started in the 1920s. These are
all autonomous Type 1 institutions. At university
level external courses had been provided at the
University of Queensland since 1911 in a model
that evolved from a Type 3 structure.

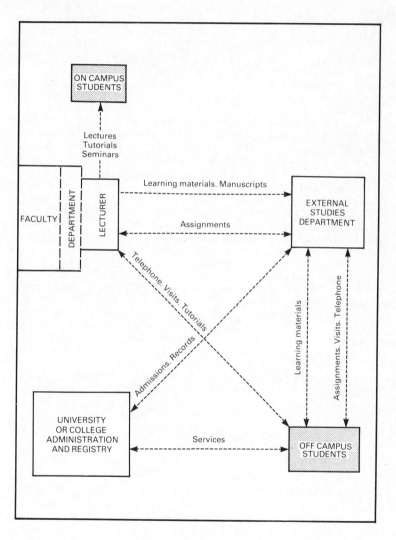

Figure 8.11    TYPE 5 The Australian integrated
mode

At individual Australian institutions there would never be sufficient students at university or college level to warrant the foundation of an autonomous institution. In 1955 the University of New England commenced teaching both on-campus and externally. A unique staffing structure and an attempt to preserve as much of on-campus provision for students as possible was evolved for the distance system. The university's lecturers were given a dual mandate and allocated groups of both internal and external students in equal numbers. Lecture notes and even audio-cassette tapes recorded live in on-campus lectures were sent to students and a requirement of compulsory periods of time on-campus was built into the distance study programme.

The system maintains that the academic staff of the university or college are to be responsible for the total teaching/learning process of writing courses, teaching them through a combination of independent study materials and face-to-face tuition and assessing the students by way of assignments and formal examinations. The external studies department is therefore an administrative one which organises for students a series of interactive activities, including at least a brief period of traditional university or college life as a full-time student in residence.

Thus external and internal teaching are integrated. The same academic staff teach and assess both sets of students. Students are enrolled in the same courses, take the same examinations and qualify for the same degrees and diplomas. Because academic staff have internal teaching commitments to conventional students, besides the responsibility of developing learning materials for external studies and then tutoring them, an External Studies Department is set up to relieve them of administrative details. This department frequently has no teaching function but looks after the production and distribution of course material, student records, statistics and student support services.

## Other institutions

Distance education institutions, as defined in this book, are institutions which teach students. They parallel ordinary schools, colleges and universities in that they enrol students, teach, assess and evaluate them and provide a total learning experience for them in every way. They also have a second function, which is not paralleled by ordinary schools, colleges and universities. They prepare for (some scholars would use the verb 'teach' here too) future students. They prepare printed, audio, video and/or computer based learning materials for students who will enrol in the future - next year or in two to ten years in the future. Precision in definition makes it impossible to include within the typology a number of institutions which have made a historical contribution to the evolution of distance education. Clearly the fact that they do not fit a particular definition in no way questions their validity or the importance of their contribution to this form of education. Three examples are considered: accrediting institutions, materials developing institutions and audio-video providers.

## Accrediting institutions

The best known example is the external degree of the University of London which has been since 1858 an examining body for degrees for which students study privately at home or by enrolling in a correspondence college or, by enrolling part-time or full-time at a face-to-face college, Of the 10,347 United Kingdom based students studying for a first degree or diploma in July 1980, at least 46% were enrolled in a correspondence college and a further 31% were studying by 'other methods' which includes independent study in their own home.

## Materials production centres

This is a model which appears to have been influenced by views on educational technology that were prevalent in the late 1960s. Full-time staff are engaged in materials development. It is hoped that by cooperative arrangements the materials developed will be made available to students studying at a distance. Two well known examples of such a structure are the Deutsches Institut für Fernstudien an der Universität Tübingen (DIFF) in the Federal Republic of Germany and the University of Mid-America (UMA) at Lincoln, Nebraska. The DIFF is a research and materials production institution which since its foundation in 1965 has made excellent contributions to distance education both in the Federal Republic and worldwide. The far-reaching research studies of Günther Dohmen, Otto Peters and Karl-Heinz Rebel are well

known and respected. The DIFF does not enrol
students nor can students apply for admission to
the course materials it developed. Cooperative
arrangements are made with other structures for
the use of the materials develops. The advantages
and tensions of such a model are well brought out
by Rebel in a recent article:

> The DIFF study units of a project are
> based on a specially developed curriculum.
> This curriculum does not simply follow
> the structure of the discipline in ques-
> tion, imparting the knowledge amassed
> through the centuries, but tries to take
> the learning needs of the target-groups
> seriously. Problem-centred structures,
> genetic learning approaches, 'subjective
> behavioural theories', implicit person-
> ality theories, everyday life problems,
> combining living and learning environ-
> ments, etc., are some of the theoretical
> approaches which have led to didactic
> structures unique to the DIFF study ma-
> terials. The price we have to pay for
> this curriculum research work in terms
> of manpower, time and costs is enormous
> but, I think, worth paying. As a compro-
> mise in academic quality is not acceptable
> - it could have fatal effects on distance
> study with regard to its academic repu-
> tation - the DIFF cooperates with scholars
> and university teachers in each of its
> projects. So-called 'academic boards'
> with an average of eight to ten members
> from different institutions of higher
> learning, research institutes etc., are
> responsible for the academic standard
> of the materials, in spite of their dif-
> ferent didactic structure. Thus each
> year about 400 German academics and ex-
> perts work for the DIFF on a contract
> basis, supporting the 133 fully employed
> staff members. As a result of this struc-
> ture, the DIFF is not a university in
> its own right, but is embedded in our
> educational system at the tertiary level,
> without being dependent on decisions
> from traditional universities (1983:101)

Similar in structure was the University of
Mid-America. Founded in 1974, it was much

publicized and quite influential but closed in
1982. It was a materials production organization
that allied itself to a grouping of other American
universities in its region in order that students
who wished to enrol might be taught. This model
is summed up in an in retrospect article by its
former directors:

> While the UMA underwent a variety of
> changes during its lifetime, its long
> range goals remained substantially the
> same: to affect substantially the access
> opportunities of adults to post-secondary
> experience, while maintaining or improving
> the quality of the teaching-learning
> system and while improving productivity
> through uses of mass communications means
> and other modern informational tech-
> nologies.
>
> A number of issues were related to de-
> veloping the best organisational frame-
> work within which to operate, and there
> was almost constant attention to re-
> definition of objectives and to staff
> reorganisation (McNeil and Wall, 1983:38)

## Conclusion

In this chapter a classification has been provided
for all those institutions which are characterised
by all the characteristics of distance teaching
institutions outlined in the previous chapters.
Within the unity of distance education, a major
divergence was posited between autonomous distance
teaching institutions and distance departments
of conventional institutions. Within these two
groupings further sub-divisions were indicated.
Certain institutional structures, some usually
associated with distance education, were found
to lie outside the typology as proposed.
It is admitted readily that distance programmes
which are taught electronically and which have
less reliance on print-based materials do not fit
easily into the typology. Well-known examples are
the Telekolleg and Funkkolleg programmes produced
by groupings of radio and television stations in
South West Germany and the intractive telephone
network of the University of Wisconsin at Madison.
Similar are a range of North American college
courses in which broadcast television is a component

from institutions such as Dallas County Community College, Miami Dade Community College and Coastline Community College. Such programmes are clearly examples of distance education, for unlike other forms of instructional television or educational technology they exhibit all the characteristics outlined in the previous chapter.

Such programmes place the focus on inter-activity and immediate feedback rather than on the permanent provision of referrable materials together with delayed feedback which is character-istic of most distance systems.

## Evaluation

Finally it is appropriate in a book designed in part for administrators of national and regional education systems in both developed and developing countries to provide some guidelines on the relative values of the two major groupings outlined in the typology: institutions which focus on the needs of distance students and are designed specifically for them as opposed to the designation of a section or a department of a conventional institution to provide for distance students.

Keegan and Rumble (1982b) tackled this problem with regard to university level institutions in the book The distance teaching universities and their proposals are reproduced here for distance institutions at all levels:

> While there are many who believe that the two approaches are so similar that mixed provision is both natural and mu-tually beneficial, we believe that:
>
> ° Autonomous DTUs are generally more advantageous for (1) external students, in that they are wholly dedicated to their needs, and (2) the nation, in that they can more readily respond to national needs which can only be met by distance means.
>
> ° Autonomous DTUs more readily cater for the needs of distance students to the extent that there are marked differences between them and students in conventional systems.
>
> ° Autonomous DTUs are administratively more efficient given the requisite

° volume of students.

° There is less likelihood of competition between DTUs because, by their very nature, they are costly to establish and hence there is unlikely to be more than one of them in all but the very largest countries.

° The costs associated with the establishment of an infrastructure for a DTU and the preparation of sufficient course materials to support a degree programme are high, and require a guaranteed annual volume of student enrolments if the system is to be cost-efficient.

° If sufficient numbers of students can not be guaranteed, a mixed system is preferable.

° The number of students at which an autonomous DTU becomes more efficient than a mixed-mode institution depends on the choice of media, the extent of the student support services, and the number of courses on offer, as well as the costs of the conventional university education in the country concerned. It lies at least in the range of 9,000 to 22,000 enrolments a year. (Keegan and Rumble, 1982b:246)

## References

Bääth, J. (1980) Postal two-way communication in correspondence education. Malmo: Liber Hermods.

Bääth, J. and Wangdähl, A. (1976) The Tutor as an agent of motivation in correspondence education. Pedagogical Reports, No. 8, University of Lund.

Carr, R. (1983) Distance education in Indian universities: a change of direction? Distance Education, 4,2,101-119.

Childs, G. (1971) The University of Nebraska Independent Study Division. In Peters, O. Texte sum Hochschulfernstudium, 57-70 as below.

Christow, J. and Mutojischiew, L. (1979). Die Entwicklung des Fernstudiums in der Volksrepublick Bulgarien. In Dietze, G. 22-30 as below.

Dahllöf, U. (1978) Reforming higher education and

external studies in Sweden and Australia. Stockholm: Almquist and Widsell.

Delling, R. (1979) Lehrbrief als Fernlehrgelegenheit, ZIFF Papiere. Hagen: Fernuniversität.

Dietze, G. (ed.) (1979) IVe Internationales wissenschaftliches Seminar zum Hochschulfernstudium. Dresden: Zentralstelle für das Hochschulfernstudium des Ministeriums für Hoch- und Fachschulwesens.

El Bushra, J. (1973) Distance teaching at university level. Cambridge: IEC.

Escotet, M. (1980) Adverse factors in the development of an open university in Latin America. In Sewart, D., Keegan, D. and Holmberg, B. (eds) (1983) Distance education: international perspectives. London: Croom Helm.

Fekete, J. and Nahlik, J. (1979) Ungarn. In Dietze 31-44 as above.

Gorochov, W.A. (1979) Hauptwege zur Verrollkommung des Fernstudiums in der USSR. In Dietze 14-21 as above.

Guiton, P. (1982) Australian distance teaching systems. Paper to conference of Universiti Sains Malaysia, Penang, Malaysia.

Harry, K. (1984) The international · Centre for Distance Learning's new computerised database, ICDE Bulletin, 6,6-7.

Holmberg, B. (1960) On the methods of teaching by correspondence. Lund: Gleerup.

Holmberg, B. (1981) Status and trends of distance education. London: Kogan Page.

Ilyin, V.V. (1983) The U.S.S.R. Financial and Economic Institute for Education. Distance Education, 4,2,142-148.

Karow, W. (1979) Privater Fernunterricht in der Bundesrepublik Deutschland und in Ausland. Berlin: DIBB.

Keegan, D. and Rumble, G. (1982) Distance teaching at university level. In Rumble, G. and Harry, K. (eds) The distance teaching universities. London: Croom Helm.

Keegan, D. and Rumble, G. (1982b) The distance teaching universities: an appraisal. In Rumble and Harry as above.

Laverty, J. (1980) Kevin C. Smith's External studies at New England. Distance Education, 1,2,207-214.

Markowitz, H. (1983) Independent study by correspondence in American universities. Distance Education, 4,2,149-170.

McKenzie, N., Postgate, R. and Scupham, J. (1975)

Open learning. Paris: UNESCO.
McNeill, H. and Wall, M. (1983) The University
of Mid-America. ICDE Bulletin. 4,31-36.
Möhle, H. (1978) Das in das einheitliche sozial-
istiche Bildungswesen der DDR integrierte
Hochschulfernstudium. Leipzig: Karl-Marx Uni-
versität.
Neil, M. (1981) The education of adults at a dis-
tance. London: Kogan Page.
Ortmeier, A. (1978) Fernstudium an Universitäten
und Fachhochschulen Australiens. Tübingen
DIFF.
Peñalver, A. and Escotet, M. (no date) Teoria e
praxis de l'Universidad a Distancia. San Jose:
UNED.
Peters, O. (1965) Der Fernunterricht. Weinheim:
Beltz.
Peters, O. (1971) Texte zum Hochschulfernstudium.
Weinheim: Beltz.
Rebel, K-H. (1982) Distance study in West Germany:
the DIFF's conceptual contribution. Distance
Education, 4,2,171-178.
Rekkedal, T. (1981) Introducing the personal tutor
counsellor in a system of distance education.
Stabbek: NKI Norway.
Schramm, W. (1977) Big media, little media. London:
Sage.
Schwartz, R. (1978) Die Konsultation in Studien-
prozess des Fernstudiums. In Möhle, H. (ed)
Hoch- und Fachschulfernstudium in der DDR
und in entwicklungsländern Afrikas. Leipzig:
KMU.
Sheath, H. (1965) External studies at New England:
the first ten years. Armidale, NSW: UNE.
Sheath, H. (1973) Report on external studies. Armi-
dale, NSW: UNE.
Shott, M. (1983a) External studies in Australia
at the crossroads? ASPESA Newsletter, 9,2,
2-9.
Shott, M. (1983b) Final report to the ASPESA execu-
tive. ASPESA Newsletter, 9,3,,15-17.
Singh, B. (1980) Correspondence education at Indian
universities. Patiala: Punjabi University.
Smith, K.C. (1979) External studies at New England:
a silver jubilee review 1955-1979. Armidale,
NSW: UNE.
Smith, K.C. (1984) Diversity down under in distance
education. Toowoomba, Queensland: Darling
Downs IAE.
TRU report (1975) An analysis of distance systems.
Stockholm: SOU.

Wedemeyer, C. and Bern. H., (1971) The independent study division of the University of Wisconsin. In Peters, Texte zum Hochschulfernstudium, 29-56 as above.

White, M. (1982) A history of external studies in Australia. Distance Education, 4,2, 101-121.

Willén, B. (1983) Distance education in Swedish universities. Distance Education, 4,2,211-222.

Zelaya Goodman, G. (no date) La administración de los sistemas de educación a distancia y sus costos. In Peñalver, A. and Escotet, M. Teoria e praxis de l'Universidad a Distancia. San Jose: UNED.

PART FOUR: DISTANCE EDUCATION IN PRACTICE

CHAPTER NINE

STUDENTS AND STAFFING


That's what I'm trying to do.  Sing a better song.
Educating Rita, 1983




## STUDENTS

### Numbers

During the late 1970s and early 1980s in many Western societies enrolments in university and college
programmes first became static and then began to
fall.  The consequences for the provision of staffing and resources were significant.  It is noteworthy that in the same period a similar loss of
enrolments was not generally experienced by distance
systems.  The figures for Australia are:

| Table 9.1: Enrolments in Australian universities and colleges of advanced education 1975-1982 | | |
|---|---|---|
| | Universities | Colleges of advanced education |
| Full-time enrolments | +  2.7% | +   1.0% |
| Part-time enrolments | + 22.9% | +  65.1% |
| External students | + 74.3% | + 196.4% |

Some traditional faculties regarded the growth
in off-campus enrolments as competition and the
external departments, in a number of cases, came
to be regarded with hostility. From the University
of Wisconsin Reid and Champness (1982:90) comment:

> Now that on-campus departments are wit-
> nessing a decline in number of full-
> time student enrolments, they view the
> expansion of the University of Wisconsin
> Extension as competition despite its

non-credit basis.

This study puts forward the view that the growth of privatisation in Western society is a major cause for the buoyancy of home study programmes. Citizens, especially those who have passed the age of twenty-five, are demonstrating a lack of enthusiasm to travel to a college or university and to join a learning group as the only method of studying for credit or for vocational advancement. Linked to this is a loss of the sense of community and of willingness to participate in the life of a college or a university by being present on its campus. If this hypothesis should prove to be correct, the implications for funding authorities are far-reaching.

## Characteristics

A major grouping of students who have chosen to study at a distance is the enrolment in the Open University of the United Kingdom. A comprehensive analysis of these students undertaken by Field (1982) signals four characteristics which differentiate these students from the traditional university undergraduate.

1. Experience. The adult student has concepts of the validity of evidence, of procedure, of accuracy and analysis, which are not part of the experience of students who transfer to university directly from high school graduation. Learning in a distance system commences with unlearning for many adults. Many of the students studied by Field were in the thirty to fifty-five age grouping and brought to their study an accumulation of experience in work, family and community which traditional students with little direct experience of employment or the application of knowledge to industrial and community settings do not have.
2. Aspirations. For many distance students work and family are the first two priorities and study comes third. In primary, secondary and tertiary education, teachers are used to dealing with people who are locked into the education system because of family and community expectations. Income and employment are seen as future consequences of the study programme. For many distance students income and economic responsibilities are a present reality, not a future hope. They may well dominate the study programme and push it into the background.

3.   Study milieu. The major factor in the enrolment
pattern of the off-campus student is distance from
the source of instruction.  It implies also distance
from the means of instruction, from the library,
from the laboratory, from the students' peers,
from the lecturer's office, from the facilities
which colleges and universities provide for students
studying on-campus.   Recreation and leisure activities are divorced from an academic environment.
There is a mismatch between the time pattern of
the student and the time pattern of the institution.
4.   Investment. Field considers that the distance
student deliberately departs from the financial
and investment pattern of his peers.  He has to
find money and time for taking on an extra work
load: the study programme.  The students' family
may find the economic cost of the study programme
is hard to bear.  For the on-campus student, enrolment in an institution of higher education has
traditionally been a sure route to a pleasant and
comfortable future job; more recently it has become
a pleasant and comfortable barrier against unemployment.
     The major components of Field's analyses of
Open University students and students generally
might be presented as in Figure 9.1.
     In general distance students tend to be gain-
fully employed, have less prior education, are
older and live comparatively far away from the
nearest place offering the same course in a different form.   Attempts to show that they also have
specific characteristics or psychological disposi-
tions have rightly been challenged by Willén (1982:
249):

> The opinion that the majority of distance
> students are autonomous, and for this
> reason choose this particular form of
> education is not supported by the investi-
> gations which have been carried out.
> On the contrary, it often proves to be
> practical reasons which have driven the
> student to choose this form of education.
> Our evaluation also clearly shows that
> most of our students had no choice, as
> no other form of education was available
> in the place where they lived, or that
> it was impossible for them to participate
> in any other form of education for family
> or occupational reasons.

| Students generally | OU students |
|---|---|
| 1. Experience ||
| People under 25, with little direct experience of employment; of the application of knowledge or techniques in service or industrial settings; of human relations or of social changes. | 75% aged 30-55 with a diverse accumulation of experience; with ideas on evidence, accuracy and analysis not gained from schooling. For many learning starts with un-learning. |
| 2. Aspirations ||
| People locked into education because of selection and training; because of family expectations; because of tied income and for whom in the current economic climate there is no attractive alternative. | For some, university studies are central as there is no other way to fulfil aspirations; or study gives a new dimension to existing work; or study is marginal with family and job responsibilities dominating it. |
| 3. Study Milieu ||
| Easy access to learning media; to fellow students; to advisers and tutors; leisure facilities are complementary to study; all within a convenient distance. | The study milieu is generally characterised by its distance from the source of instruction; the distance in time caused by the mismatch between student-system time and institutional time. |
| 4. Investment ||
| Traditionally a paid-for place in an institution of higher education has been the surest route to a clean, pleasant and interesting job. More recently it is a postponing of unemployment or work experience. Graduates emerge not very useful immediately to employers but they can be developed and exploited by employers. | The student takes on and finds money for an extra workload, a departure from most of his peers. To the family of the student the return may be less tangible than from other activities. The graduates are older, expensive and less mobile but with extensive experience of life. |

Figure 9.1 Differences between OU students and
students generally (Field)

> Our data shows that distance students
> at the university do not constitute any
> special group compared to other adult
> students at the university. The extension
> of this discussion, suggests that it
> could be harmful for students if one
> were to hypothesize that students are
> autonomous learners who know how to
> proceed through each of the learning
> events. Such an opinion could be misused,
> so that the planner and the teacher do
> not take the needs and capabilities of
> the students seriously enough when organ-
> izing education. (1982:249)

Privatisation of the study process and isolation
from teacher and peer group remain the central
distinctive features of distance students. These
are factors that make studying at a distance a
perilous task for those who cannot benefit from
privacy. They place large burdens on institutions
to provide compensatory learning mechanisms for
those who study in this way.

## Drop-out

Pre-occupation about drop-outs is a constant feature
of distance education literature and practice,
though not at primary and secondary school level.
Rekkedal (1971, 25) sums up the position:

> Comparing drop-out rates within different
> correspondence courses in different in-
> stitutes is very difficult. The courses
> vary in content, level, quantity of work,
> degree of difficulty and organization.
> Also the educational methods and media
> involved differ from course to course.
> Further, there are also large differences
> between criteria used in connection with
> course drop-out and cancellations and
> how drop-out and success are defined.
> In some surveys all students enrolled
> are taken into consideration. In other
> studies only individuals who really have
> started submitting assignments are defined
> as students. Nevertheless, the quanti-
> tative data published seem to indicate
> that the rate of drop-out in correspon-
> dence education normally is considerably
> higher than in full-time face-to-face

education, and that the number of students dropping-out is especially high in the beginning of the studies (see for example Glatter and Wedell 1970), but not generally higher than in other forms of part-time studies.

On the OUUK Woodley and Partlett (1983: 20-21) provide a balanced picture:

We have tried to take a system-wide look at student drop-out. This global approach has led us to consider general trends, patterns and explanatory models and to make suggestions for changes to the system as a whole. However, if we are to reach a more complete understanding of the drop-out process, we must complement the approach with more detailed microanalysis. On the individual student level we need to know far more about the psychological processes involved in becoming, then ceasing to be, an Open University student. By looking closely at individual courses and how students study them, we can perhaps make more detailed and concrete proposals for change.

In trying to understand why some students succeed while others drop out we must acknowledge the complex interplay of certain 'push' and 'pull' factors. 'Push' factors encourage them to continue while 'pull' factors lead to withdrawal. Below we give an over-simplified picture of the 'pull' factors acting on an imaginary individual:

| Push | Pull |
| --- | --- |
| Wants degree to get promotion. | Wants to spend more time with family. |
| Likes to finish something started. | Course is very difficult. |
| Very interested in the subject matter. | Fees are high. Doesn't like course tutor. |
| Spouse is very encouraging. | P/t degree course available nearby. |
| Allowed time off for summer school. | |

Each of these factors will have different strengths and drop-out will occur when the 'pull' factors barely outweigh the 'push' factors. Some students begin their course with the 'pull' factors and they are very vulnerable. In other cases the 'push' factors greatly exceed the 'pull' ones and it takes a dramatic new 'pull' factor such as a death in the family, or being sent abroad to work, to cause withdrawal.

A possible theoretical basis for an analysis of drop-out in distance education might be an adaptation of Tinto's work on drop-out in on-campus courses to the problem of studying at a distance. Tinto developed a theoretical model, based ultimately on Durkheim, in which it was hypothesised that weakness of integration of the student into the social fabric of the institution was an indicator of possible drop-out.

If one were to accept this theory, virtually all distance students would be 'at risk'. Their integration into the structure of their university or college is fragile and continually so throughout the length of the study programme. The distance student, almost by definition, does not take part in the life of the institution and the industrialisation of distance systems works to produce a customer/business atmosphere which negates the integrative support mechanisms which Tinto hypothesises as vital. The privatisation of learning at a distance tends further to provoke lack of integration.

This study suggests that there is a propensity to drop-out by enrollees in distance education. This propensity can be attenuated by the provision of quality learning materials but above all by the provision of adequate student support services for the avoidance of avoidable drop-out. Where student support of an adequate nature is not provided, students should understand that distance study may be constantly fraught with the risk of discontinuation.

Time
----

Time available for study is closely related to success or failure in distance education; it is also closely related to drop-out. The German scholar Schwittmann studied the relation between time avail-

able for study and success at both the Funkkolleg
programmes by radio in Southern Germany and the
courses at the Fernuniversität in North-Rhine West-
falen.  Schwittmann (1982) claims that 'time available for study' is the only important variable
for predicting success or failure in a distance
study programme.  He goes further and forecasts
that from a multi-media study package including
visits to study centres, watching television programmes, listening to radio programmes, studying
course materials, doing assignments, one can forecast which element of the multi-media study package
will be dropped first when one knows the relevance
of each element towards the final examination and
the amount of time available to the student. There
is food for thought here for those who complain
that distance students do not attend study centres
nor watch television broadcasts with the frequency
that they should.

Staffing analysis

In the literature of distance education one finds
little analysis of the staffing of distance institutions.  The typology presented in this book provides a framework for an initial study as Type
1 and Type 2 institutions (correspondence schools
and distance teaching universities) have the possibility of appointing full-time staff to both administrative and academic positions; mixed institutions
(Types 3-5) normally function with part-time staffing with only the top management working full-
time in distance education.
    Carr (1984:16) has analysed author employment
in distance teaching universities and discussed
the relative merits of a high level of full-time
staffing or a high level of part-time staffing
for the course development part of a distance institution.  In favour of a high level of full-time
staffing he lists:

(i)    Commitment (he quotes Perry that academics
       give their loyalty and commitment to the uni-
       versity that employs them full-time).
(ii)   time availability
(iii)  continuity - availability for course main-
       tenance
(iv)   communication
(v)    contribution to research.

    In favour of a high level of part-time staffing

he lists:

(i)   Cost - both in finance and facilities
(ii)  breadth of contribution
(iii) flexibility of contribution
(iv)  status - well known externals can bring status
      to the DTU.

Autonomous distance teaching institutions (Type 1-2). Three patterns of staffing can be identified and these will be labelled here (i) full-time staffing, (ii) full-time/part-time staffing, (iii) part-time staffing.

Full-time staffing.   Full-time staff are involved in both the development of learning materials and in the provision of student support services, sometimes including the marking of assignments. Portions of the course writing and the overflow of students' assignments are handled by part-time contract staff or marked by computer.

Examples of institutions which use this model of staffing are the Australian and Canadian correspondence schools and colleges of external studies, the Centre National d'Enseignement par Correspondance in France and Athabasca University in Alberta, Canada.    All of these institutions use full-time staffing for both of the characteristic operating subsystems of distance education: course development and student support services.

Full-time staffing is usually justified on academic grounds and on the greater effectiveness and commitment of staff when they are trained. In higher education a valid contribution to research is also possible.   Full-time staff in such institutions have a demanding role because the attempt to write creative course materials can be interrupted daily by the constant flow of assignments and telephone calls from students at present enrolled.

Disadvantages frequently cited are cost and inflexibility.    Many distance institutions pay only a few dollars per assignment to contract staff (Markowitz, 1983) and get course materials written on contract for fees which can with difficulty cover the overheads of full-time appointments.

Full-time/part-time.   Learning materials are developed by full-time academic staff (with some portions of the writing contracted out to specialists) and the marking of assignments and counselling

177

of students is conducted by part-time staff. The OUUK at Milton Keynes is a well known example of an institution which uses full-time staff almost exclusively for course development (with some contribution to research) and part-time staff for student support services.

In the first years of the OUUK full-time staff shared the course writing with contract authors from other universities and were assisted in the course development process by instructional designers (educational technologists) from the university's Institute of Educational Technology. Today both these processes are greatly diminished. The full-time academics are assuming more and more of the course development and as they themselves learn the skills of instructional design they tend to dispense with advice from educational technologists.

Full-time OUUK academics do not normally have responsibility for a group of students studying a course, though they do meet students at residential summer schools. Nor are they usually available for telephone tuition. Once they have finished the development of a course, they tend to move on to developing the next course. Much reflection on this staffing structure has taken place within the OUUK and it is generally agreed that the full-time faculty have provided the university with:

° a resident faculty on a par with many other universities;

° a nucleus by whom research grants and other educational, government and public commissions have been won.

° a group of course developers who have contributed to the production of highly acclaimed multi-media teaching packages.

The part-time and computer marking of students' assignments (TMAs and CMAs) has allowed the OUUK to provide an efficient and cost-effective teaching structure, plus representatives of the university close to the students' home and ambassadors of a correspondence university in every corner of the country and in most of its educational institutions.

Also commented upon have been:

° the lack of connection between the course development subsystem and the student support subsystem

◦ the occasional lack of interest of the full-time authors in the course in presentation and feedback on the course materials.
◦ low productivity in terms of units written per academic year
◦ lack of interest in research in distance education
◦ lack of flexibility of staffing once a course in a particular discipline has been written and is established for the next 8-10 years.

Part-time staffing. The development of learning materials and the marking/commenting on students' assignments is undertaken by part-time staff on contract. This may be their only occupation or they may have responsibilities to other (face-to-face) educational institutions or they may work in other professions (law, accountancy). Many Type 1 institutions, for instance the Rapid Results College at Wimbledon, use this model.

Apart from a group of administrators many correspondence schools and colleges use only part-time contract staffing. The contract writer may produce the full text or the institution may employ an editor who re-structures or adapts the materials. Similarly the part-time tutors can range from the dedicated individual who has the ability to set up a privileged one-to-one tutorial structure by correspondence, telephone and audio cassette, to the anonymous marker who mechanically grades assignments for unseen and never-contacted students.

Staffing in mixed institutions (Type 3-5) The three major groupings of traditional institutions which also teach at a distance, independent study divisions (Type 3), the consultation model (Type 4) and the integrated mode (Type 5), have normally extensive staffing for face-to-face lecturing. How do they provide for their external students?

It is difficult to generalise about the provision of staffing for the distance education departments of conventional colleges and universities as the possibilities are numerous. Markowitz (1983) shows that a staffing structure much favoured in independent study by correspondence divisions in the United States is to pay faculty staff overload to develop learning materials for distance students and then to pay faculty staff or other academics overload to teach the students once the courses are presented.

In the consultation system, at least in its

179

most typical development in the German Democratic Republic, course development is a centrally controlled and planned process. A central government institute for distance education brings together teams of academics from institutions throughout the nation to develop the materials providing also distance education expertise and design services. Once developed the materials are used in all the institutions authorised to offer the course throughout the country.

When the course is in presentation, the onus falls - as in many Western systems - on the small administrative distance education departments in the universities and on the administrators of the consultation centres (who have a role which in some aspects parallels that of the OUUK staff tutors). As there is no assignment submission and return structure, much of the student contact falls to the lecturer who holds the consultations. These tend to be academics either of the university or of other higher education institutions.

In the Australian integrated mode the course materials are developed by the professor or lecturer who teaches the on-campus students enrolled for the course. At the best this provides the external student with a fair approximation both in content and feedback to what is occurring on-campus. At the worst it can result in hastily prepared lecture notes being handed to a secretary for typing and dispatch or an audio-cassette recorder placed in the lecture room to record the lecture and students' reactions.

Shott (1983) analysed the staffing of the integrated mode and his queries are relevant for all mixed institutions that teach also at a distance. He suggests that such systems have four weaknesses:

°     a conflict of loyalties for the lecturer between the two types of students
°     insufficient recognition of the specific problems and needs of external students
°     a difficult relationship between the department of external studies and the academic faculties
°     fragmented provision of course offerings and awards for external students.

Shott feels that much of the progress in distance education in the last decade has been achieved by the full-time academics of Type 2 institutions and that this is a resource that institutions of

Type 3 - 5 do not have.

## Conclusion

The entry of large numbers of full-time staff in the distance teaching universities has been one of the striking features of distance education in the last decade. It has provided the possibility of training full-time staff for teaching at a distance; it has enabled academics to become competent in all the skills of the design of learning materials whether print, audio, video or computer based; it has provided a nucleus of permanent staff for research.

The foundation of the Dutch Open University at Heerlen, one of the most recent of the Type 2 institutions, has highlighted the question of full-time staffing for distance systems. Founded in a country with small distances and a comprehensive higher education provision, it had nevertheless the support of all political parties in the country and 85,000 enquiries for application prior to its first intake of students in September 1984.

The Dutch Open University was founded with a philosophy which stressed the specific nature of distance education which has far-reaching consequences for the appointment of full-time staff. Logically worked out this philosophy would imply that full-time academics from other universities who accept a permanent, full-time position at the Open University would have three major commitments to distance education: (i) the need for retraining to accept the philosophy of the distance university, to work in multi-media course team situations and to learn the skills of course development and student provision, (ii) the learning of the skills of author, instructional designer, editor and layout specialist so that with time the academic becomes a specialist in all aspects of print and non-print development of distance learning materials, (iii) a commitment to research - not only the maintenance of national standards of research in one's discipline but also research specifically on how to teach that discipline at a distance.

## References

Carr, R. (1984) Course development procedures. ICDE Bulletin, 5,21-27.
Field, J. (1982) Characteristics of OU students. Teaching at a Distance Research Supplement

No.1. Milton Keynes: OU.

Markowitz, H. (1983) Independent study by correspondence in American universities. Distance Education, 4,2,149-170.

Reid, J. and Champness, D. (1982) The Wisconsin Educational Telephone Network. British Journal of Educational Technology, 14,2,80-100.

Rekkedal, T. (1971) Correspondence studies - recruitment, achievement and discontinuation. Epistolodidaktika, 2,3-38.

Schwittmann, D. (1982) Time and learning in distance education. Distance Education, 3,1,155-171.

Shott, M. (1983) External Studies in Australia at the crossroads? ASPESA Newsletter, 9,2, 2-9.

Willén, B. (1981) Distance education at Swedish universities. Stockholm: Almqvist and Wiksell.

Woodley A. and Partlett, J; (1983) Student dropout. Teaching at a Distance, 24, 2-23.

# CHAPTER TEN

## CHOICE OF MEDIUM

> The motion picture is the great educator of the poorer people. It incites their imagination by bringing the whole world before their eyes. It sets spectators thinking and raises their standard of living. Books will soon be obsolete in the public schools. Scholars will be instructed through the eye. It is possible to teach every branch of human knowledge with the motion picture. Our school system will be completely changed inside of ten years. Thomas A. Edison, 1913

## Context

In the distance education university of the early 1980s the lecturer sits all day long at his or her word processor. The content of the course is inputed into the word processor and the lecturer prints out a hard copy from the printer. No secretary or typing pool support is needed and the need to proof read for other person's errors is eliminated. The lecturer corrects the hard copy, puts in the corrections himself and prints out a final version of the course materials to ensure that the text is correct. He then inserts the university's house style instructions for headings, subdivisions, choice of type-face and layout.

The lecturer then turns to his or her mouse to prepare the computer-designed illustrations, graphs, diagrams and other illustrative features that he wishes to use as part of his teaching. When these are completed to the lecturer's satisfaction, they are blended electronically into the text. The text and illustrations are printed out and the printed materials for the course are now complete. They can be distributed to the students' computers by satellite and the student can decide whether to study them on screen or print himself a hard copy. Alternatively the materials can be photocopied or plates can be made for conventional printing. The whole process of teaching at a distance has been industrialised and rationalised with the elimination of intermediary persons between the lecturer and the students.

As the lecturer spends much of his or her time at the word processor or in the audio, video or computer design laboratory when not working at the word processor, the teaching style of the distance education lecturer has evolved far from that of the on-campus university and the skills and training required are quite different. The lecturer needs the skills of a word processor operator, of an instructional designer, graphic artist and layout expert for print materials and extensive skills in the development and evaluation of audio, video and computer-based materials.

In such a context, (the technology for which is available at the time of writing) the choice of medium to be used is of vital importance. The range available as presented in a recent study by Ruggles (1982) includes: print, radio, audio-cassettes, television (TAGER, telecourses, slow scan, video-tapes, teleconferencing), satellites, videodiscs, videotex and microcomputers. Daily repercussions of an educational, political and financial nature are set up by the choice made from the various forms of new communication technology available. Many studies have shown that choice of medium is one of the major cost-inducing variables in a distance system and that the choice of certain media can rapidly and permanently increase total system costs.

A good summary is provided by Rumble (1984):

> In conventional universities geared to the lecture, seminar, and tutorial, there is a clear and almost linear relationship between staff and student numbers, and it is this relationship that is the primary determinant of cost. Media-based distance education, however, changes the production function of higher education. This change occurs not where media is used to supplement the teachers' role - this merely increases total costs, but where it is used as a substitute for teachers. In essence, capital replaces labour, offering to the educationalist what Leslie Wagner (1982:ix) has described as 'a mass production' alternative to the traditional craft approach.

The literature on choice of media for distance systems is quite noteworthy, so that this chapter looks only briefly at history, practice, literature, theory and the future of media in distance systems.

## CHOICE OF MEDIUM

### Historical development

Distance education began with print-based materials one hundred years ago. Over the last fifty years many new forms of communication technology have become available to educators both on-campus and at a distance with a tendency in the literature being to equate the latest with the best.

There were periods of great interest in educational films and educational radio in the 1930s and 1940s, programmed learning in the 1960s, educational television in the 1970s and educational computing in the 1980s. But the 1970s and 1980s were noted for a new sophistication in the use of print (Daniel and Stroud, 1981).

### Practice

Despite the claims made for many of the forms of new communications technology it is clear from studies of practice in the 1980s that most institutions remain print-based. The OUUK marked itself out as sui generis from the rest of the distance teaching universities by its insistence on broadcast television as a medium for distance education. The chapters of the 1982 book The distance teaching universities, each written by an individual from the institution concerned, show clearly the almost complete dominance of the print-based materials in the 1980s and in general that institutions at lower levels would use even less non-print materials. For the OUUK, the teaching package in the early 1980s, before the severe budgetary restrictions of the mid 1980s, was usually analysed thus:

- 80% correspondence, print-based materials
- 10% face-to-face sessions, either compulsory or voluntary
- 7% broadcast television
- 3% broadcast radio

The leading OUUK authority on non-print media concluded (Bates, 1982):

> television and radio in particular are proving to be of less significance in teaching systems or more difficult to use successfully than was originally expected.

## Literature

There is a rapidly growing literature on the use of new communications technology in distance education and from it six studies or groups of studies have been chosen for comment because of their authority and influence.

° McKenzie, N., Postgate, R. and Scupham, J. (1975) Open learning. Paris, UNESCO. French edition (1976) Etudes ouvertes.
° Swedish Broadcasting Corporation (1975) The TRU report. A programme for sound and pictures in education. Stockholm: SOU.
° Reports from the OU Media Research Group (1975 - 1980). Milton Keynes: OU (IET).
° Eicher, J.C. et al. (1977-1982) Economics of new educational media. Paris: UNESCO, 3 vols.
° Articles by A.W. Bates, Head of the O.U.U.K. Media Research Group 1980-1983.
° Ruggles, R. et al. (1982) Learning at a distance and the new technology. Vancouver: Educational Research Institute of British Columbia.

1. Open learning

The UNESCO study Open learning and the TRU Report are rightly acknowledged as the two major comparative studies of distance systems published in the 1970s. Both studies, however chose to ignore the painstaking comparative studies of Peters in the 1960s and his 1971 synthesis Texte Zum Hochschulfernstudium. Both studies chose not to acknowledge Peters' conclusion that western and socialist distance systems were fundamentally print-based systems with the possibilities of an admixture of face-to-face sessions.

Nevertheless the UNESCO study has been influential and its presentation can be found in planning documents and research studies in many countries. Particularly surprising is the emphasis on broadcast radio and television in Australia (a country which has had print-based systems at university level since 1911 and at primary and secondary level since 1919 and in which geographic and demographic considerations make broadcasting problematical) and in France where the comprehensive government systems have been print based since 1939 and the perfectionist, academic atmosphere of education at all levels make interest in the technology of education at most peripheral (Ardagh, 1975). The chapter on France was, in fact, rewritten for the French translation with an explanatory foot-note. (Etudes Ouvertes, 1977). Educational research takes place within a context and a tradition and without feedback from this structure it is fraught with danger.

2. <u>Distance education. An outline of the present situation and some organisational alternatives for post secondary education</u>, the contemporary Swedish study often referred to as the 'TRU Report' took a similar line and concentrated on the use of broadcasting in education. Although influential outside Sweden, Willén shows that Swedish distance education at university level took a quite different direction:

> In spite of the Committee's brief to deal with the university level, they have chosen to describe many distance education systems at lower educational level and have not discussed the differences in distance education between different educational levels. But the most severe shortcoming is in the description of the international scene given by the working group; it is characterised by an obvious bias toward systems based on radio and television. To take one example, the information about Australia is completely distorted, as only one limited experiment in broadcasting is described, while the basic model used there for many years has been ignored, even though the bibliography refers to work describing in detail the development of distance education in Australia (1984: 101).

3. In the period 1970-1979 researchers in the Audio-Visual Media Research Group at the OUUK, among whom were A. Bates, M. Gallagher, J. Meed and L. Kern, built up an exhaustive documentation on the use of non-print media by students in a major distance system. No study of the use of media in distance education

can afford to ignore these data.

4. The three volume UNESCO study <u>Economics of new educational media</u> published from 1977-1982 by J. Eicher, D. Hawkridge, E. McAnany, F. Mariet and F. Orivel gave an authoritative analysis of costing structures for the use of new media in education. The authors, however, tend to ignore the setting in which such media are used and miss the important distinction made by Neil (1981) between those media which <u>support</u> the work of teachers and lecturers (use of educational technology in conventional education) and those institutions in which media <u>replace</u> and render un-necessary face-to-face teaching (distance education). Hence, the study is frequently unclear on whether plant, buildings, salaries of school teachers and administrators form part of the costing mechanisms or not.

5. A Canadian study by R. Ruggles, J. Anderson, D. Blackmore, C. Lafleur, J. Rothe and T. Taerum entitled <u>Learning at a distance and the new technology</u> provides an up-to-date listing of the various media available to distance systems and the reader is referred to this book for details of the availability and use of media in distance education.

6. In the period 1980-1983 A.W. Bates, the leader of the (by then dispersed) group of researchers of the Audio-Visual Media Research Group summarised the work of his colleagues in a series of seminal papers (Bates 1980, 1981, 1982, 1984) which provided a new theoretical overview of the use of non-print media in distance systems based on an evaluation of the first decade of the OUUK's teaching. His presentation to the ICCE Vancouver conference 'Trends in the use of AV media in distance systems' (Bates, 1982) came as a disappointment to many. In it he states:

   ° There is a clear movement away from using broadcasting by distance learning systems.
   ° Video material produced right from the beginning for use only on cassette requires a different style of production from broadcast television.
   ° In the OUUK the greatest media development

during its 12 years of existence has been the humble audio-cassette.

If distance education systems wish to provide a wide range of courses to students who are often scattered or isolated, telephone tuition is the only practical way of providing two-way, interactive tutorials.

He suspects that many of the educational functions of computer-aided learning can be done more easily, conveniently and cheaply through a combination of audio-cassettes and print.

Many of Bates' conclusions had been foreshadowed by Schramm's (1977) Big media, little media.

## Theoretical framework

Bates (1982) gives us a five-point guideline for the choice of media for a distance system:

1. Accessibility: available in most students' homes?
2. Convenience: can the student use the medium?
3. Academic control: can the teacher design the material himself?
4. 'Human' touch: can the learner relate to the teacher via the medium?
5. Availability: what is available now?

Further indicators that influence the choice of medium are: pedagogic effectiveness, costs, political influences, research pressures, student access and privatisation of living.

The twenty-year long debate on the pedagogical effectiveness of various media was summed up by Schramm (1977) with the conclusion that any media is all right if well used.

Rumble (1982), Eicher et al. (1977-1982) have provided adequate costing mechanisms for calculating the costs of various media chosen:

Broadly speaking, very significant costs are incurred in the preparation of materials irrespective of student numbers. The level of cost incurred will vary depending on the choice of media. Production costs of television are high

189

but not as high as for film. The production cost of radio is relatively low.
Print production costs vary depending
on the level of sophistication, but overall are not normally significant in themselves within the context of a particular
project. Where print is the principal
medium the cost of academic staff time
in its design and development may be
significant. (Rumble, 1982:119).

Political considerations have frequently influenced decisions on the choice of media. The
OUUK/BBC relationship in the provision of television
programmes for the UK Open University system is
well known, with both the educational institution
and the broadcasting station cooperating in the
production of programmes. Similarly the government
of British Columbia when founding the Open Learning
Institute seem to have anticipated the use of new
developments in communications technology - when
the first administrators designed a system based
essentially on print and telephone, the politicians
devised a new institution, The Knowledge Network
of the West, to concentrate on the new technology.
The powerful impact of the influence of educational
television researchers on decision-makers has already been referred to.
    Student access to media influences educational
decisions. It may limit the use of what might
be an excellent pedagogical medium - the video
disc, and proliferate the use of the home computer.
If the hypothesis of the privatisation of institutional learning put forward in this book proves
correct, then teaching choice will be influenced
by the potential availability of the medium in
the students' homes rather than in study centres
or other local buildings.

## Conclusion

What medium then should be chosen? It often comes
as a surprise to those who do not know distance
systems that there are two answers to this question.
Print can be pretty useful for the course content,
but pretty hopeless for the student support services
which accompany the course materials one, five
or ten years later. The reasons why print is the
great survivor of distance systems were given by
Peters (1979) and as the OUUK decided in the mid-
1980s that its courses were to remain unchanged

for 8-10 years, it is clear that a durable medium is needed. But when the course is in presentation students need instant feedback by telephone, electronic mail, on-line computer or teleconference. Print is too cumbersome. 'The great weakness of distance education has in most cases been the slowness of the communication process caused by the correspondence method dominating this kind of education' (Holmberg 1984:50). Improved and cheaper telephone services should lead to the wider use of the telephone for immediate two-way communication when the student is in difficulties.

## The future

The world of distance education cannot remain remote from the developments in city living that have taken place from the late 1970s to the early 1980s in many societies.

The house of the late 1970s (which still remains the typical home for many) featured telephone, radio, television, heating, lighting and washing machines as the main systems. The changes available by the mid 1980s are striking: in addition to the radio, a hifi system has become standard, cable television has been added with the number of sets increased and with video games, a VCR and a video-camera. An alarm and air-conditioning system is now standard but the greatest development is around the telephone, with facsimile, recording, telex/teletex, videotex and telephonic secretary being newly available. The home computer, the latest arrival, will soon be used for home administration.

With these electronic developments in the home has come a privatisation of living and a loss of a sense of community involvement in many Western societies. Some or all of the former community based activities have been transferred in full or in part to the home:

| COMMUNITY ACTIVITY | HOME ACTIVITY |
| --- | --- |
| the restaurant | the home barbecue |
| the theatre | the video-cassette recorder |
| the church | - |
| the seaside | the home swimming pool |
| the sports stadium | the television set |

The development of home based universities

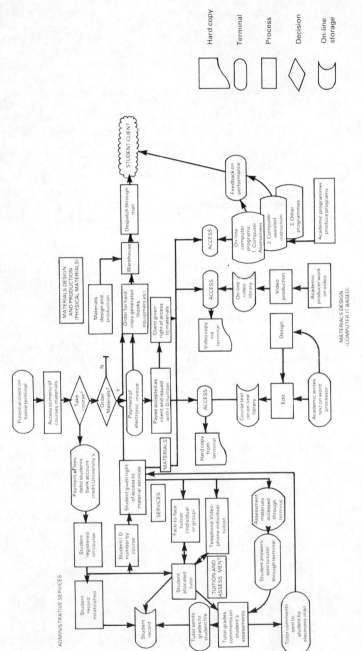

Figure 10.1 The information technology university (Rumble)

in the last decade and the privatisation of institutional learning that is a characteristic of distance education are logical consequences of these developments in the patterns of many communities. That is not to say these developments pose any threat to conventional education. Conventional education will, doubtless, remain oral and group-based and take place in educational institutions, but side by side with it - and complementary to it - there is ample space for developments in distance education courses, designed especially for those who work and for those for whom there is no work.

Side by side with the electronic developments in the house of the 1980s come developments in what has been called (Rumble, 1984) the information technology university. Rumble's drawing shows the integration of the main systems of a distance teaching university integrated into one information technology network (See Figure 10.1):

    Materials design
    Production of physical materials
    Student services
    Tuition and assessment
    Administrative services.

## References

Bates, A. (1980) Towards a better theoretical framework for the use of audio-visual media. Instructional Science, 10, 41-55.

Bates, A. (1981) The unique educational characteristics of TV and some consequences for teaching and learning. Journal of Educational Television, 141-149.

Bates, A. (1982) Trends in the use of audio-visual media. In Daniel, J. et al. Learning at a distance. A world perspective. Edmonton: ICCE.

Bates, A. (1984) Broadcasting in education: an evaluation. London: Constable.

Daniel, J. and Stroud, M. (1981) Distance education: a re-appraisal for the 1980s. Distance Education, 2,1,35-51.

Holmberg, B. (1984) On the educational potentials of information technology with special regard to distance education. ICDE Bulletin, 6, 49-54.

Peters, O. (1979) Some comments on the function of printed materials in multi-media systems. Epistolodidaktika, 1, 10-20.

Ruggles, R. et al. (1982) Learning at a distance and the new technology. Vancouver: ERICB.

Rumble, G. (1984) The cost structures of distance education: when it is cheaper and what can go wrong. Open University, mimeograph.

Schramm, W. (1977) Big media, little media. London: Sage.

Willén, B. (1981) Distance education at Swedish universities. Stockholm: Almquist and Wiksell.

CHAPTER ELEVEN

ADMINISTRATION


"I've taught the dog to whistle".
"I can't hear him whistling".
"I didn't say he'd learnt to whistle".
From a cartoon strip. 1977.


## Administration

An overview of the characteristics of educational administration is given by Fielden and Lockwood's summary:

> Universities differ significantly from many other forms of organisations. They are multi-purpose organisations, undertaking teaching, research and public-services, and it is extremely difficult to separate the contributions made to each purpose. It is even more difficult to measure the outputs in meaningful terms. The composition of membership also provides differences; for example, most of the academic and administrative staff in effect possess virtual life tenure whereas most of the student population is replaced every three or four years. These and many other features distinguish universities from most other forms of organisation. (1973:20)

In administrative theory the process of administration is created to achieve the output. Educational administration is distinguished from most other forms of organisation because it is 'difficult to measure the outputs in meaningful terms'. It is difficult to reach agreement on, let alone measure, the 'advancement of knowledge' or 'the preparation of a student for life'. The administrative answer has usually been to suboptimize, that is to establish a level of output which can be measured ('how many students pass the examinations',) but there is always the danger that

195

such sub-optimizing will block the educational system from achieving its real goal.

The administration of distance systems comes closer to general administative theory than administration of conventional educational systems. It represents an industrialisation of the process of educational administration and requires administrative skills that are akin to those of an industrial enterprise. The distance system has daily preoccupations with lead times, deadlines, print runs, job schedules, type-faces, delivery and dispatch. Although motivation of staff and students remains a prerequisite for student learning, to it are allied a whole range of processes in which administrative efficiency is essential if successful learning is to take place: deadlines for learning materials, layout formats, production schedules, timing of dispatch, turn-around-time for assignments, communication of guidelines and instructions by mechanical or electronic means.

Administrators of distance systems, or the distance departments of conventional education institutions, depend for their success on their ability to manage quasi-industrial processes. As a result some distance institutions (mainly of Type 1 - correspondence schools and colleges) seem able to dispense with the employment of educationists, and rely on managers, typists and clerks for their administration.

Miller and Rice (1967) in their Systems of organisation. The control of task and sentient boundaries show how organisations can be characterised by their essential operating activities and the importance of analysing task boundaries and sentient (personal) boundaries in administration:

> Any open system exists, and can only exist, by exchanging materials with its environment. It imports materials, transforms them by means of conversion processes, consumes some of the products of conversion for internal maintenance, and exports the rest. Directly or indirectly, it exchanges its outputs for further intakes, including further resources to maintain itself. These import-conversion-export processes are the work the enterprise has to do if it is to live. An educational enterprise, imports students, teaches them and provides them with opportunities to learn; it exports

ex-students who have either acquired
some qualifications or failed. (1967:3)

In Miller and Rice's terms it is important
to identify the 'operating activities' that characterise the enterprise. The operating activities
are those that directly contribute to the import/
conversion/export processes which define the nature
of the enterprise and differentiate it from other
enterprises. Miller and Rice's theory of system
organisation was applied to the organisation of
distance education systems by Kaye and Rumble
(1981). They had little difficulty in identifying
two characteristic operating subsystems 'course
development' and 'student support services' and
the task boundaries that separate these activities
within the organisation from other activities.
The course development sub-system comprises the
planning, designing, crystallising and recording
of the teaching (together with the proposed methodologies and structures for presenting the teaching
at a future date) in mechanical or electronic form.
The student support sub-system comprises the activities designed by the institution to focus on
the student's home (or institutional centre near
the student's home) that will provide a private
and individualised presentation of the pre-recorded
course content together with the stimulation of
teacher and peer-group clarification, analysis,
motivation and non-verbal atmosphere that normally
accompany the presentation of the course in oral,
group-based educational provision.
Kaye and Rumble's conclusion seems inevitable:

> It is one of the tenets of this book
> that the management of distance-learning
> systems is qualitatively different from
> that of conventional, classroom-based
> teaching systems. (1981:26)

Distance education enterprises have clusters
of task and sentient boundaries which focus on
the process of 'course development' and others
which focus on the process of 'support services
for students studying at home' in a way which cannot
be found in other educational institutions. These
two characteristic operating sub-systems define
the nature of a distance system and differentiate
it from other forms of educational administration.
In Miller and Rice's (1967:6) analysis, organisations have two other types of activity besides

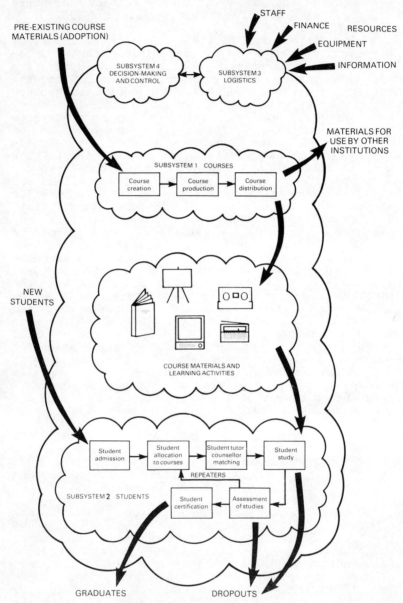

Figure 11.1  A systems view of distance education
(Kaye and Rumble)

Note Copyright approval.

operating activities:

> Maintenance activities procure and re-
> plenish the resources that produce op-
> erating activities. Thus not only the
> purchase, maintenance, and overhaul of
> machinery, but also the recruitment,
> induction, training and motivation of
> employees come under this heading.

> Regulatory activities relate operating
> activities to each other, maintenance
> activities to operating activities, and
> all internal activities of the enterprise
> (or unit) to its environment.

To these may be added in some Type 2 (Distance
teaching universities) institutions a fifth sub-
system for research activities. Kaye and Rumble
present their analysis in Figure 11.1.
    The remainder of this chapter treats briefly
the five administrative structures of distance
systems: course development and student support
services together with the maintenance, regulatory
and research sub-systems.

## Course development

There have been few studies of the administration
of course development activities. In distance
education course development does not imply just
the preparation of print and non-print learning
materials but the production of a total learning
experience for the distance student that will parallel all the facilities that are characteristic
of oral, group-based education including the additional homework, laboratory practicals and library
research periods that are the characteristics of
face-to-face study. Useful contributions to good
practice have been provided by Holmberg (1981)
and the South Australian College of Advanced Education (1983).
    On the administration models of course develop-
ment there are two studies by Mason and Goodenough
(1981) and K.C. Smith (1980):

| Smith (1980) | Mason and Goodenough (1981) |
|---|---|
| 1. Course team model | Course team |
| 2. Author/editor model | Content specialist and |

|                              | editor                             |
| 3. Author/faculty model      | Content specialist and transformer |
| 4. Educational adviser model | Instructional design               |
| 5. Intuition model           | Content specialist only            |

1. <u>The course team model</u>. Perry (1976) presents the course team approach as expensive, essential for the success of the OUUK, and as that institution's major contribution to higher education. K.C.Smith, however, isolates the OUUK as <u>sui generis</u> because of the size of some of its course teams (sometimes with more than 20 members from OUUK full-time staff, BBC staff and representatives of other institutions). If distance education is an industrialised form of teaching then there are strong justifications for a course team approach in that the materials become institutionalised, in that it is the institution rather than an individual who teaches, and the materials can continue to be used when the authors have moved to other tasks or left the institution. Difficulties arise in maintaining dynamism, avoiding a stereotyped middle-of-the-road approach and the possibility of personality clashes. Smith seems to favour a smaller group of 5-6 persons and cites Athabasca University (Canada) and Deakin University (Australia) as examples.

2. <u>Author/editor model</u> (similar to Mason and Goodenough's 'Content specialist and editor'). Smith (1980:63) gives this as the usual model adopted by north American Independent Study Departments (Type 3 institutions) and describes it as follows:

> The most common model for course development for correspondence students at all levels of education and especially in America is what I call the author/editor model. In this approach authors are contracted to write a course, that is supply the content, and have it edited by specialists within the corespondence school or department of independent studies. This model has been used in the University of Wisconsin extension department and Pennsylvania State University.

3. <u>Author/faculty model</u> (similar to Mason and

Goodenough's 'Content specialist and transformer').
Mason and Goodenough (1981:107) comment:

> a more sophisticated role is one in which
> an editor acts as a transformer of aca-
> demic subject-matter making it more suit-
> able for the distance learner by introduc-
> ing instructional design elements.

Successful use of structures similar to this have
been made by the National Extension College (Cambridge) and the Open Learning Institute (Vancouver)
in which a full-time staff member is allocated
a group of subjects and 'transforms' materials
written by contract authors into distance learning
courses.

4. Educational adviser model (similar to Mason
and Goodenough's 'Instructional design'). Mason
and Goodenough (1981:109) describe this from UNED,
Spain as:

> external writers are contracted to develop
> content from a brief devised by a team
> of educational technologists, curriculum
> designers and internal academics or sub-
> ject-matter experts.

and comment that the freedom traditionally experienced by academics is not easily handled in this
model.
   Smith describes it from Australian Type 5
(integrated) institutions where the Departments
of External Studies have educational advisers who
have wide academic experience and a special interest
in distance education techniques enabling them
to work closely with the institution's faculty
academics.

5. Content specialist only. Mason and Goodenough
(1981:105-106) list the advantages and limitations
of one academic/content specialist working alone
to produce a course. This can have advantages
of speed, uniformity and cheapness as well as pro-
tecting the freedom of the academic that is central
to a number of national university systems. Courses
developed in this way can be found in Type 1 (correspondence schools and colleges), Type 2 (Distance
teaching universities) and Type 5 (Integrated mode)
institutions.

## Student support services

The provision of student support services achieves for distance systems the essential feedback mechanisms that are characteristic of education. It is mainly through them that two-way communication is established between student and institution, though the better course materials have inherent feedback mechanisms as well. Provision of student support services distinguishes distance education institutions from publishing houses and other producers of learning materials.

The link that is provided between the learning materials that have been developed and the learning that it is hoped will take place from the materials is central to the concept of distance education. Fraught with danger is the idea that distance teaching is complete once the learning materials have been developed and mailed to the students. Too often they remain unopened, or, if opened, unread.

The OUUK developed a particularly rich structure of student support services which was in many ways the central innovation of the system (Keegan, 1979). The system, providing linking between materials and learning, included at least nine interlocking components, many of which were optional to the student. These structures came under the control of the OUUK's Regional Tutorial Services department and were described by Sewart (1978) as a 'continuity of concern for the student studying at a distance':

  ° the tutor-counsellor who follows the student throughout his/her university career
  ° the tutor available for consultation on an individual course
  ° 13 regional offices providing a decentralised focus for the administration of tuition, counselling and student support systems
  ° a study centre within easy travelling distance where the student can meet other students and use facilities
  ° tutorials at regular intervals
  ° computerised student records that can pick up problems in students' progress and anticipate drop-out.
  ° Kosmat analysis - a computerised weighting of the grades given by tutors on all

> °  assignments against the national average
> °  residential summer schools
>    a student association with regional
>    branches

The five major groupings in the typology developed for this book have, in general, different
approaches to the provision of student support
services.  Two of the groupings of institutions
have heavy involvement in this provision:

° Type 4: the consultation system of the central
  and Eastern European socialist democracies.
° Type 5: the Australian integrated mode.

Two groupings of institutions have tended to rely
on the development of learning materials as central,
with student support focusing on attentive correction and comment on assignments:

° Type 1: the correspondence schools and
  colleges.
° Type 3: the independent study model.

The fifth grouping (Type 2, the autonomous distance
teaching universities) varies widely in the
financial dimension and theoretical commitment
to support services.  By measuring and weighting
the volume of compulsory and optional face-to-
face services provided by different educational
structures it would be possible to draw up a continuum on which institutions might be placed ranging
from conventional education to private reading. (see
Figure 11.2.)

The administration of maintenance (or logistical)
activities. Kaye and Rumble list purchasing, maintenance and repair of buildings and equipment,
staff recruitment, induction, training and motivation under this heading (1981:22).  Of particular
importance in the administration of distance systems
is the characteristic plant that those institutions
require.  The cost effectiveness of distance teaching systems has often been referred to because
new educational buildings are not needed: there
are no lecture theatres, seminar rooms, laboratories, playing fields, cafeterias and student
facilities.  Library and office accommodation is
needed for staff only, though one institution (CNEC
in France) dispenses with office accommodation
for all but senior staff by having full-

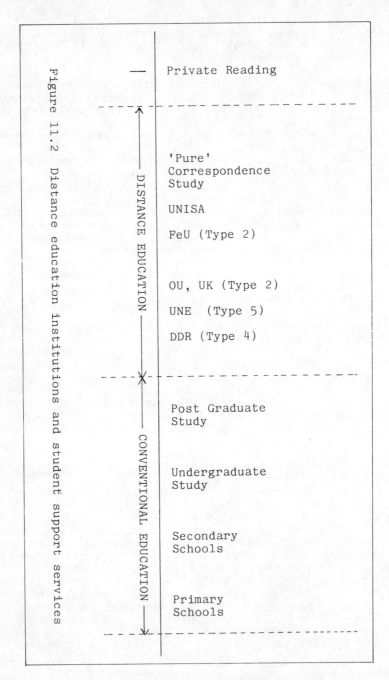

Figure 11.2 Distance education institutions and student support services

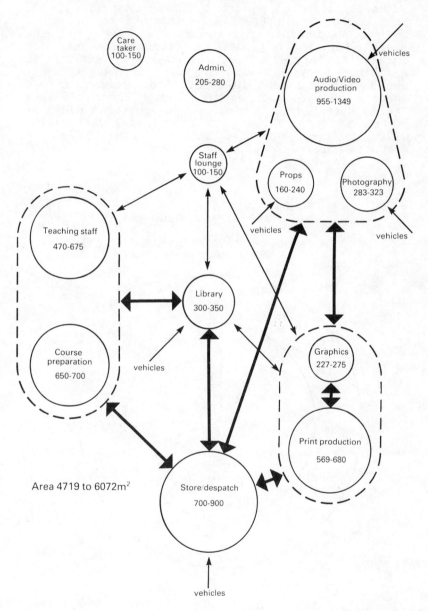

Figure 11.3 Proposed design for distance institution
Note copyright approval.

time teachers work from home. Local centres and
tutorial rooms are often provided free by local
authorities or hired from other institutions. Yet
Keegan and Rumble (1982:226) hesitate to recommend
the foundation of an autonomous distance teaching
system for small groups of students because the
industrial infrastructure can be costly, production
facilities have to be purchased or budgeted for
and a long lead-time in course production is needed
before students can be enrolled. These tensions
are illustrated by a proposed design for a distance
system (Figure 11.2) and the actual allocation
of space from an existing institution, UNISA in
Pretoria (Figure 11.3).

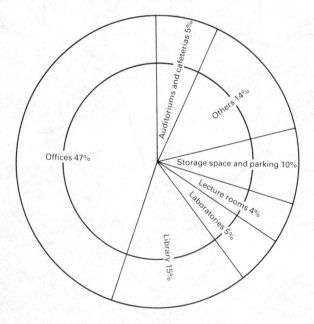

SUBDIVISION OF TOTAL FLOOR SPACE
ACCORDING TO SPACE CATEGORIES

Inner circle:   56 200 students (1980)
Outer circle: 140 000 students (2012)

Figure 11.3 Allocation of plant at UNISA, Pretoria
Note copyright approval.

Research subsystem. Type 2 institutions (distance teaching universities) with large full-time academic staffs need an administrative sub-system for research activities.

Regulatory subsystem. The regulatory activities relate the operating activities to each other, the logistical and research activities to operating activities and the activities include decision making structures, planning, financial management and evaluation. Certain aspects of financial management are treated in Chapter 11 and evaluation in Chapter 12. This chapter concludes with a comprehensive guide to the planning of a distance system provided by Dodd (1984:147-150):

PLANNING A DISTANCE EDUCATION SYSTEM

| STUDENTS | Age | Minimum age for entry:<br>Maximum age<br> restriction?:<br>Majority age range: |
| --- | --- | --- |
| | Sex | male          female |
| | Geographical distribution | Where<br><br>Regional quota?:<br><br>          urban          rural |
| | Educational entry conditions | Open entry:<br><br>or restricted entry: |
| | Study time | Full-time or part-time:<br><br>Study time available<br>each week:          (hours) |
| | Occupational groups | Occupation quotas?: |

| STUDENTS (Contd.) | Lifestyles | Income (to pay fees):<br><br>Housing (study environment):<br><br>Possessions (TV, radio, cassette player, tleephone etc.):<br><br>Transport (to attend local centres): |
|---|---|---|
| | Study motivations | e.g. vocational, educational, personal |
| | Student population | New entrants Year 1  Year 2  Year 3  Year 4 |
| | | Continuing Students |
| | Level | e.g. elementary, secondary, undergraduate, postgraduate, continuing education: |
| | Purpose | e.g. functional, vocational, inservice training and updating, educational: |
| | Number | How many different programmes: |
| | Priorities | Which programme(s) first: |
| COURSES | Type | Traditional:<br><br>Non traditional (e.g. multi-disciplinary): |
| | Levels | How many course levels in each programme: |
| | Number | How many courses at each level: |
| | Student choice | What freedom of student choice: |
| | Time | How many years  for graduation: |

| TEACHING YEAR | Structure | How many semesters:<br><br>How many student weeks per semester: | |
|---|---|---|---|
| MEDIA | Range | Print, Broadcast, Non-broadcast | |
| | Mix | print    broadcast    non-broadcast | |
| PRINTED | Academic creation | Who writes (e.g. on campus faculty: external authors):<br><br>Where:<br><br>When (time availability):<br><br>How (single authors or course teams):<br><br>Why (incentive): | |
| | Physical production | Where (on campus; off campus):<br><br>How many copies initially: | |
| | Distribution | Method (post; road):<br><br>Frequency (weekly; monthly):<br><br>Destination (student home; local centre): | |
| BROADCAST MEDIA | Television and Radio programmes | Allocation | All courses or only some courses |
| | | Role | Supportive or new study information:<br>Institutional: |
| | | Production | Who produces:<br>Where: |
| | | Reception | Home-based or local-centre-based: |

| NON BROAD-CAST MEDIA | e.g. video tapes, audio-cassettes, equipment for experiments | Allocation | All courses or only some courses |
| | | Role | Supportive or new study information: |
| | | Production | Who produces:<br><br>Where: |
| | | Reception | Home-based or local-centre based: |
| FACULTY SUPPORT | Avail-ability of specialist staff support | e.g. text editors and designers:<br><br>broadcasting personnel:<br><br>audio-visual specialists:<br><br>educational technologist:<br><br>course administrators: | |
| | Purposes | e.g. tuition and counselling:<br><br>local study activities: | |
| | Locations | Where: | |
| | People | e.g. campus faculty:<br><br>part-time local staff: | |
| ASSESSMENT | Type | e.g. oral, written | |
| | Frequency | How often | |
| | People | Who will assess | |
| | Location | Where | |
| EXAMINATION | Type | e.g. oral, written | |
| | Frequency | How often | |
| | People | Who will examine | |
| | Location | Where | |

| ADMINISTRATION | Who will be responsible for student and institutional administration | |
|---|---|---|
| MANAGEMENT | How will the faculty and other personnel be organised and managed | |
| FINANCE | Institution-al | What finance is available in the first year and in subsequent years: |
| | Students | What fees will students pay |
| DATE OF OPENING | When will the first students be enrolled? | |

Figure 11.4 Planning a distance education system (Dodd)

References

Dodd, J. (1984) Progettare un sistema di istruzione a distanza in Italia. In Keegan, D. e Lata, F. (edd) L'Università a distanza. Riflessioni e proposte per un nuovo modello di università. Milano: Angeli.

Fielden, J. and Lockwood, G. (1973) Management of universities. London: Chatto and Windus.

Holmberg, B. (1981) Status and trends in distance education. London: Kogan Page.

Kaye, A. and Rumble, G. (1981) Distance teaching for higher and adult education. London: Croom Helm.

Keegan, D. (1979) The Regional Tutorial Services of the Open University. Hagen: Fernuniversität (ZIFF).

Mason, J. and Goodenough, S. (1982) Course development. In Kaye and Rumble as above.

Miller, E. and Rice, A. (1967) Systems of organisation. The control of task and sentient boundaries. London: Tavistock.

Perry, W. (1976) The Open University. A personal view. Milton Keynes: OU.

Sewart, D. (1978) Continuity of concern for adults studying at a distance. Hagen: FeU (ZIFF).

Smith, K.C. (1980) Course development procedures. Distance Education, 1, 1,61-67.

South Australian College of Advanced Education (1983). Course development. Unit 3 in Graduate Diploma in Distance Education. SACAE: Adelaide.

PART FIVE: EVALUATION

# CHAPTER TWELVE

## ECONOMICS

'Put yourself in my place,' said the Minister. 'You're asking me to make a tough decision, but you're not giving me the facts.'

The Secretary for Education shuffled through his papers, as if he might find the answers there, like a joker in a pack of cards.

'You see, sir, we aren't sure how much this technology will cost in real terms, but we hope it will be less than we'd have to spend providing the same education by other means.'

'You really expect me to believe that these new machines can teach just as well as my teachers? Where's your proof? What's happened in other countries?'

'Well, sir, we certainly don't know much yet about what children learn this way, but there's a similar project starting in Bothana in 1980.'

The Minister frowned and said, in a snarling tone, 'So, we don't know what it costs and we don't know whether it works, but you still expect me to risk my political reputation on it. What's the alternative?'

'More and more children not being educated sir,' the Secretary said quietly.

'Why's that?'

'We can't afford the usual education any more, sir. We simply must try to increase our cost-effectiveness by using technology.'

'But can technology increase the cost-effectiveness of education?'

'There's some doubt if you will ever know whether technology can increase education's cost-effectiveness,' interjected the Professor, unable to restrain himself any longer.

Across the table, the Minister looked even more annoyed. He really needed an answer.

'We haven't had great success in judging cost-effectiveness in education,' the Professor went on, puffing on his pipe. 'Many of the assumptions underlying this type of analysis simply don't apply in the field of education. You can't treat education as an industry, for example'.

'But surely the chances of carrying out this analysis are increased when technology is introduced on a grand scale?' asked the Secretary.

'Well, the problems lie in identifying costs

215

and effects and then in measuring them. We're getting better at it, but it isn't easy.'
   'My members want to know how this new technology will improve their working conditions. They
want the money to be spent on employing
more teachers, to reduce class sizes. That would
be the best way to increase their cost-effectiveness,' claimed the President of the Union
of Teachers.
   'Hmmm,' said the Minister, 'if we can't measure
the cost-effectiveness of technology, we'll have
even less chance of measuring the cost-effectiveness
of that strategy.'
   'You see what I mean', the President trumpeted,
'if you can't tell how cost-effective the teachers
are, how can you compare them with the new educational media?' Jean-Claude Eicher, David Hawkridge, Emile McAnany, Francois Mariet, Francois
Orivel. 1982.

## Pre-1970s

Prior to 1970 the economics of distance teaching
at university level in the West revolved mainly
around the distance/external/independent study
departments of conventional universities. In the
main, these departments were funded, as was conventional education, by government Ministries of
Education from public monies, though the weighting
for an external student was normally lower than
that of an on-campus student. In many American
universities, distance departments (even when
students were studying for college credit) were
grouped with continuing education departments and
had to be self-supporting. Much of the rest of
the world of distance education was proprietary
in the early 1970s, if one excepts the correspondence schools and colleges of external studies
run by the Australian state and Canadian provincial
departments of education and the French CNTE (now
CNEC).
   Prior to 1970 a cost equation for some proprietary distance education institutions seemed
to take the form as illustrated in Figure 12.1.
   There was little protective legislation at
this period and the national accrediting agencies
were not as influential as they were later to become. Malpractice was possible and education
at a distance had, in general, an unenviable reputation from which it has not fully recovered even

| PRODUCE LEARNING MATERIALS AS CHEAPLY AS POSSIBLE | + | ENROL AS MANY STUDENTS AS POSSIBLE | = | SUCCESS |

Figure 12.1  Some proprietary correspondence schools

in the mid-1980s.  Documentation on malpractice is difficult to establish but there is enough evidence in McKenzie and Christensen (1968), White (1975), Karov (1978), Weinstok (1975) and Ehmann (1981) to convince the interested reader that something was amiss.

There were, of course, many excellent proprietary institutions in the 1970s and earlier - one thinks especially of the members of the NHSC, the CEC, the EHSC, the B.A.C.C. and similar accrediting associations - and for these an analysis of costs would need to be re-established thus:

| PRODUCE LEARNING MATERIALS OF QUALITY | + | ESTABLISH REPUTATION FOR STUDENT SUCCESS | = | SUCCESS |

Figure 12.2 Quality proprietary correspondence schools

## Cost analyses of the OUUK

Wagner (1972) provided the first cost analysis of a distance teaching system with the entry of the OUUK into the field of distance education. He applied the cost structures of conventional universities (CU), taken largely from the Robbins Report, to the budgetary data of the OUUK. The results were impressively in favour of the OU:

°  the average recurrent cost per equivalent undergraduate at the OU was only 25% of that of CUs

°  the capital cost per student place at the OU was only 6% of the conventional figure

°  the average recurrent cost per graduate - which depends on drop-outs - would be in favour of the OU unless its drop-out rate went over 85%

° the resource cost per equivalent undergraduate at the OU was only 16% of that of CUs.

Wagner accepted the statement of Perry and the OU administration that the output, the OU graduate, would be similar to that of conventional universities; admitted that there was a problem with research as OU academics did less; costed the OU teaching package in 5 sections: correspondence materials, TV, radio programmes, classes at study centres, and residential summer schools. He regarded the course development components as fixed costs 'the expense of the impersonal components is in effect a fixed cost' (1972:165) and the major variable cost 'is that concerned with the provision of personal tuition services'. (1972:167). He showed that in capital costs at the OU, student, cultural, recreational, library and catering facilities do not have to be provided. He realised the central importance of drop-outs on average recurrent costs per student - if one designs a system for 50,000 students one may have a cost-effective system; however, if most drop-out one has a very costly system. Wagner, however, even in 1972 refused to accept traditional drop-out statistics for correspondence schools as relevant to his cost structure for the OU:

> the OU is an innovation ... the OU is much more than a correspondence college, since it offers an integrated system of teaching in which TV, radio, personal tuition and correspondence all play a part. (1972:177).

Carter (1973) objected strongly. A university exists to provide an educational experience, not just to turn out equivalent graduates. Wagner was costing two quite different kinds of educational experience (1973:69). Wagner had not costed CU faculties like medicine, nor was his allowance for research at CUs adequate. OU courses were all low-level; much of the costs of CUs were for laboratories for post-graduate students. Wagner had forgotten to cost all the services that CUs were doing for the OU (residential schools, study centres, libraries).

Wagner replied by recalculating his costs to include science and he adjusted for research but did not accept most of Carter's other claims. The revised costings came out with little difference from his previous analysis because Carter was confusing consumption and investment benefits (1973: 72).

Although the 'educational experience' of the OU and the CUs was different, the social benefit to the community as measured by future earnings of OU graduates would be the same. The present writer has interviewed too many OU graduates about their use of their OU degree fully to accept Wagner's position here. Too often one meets the pattern of an employee of a British company, whose, education was neglected as a child, who did an excellent science or technology degree at the OU, who sought unsuccessfully for a lecturing position at a college or university on graduation, who then sought unsuccessfully for a part-time lecturing position and who today works for his company making no use of his/her B.A. (Open). Such patterns do not support Wagner's position, though one has to admit that in the British employment situation of the mid-80s it is unlikely that a 40+ year old graduate from any university would receive an immediate degree-related position upon graduation. Swift (1980:23) carried out the first official OU research on the success of OU graduates in gaining employment but the results, though positive, are as yet too tentative to give clear indications on the value of OU degrees in the labour market. In a 1973 paper in <u>Universities Quarterly</u> Wagner re-presented his arguments in the context of a national goal of expanding the 15% of each age cohort who in 1971 entered higher education in the U.K. He suggested the substitution of capital for labour by increasing the role of impersonal tuition by means of correspondence and broadcasting. This and the often recommended 'multi-mode' (half on-campus and half off-campus), have often been suggested but rarely taken up in the succeeding decade. In Wagner's words

> educational technology remains in CUs a <u>complement</u> to existing methods of tuition instead of a <u>substitute</u>. (1973: 404)

Wagner now admitted the validity of more of Carter's claims and re-presented his figures in slightly modified form, with the general conclusion on the cost effectiveness of the OU unchanged. 'Academic salaries', we are told, 'which are the main item in costs at a conventional university take up less than 15% of OUUK costs and are unrelated to student numbers'. (1973:398) Wagner pointed out that the OUUK system was devised for its educational effectiveness as a distance teaching system, not because it was cheap (1973:400). Various ways of making it cheaper are considered: reducing personal tuition and increasing correspondence being the basic one.

Laidlaw and Layard in 1974 moved the analysis from the cost of the OUUK to the costs of courses at the OUUK, seeking to throw light on the costs of OU teaching methods as against conventional 'live' instruction.

They distinguish between four 'types of cost' at the OU (1974:445)

(i) <u>fixed course costs</u>: inescapable if the course is put on

(ii) <u>variable course costs</u>: costs which are dependent on student volume

(iii) <u>fixed central costs</u>: inescapable if the OU is to exist

(iv) <u>variable central university costs</u>: which alter with the volume of students.

They conclude, like Wagner, that the real strength of the OU system is (1974:452) 'the potential economies of scale which can be reaped by substituting capital for labour'. This means that a major part of the costs of the course become fixed and invariant with respect to student numbers. By contrast, campus universities' courses have low fixed costs but high marginal costs. For low levels of operation the campus university is the more efficient system and for high levels the OU is.

The breakeven point in 1971 was calculated at 21,691 students, at which point the OUUK average cost per student would be lower than that for CUs.

In 1975 Lumsden and Ritchie presented a survey and cost analysis of the OUUK. Their argument tends to support the position taken up by both Wagner and Laidlaw/Layard. In particular they attempt to answer the question 'What is the contribution towards the final degree of an average student year in the OU compared to an average student year in a conventional university?' and provide four different sets of answers. The article speaks of 'mass-media lectures' (1975:238) on radio and television as central to the system and concludes with a discussion of the costing of a television university in the U.S.A.

In 1977 Wagner returned to the debate with

a well-known article 'The economics of the OU revisited'. His appraisal of his forecasts of expenditure in the earlier articles was that they
were generally accurate but that the OU had admitted
more students than planned so that some costs were
in fact marginally lower. The input is weighted
even more heavily in favour of the OU by claiming
that costings should not be of graduates, but of
what is value-added to produce the graduate. Thus
in British CUs one starts with at least
2 'A' levels; at the OU one starts normally with
much less. No re-evaluation of output (the value
of the graduate from OU or CU, to employers, the
community, postgraduate research) is, however,
considered necessary.

The 1977 article introduces data for forecast
and more sophisticated analysis of distance systems.
Thus: the drop-out rate of finally enrolled students
is set at 25% per course; the costs of course production are rightly assigned to the years before
presentation (1977:366); the equation $C = a + bx
+ y$ where $C$ = fixed costs; $x$ = number of courses;
$y$ = number of students, is introduced from Laidlaw
and Layard (1974) and Rumble (1976). A new distinction is made between new course production
and maintenance of existing courses.

Wagner presents two major conclusions:

(i)   most of economies of scale of the OU
      had been reaped within the first few
      years and there was little hope of further
      reductions. This was because the econ-
      omies of increasing student numbers had
      been used by the OU to increase the number
      of courses in development and on offer
      rather than to reach the steady state,
      and because it proved impossible to im-
      prove academic productivity especially
      for full-time tenured staff once the
      institutional patterns had gelled.
(ii)  his analysis can offer little guidance
      on policy changes within the OU or on
      the planning of other distance systems.

It is a little disappointing that Wagner offers
no comparisons with other systems or with variants
on the OU system. Some suggestions are made (1977:
371), however, on reducing face-to-face tutoring,
reducing summer school attendance, lowering the
quality of printing or layout of materials - the
normal suggestions that distance systems face when

they need to cut costs. Wagner claims that all of these would change the nature of the product the OU offers to students.

Carnoy and Levin (1975) and Mace (1978) were the first to challenge these conclusions. Carnoy and Levin show:

> the limited nature of the Open University education as well as the credential effect of particular institutions on earnings and occupational attainments would suggest that the Open University graduate is not likely to receive either consumption or income benefits from his education that are as high as those of the person from the more conventional university setting. (1975:231)

Mace considered that the claim of the OU to be more cost-effective than CUs was not substantiated. His OU article challenged the economic analysis of Wagner and the 'openness' of the OU as it had been presented in a number of articles, especially by a former OU pro-Vice-Chancellor, Naomi McIntosh (1976).

Mace's position is clear (1978:295):

> It is concluded after an examination of the methology and the evidence, that neither the economic case nor the social case is substantiated. Moreover, this view of the OU's performance may constitute a dangerous myth, because it may well inhibit further attempts at economic evaluation of the OU.

Mace bases much of his criticism of Wagner on the evaluation of the output of the OU system: earnings forgone, competivity on the labour market and the value-added by the OU: do the same changes in earnings result and are these increased earnings enjoyed over the same period? He accepts Wagner's costing that it takes one half of CU costs to produce a graduate at the OU and one third of CU costs for the average recurrent annual cost per student but asks whether the measure of output (graduates), could be produced more cheaply by reducing or re-allocating resources between the various items in the OU budget? (1978:305)

The answer is that, of course, it could but that you produce a different teaching package and this alters the quality and possibly the quantity of the output. Mace's main candidates for reduction are television broadcasting and class tutorials which he suggests, without proof, could be reduced without affecting the quantity, quality and status of the output.

## Cost analyses of distance systems

The economics of distance systems takes on a new dimension with the chapter by Neil, Rumble and Tout in the 1979 book Fernstudien an Universitäten edited by Dörfler and published in Vienna. It is clear from the opening sentence that the parochialism of the Wagner-Mace debate has been left behind:

> In numerous instances, we have observed the launching of distance learning systems for which the fundamental variables which affect costs to a significant extent have either not been made explicit or have not been given explicit working values in initial budgeting exercises. The effects of such omissions are serious. For example, costs of preparing course materials can escalate alarmingly way beyond the financial resources provided; production schedules repeatedly go awry; the resources which are marshalled may be critically insufficient in kind, amount and timing; students can be set wholly unrealistic workloads. (1979:93)

Valuable as the economic analyses of the OU had been, they had not extrapolated from the context of a single institution which has been described as sui generis (Daniel and Stroud 1981:148) and which offers an unusual, if highly successful, costing mix of extensive television broadcasting with large amounts of compulsory and optional face-to-face sessions - a costing structure characteristic of none of the five models in this book's typology, not even Type 2: the distance teaching universities.

Neil, Rumble and Tout base themselves on the economic analyses of distance teaching systems outlined above plus the work done on the economic analysis of media in education during the 1970s by Eicher, Jamison, Klees, Wells and others. As a result they seek to provide costing processes that will be of value to all working in distance systems:

>Our interest is not primarily in the economics, in the classical sense, of distance learning systems, but rather in modelling. A financial management approach involving firstly, <u>decision accounting</u>: that is, making reliable and appropriate estimates on the basis of explicit models, of the costs and revenues associated with particular alternatives at particular levels of operation; and secondly, assuming that the models evolved ensure a high level of effectiveness, <u>control accounting</u>: that is, providing information to assist management in maximizing efficiency.

Their contribution begins with a brief resume of studies so far:

>The studies tend to analyse costs along the following lines: firstly, historical cost information on the system is collected; secondly, the historical relationship between these costs and the system variables that influence them are specified; and finally, future system costs are projected, based on hypotheses concerning the future configuration of cost influencing system variables. Future system costs are derived on the basis of cost functions which seek to identify fixed and variable costs within the system, leading to the derivation of <u>marginal costs</u> (important when costing plans for expansion) and <u>average costs</u> (important as a cost index) per unit of output. These are usually expressed in terms of the marginal costs per student and average cost per student respectively, but sometimes expressed as the cost per student-hour (1979:96).

The cost functions so identified have tended to be linear in form, expressed in their simplest form as:

$$TC = F + VN$$

where:

TC = total costs

F = fixed costs

V = variable cost per unit of output(N)

N = number of units of output (students/ student hours, etc.)

When the total cost function is linear, the average cost (AC) is simply equal to the fixed cost divided by N plus the variable cost (V), so that

$$AC = F/N + V$$

and the marginal cost is equal to V.

They confirm the previous studies, especially that of Laidlaw and Layard, that:

- the cost structures of distance learning systems differ significantly from those of traditional instructional systems (1979:98)
- distance systems have high fixed costs and low variable costs relative to conventional campus-based universities (1978:98)
- distance systems have potential for effecting economies of scale: as the number of students increases so the average cost declines by spreading the fixed cost over more units (1979:98)
- for smaller numbers of students, campus-based universities using traditional instructions are more efficient, but for higher numbers a distance system is more efficient (1979:100)
- design and production costs are generally much higher than the costs of transmission and reception (1979: 100)
- there must be sufficient students to allow economies of scale to be reaped (1979:102).

They note finally that 'these conclusions have nothing to say about the learning effectiveness of the various methodologies which are compared', (1979:102).

The three authors then present their own financial model of a distance system based on three major areas of costing: (i) the organisation, (ii) the number of courses, (iii) and the number of students.

The model itself is built up from 10 functional lines for organisational data, 12 on creating course materials (lesson writers; video producers; audio producers; lesson texts, video components, audio components per main planning period; maintenance rates; creation ab initio and remaking; number of units produced per planning period; components purchased, and average costs per standard unit.) There are 6 entries for course tutoring comprising marking assignments, face-to-face sessions, and counselling of student learning problems.

The model is further developed and rewritten in 1981 as Chapter 13 of Kaye and Rumble (eds.) Distance teaching for higher and adult education. In this version the cost functions identified are increased to 37 and their own assessment of the model is given as:

> a first attempt at developing a framework within which to derive a series of cost functions reflecting some of the major cost-inducing variables in distance-learning systems. (1981:230)

The study is important because it transformed what had been a series of studies of a particular institution into a modelling process for distance systems in general; it used the work of Eicher, Jamison and others on the costing of educational communications media, and it separated clearly the analysis of cost-inducing variables in distance education systems from the economics of conventional institutions.

## Canadian small distance education systems

North American financial and management practice was brought into the economics of distance education as a result of studies at Athabasca University, Edmonton, Alberta by Snowden and Daniel. They present (1980:78) a cost equation for small distance education systems based on the two functions of course development and services delivery:

$$TC = a_1(x_1 + x_2/1) + by + c$$

where

$x_1$ = course credits 'in development'

$x_2$ = course credits 'in delivery'

1 = the lifetime of a course in delivery, where it is assumed that the total cost of maintenance over the life of a course is equal to that of developing a course. 1 is taken to be 5 years in practice

y = weighted course enrolments. Course enrolments are on the basis of a standard 6-credit course, such that a student enrolled on a 3-credit course is equal to 0.5 of a standard course enrolment

$a_1$ = course development costs per credit

b = delivery costs per weighted course enrolment

c = costs of institutional overheads.

This model differentiates costs for courses in development which will be taught in the future from courses already developed which are now being taught. Snowden and Daniel show that the average recurrent cost per course enrolment declines as the number of course enrolments increases, but at a declining rate, so that once a small distance education system reaches about 10,000 course enrolments, with a media mix and student support services similar to those of Athabasca University, then further economies of scale cannot be expected to be important.

Costing of educational technology

The economics of new educational media have been studied by a number of leading experts in the field

of the use of new communications technology in
education: J.C. Eicher, D.T. Jamison, S. Klees,
E. McAnany, J. Mayo, F. Orivel, H. Perraton and
P. Suppes. Schramm's overview Big media, little
media is also well known. These studies have been
summarized in a three volume UNESCO study (Eicher
et al. 1977, 1979 and 1982) and a volume edited
for the World Bank by Perraton (1982).

These studies deal with the costing of the
use of certain new communications media in education
and not with whole distance education systems costs.
Many of the programmes which are central to the
economic analyses of these studies would not be
covered by the definition of distance education
adopted for this book:

>     The Minerva Madureza project (Brazil)
>     The Radio Mathematics project (Nicaragua)
>     The Mauritius College of the Air
>     The El Salvador Educational Television Project
>     The Telesecundaria program (Mexico)
>     The Maranahão FMTVE (Brazil)

These were all innovative programmes, justly famous
for the use of educational technology in development. They deal with projects like the introduction
of radio into formal education (Nicaragua), the
use of educational television to provide instruction
for the last four years of fundamental education
(Maranahão), or broadcast programmes to support
the small private colleges which try to maintain
standards with the Royal Colleges and large Roman
Catholic secondary schools in Mauritius. For a
true costing of such projects one would have to
include the school buildings, other plant and some
of the payment to the face-to-face teachers. This
would confuse the functional basis for the economics
of distance systems.

In 1982 Perraton published The cost of distance
education, a 65 page summary of the. evidence to
date analysing the Wagner, Laidlaw-Layard, Snowden-
Daniel, Rumble series of studies, together with
the work of Eicher, Jamison and the UNESCO/World
Bank series, and providing his own synthesis.

## Whole distance education system costs

Rumble had established his cost analysis and
financial modelling structures by the late 1970s.
In the early 1980s he set about applying his structures to actual situations. This produced two

major economic case studies of UNED in Costa Rica (1981, 375-401) and of UNA in Venezuela (1982, 116-140) and an overview of economics and cost structures (1981, 220-234) which was published as Chapter 12 of <u>Distance teaching for higher and adult education</u>.

In his 1982 article Rumble presented a 'state of the art' analysis of the economics of distance education as it was in 1980. The presentation is so nuanced, qualified and comprehensive that it is best to present here his conclusions almost in full:

○ Broadly speaking, very significant costs are incurred in the preparation of materials irrespective of student numbers. The level of cost incurred will vary depending on the choice of media. Production costs of television are high but not as high as for film. The production cost of radio is relatively low. Print production costs vary depending on the level of sophistication, but overall are not normally significant in themselves within the context of a particular project. Where print is the principal medium the cost of academic staff time in its design and development may be significant.

○ Transmission and duplication costs are very high for video systems. The cost of film and of video-cassette based systems increases with the magnitude of the project. The cost of distributing print and audio-visual materials to students depends on the means of distribution used, population dispersal, and difficulty of access to the target population.

○ In conventional educational systems teaching costs are traditionally held to be a recurrent cost that is variable with the number of students in the system. In contrast, in distance learning systems the cost of developing the materials can be regarded as a fixed cost that can be written off over the life of the course of which they form a part. This investment has been seen as analogous to capital investment in business, representing a move away from the labour intensive nature of conventional teaching systems. It follows that the more students there are using the materials, the lower the average cost per student of the materials. Hence at some point, and this depends on the choice of media, a distance teaching system should become cheaper per unit of output than a traditional system.

The use of face-to-face tuition tends to undermine the cost advantage of distance teaching by re-introducing a cost element that is directly variable with student numbers. As a result, face-to-face contact is usually restricted particularly at the higher levels and has a different function to that found in conventional systems, where it is a major teaching medium.

From an economic point of view the investment in course materials is not normally warranted where student numbers are small. As a result the choice of courses in distance teaching systems may be restricted, at least in comparison with conventional systems.

Administrative systems for the control of course design, production and distribution and for the teaching of students at a distance tend to be more clearly differentiated from the academic functions than is the case in conventional systems, as well as being more complex in themselves. The initial investment in administrative systems prior to the enrolment of any students is likely to be signficant and on the whole more costly than is the case in conventional systems.(1982: 119-120).

Rumble's work in a number of distance systems enabled him to identify the main generators of costs in a distance system and to show how the costs change as key input or output variables change. Examples of the main cost-inducing variables are:

course design, including design staff,

       external course writers and costs of
       re-presentation of courses.

°   Production costs of printed course ma-
       terials, audio visual materials and exper-
       imental equipment.

°   courses being presented - transmission,
       distribution, examination and assessment.

°   Local centres - library and audio-visual
       facilities, counselling and administrative
       staff.

°   Students - tuition and counselling, admin-
       istration of student records.

The most significant factors that bear upon the
cost structures of distance learning systems are
identified by Rumble as (i) the choice of media
(ranging from roneod-notes to television broadcasting) can significantly affect the cost of the
system, (ii) the size of the academic programme
- the number of courses to be developed, especially
when these are linked to face-to-face tuition,
and (iii) the number of students in the system.
    Rumble provides two clarifications to conclude
his work:

> Distance learning is not necessarily
> a cheap way of teaching. The level of
> initial investment required to establish
> an institution and to develop and produce
> course materials is considerable and
> will only pay off, in cost-efficiency
> terms, if there are sufficient students
> in the system to warrant the investment
> and to reap the economies of scale that
> are there to be achieved (1982:138)

and on planning a distance project:

> It is clear that the absolute costs of
> a project (both in terms of the fixed
> expenditure on capital items and over-
> heads, as well as variable expenditure
> per student or student-hour) are criti-
> cally dependent upon the choice of media
> and their distribution or transmission
> systems. This suggests that before plan-
> ners and decision-makers embark on the
> establishment of a distance learning-
> system, very careful consideration must
> be given in the light of student number
> projections to the cost implications

> of media choices and the number of courses
> to be developed and presented. Certainly,
> for low student populations, conventional
> teaching methods are likely to be more
> cost-efficient than high-technology dis-
> tance learning systems. (1981:233).

He attempts to quantify the student population
by suggesting that distance institutions with 10,000
- 20,000 enrolments annually are critically balanced; below 10,000 the autonomous distance system
cannot be financially justified; beyond 20,000
the economics favour the distance system against
a conventional one but that above 40,000 students
the economies of scale cease to be as significant
because the average student cost curve flattens
out.

## Costing of distance teaching universities (Type 2 institutions)

Keegan and Rumble applied these economic analyses
to the distance teaching universities with the
following conclusions:

> Distance teaching universities (DTUs)
> can be cost effective in comparison with
> conventional universities, but this may
> not necessarily be the case. Their cost
> advantage can be undermined if:
>
> 1. The investment in media and materials
>    is excessive, relative to the number
>    of students in the system.
> 2. The direct student costs (or variable
>    cost per student) is above or on
>    a par with those at conventional
>    universities - in which case the
>    DTU will never achieve economies
>    of scale relative to conventional
>    universities.
> 3. The variable cost per student in
>    a DTU is only marginally lower than
>    that in a conventional university,
>    since in this case the DTU will
>    need proportionally more students
>    if its average costs are to drop
>    significantly below that of the
>    conventional universities.
> 4. The DTU cannot attract sufficient
>    students to warrant the investment

in the development of its materials
and systems. (1982:220)

These factors have important implications for the
provision of face-to-face tuition. The more face-
to-face tuition built into a distance teaching
system, the nearer variable student costs will
be to those found in conventional universities.
Yet, if one considers that the quality of academic
provision makes an extensive face-to-face element
essential in a distance teaching university, then
DTUs with relatively low student numbers may not
be able both to improve the quality of their provision and retain their present level of cost-
efficiency relative to conventional universities
in their country or province.

Keegan and Rumble (1982:245) proceed with
an attempt to compare the cost structures of autonomous distance teaching institutions (Type 1 and
2) and mixed institutions (Type 3,4 and 5):

1.  Once an annual minimum of enrolments
    is guaranteed there are some indicators
    in favour of an autonomous institution.
2.  The costs associated with the establish-
    ment of an infrastructure and the prep-
    aration of sufficient course materials
    are such that a mixed system is prefer-
    able, if an annual minimum of enrolments
    cannot be guaranteed.
3.  The annual minimum number of enrolments
    probably lies in the region of 9,000
    - 20,000,

and that these financial indicators depend always
on the choice of media, the extent of student support services, the number of courses on offer and
the costs of conventional education in the country.
Even so a government may decide that financial
indicators, one way or the other, are not normative
in the choice of an autonomous of mixed distance
teaching system.

Conclusion

From an analysis of all the studies presented in
this chapter certain economic indicators on the
costing of distance systems can be put together:

°   The economics of conventional education is
    of little value for the cost analysis

233

° of distance systems.

° The equation frequently used in conventional education:

$$\text{Faculty salary expense} = \frac{\text{Weekly student hours x average faculty salary}}{\text{Average class size x average faculty load}}$$

has little relevance in distance education.

° The proportion of fixed costs to total costs in conventional education (schools, colleges and universities) is small; this is not true of distance systems.

° Distance systems, like industries, have high capital investment in the production of courses; conventional education is labour-intensive.

° The number of drop-outs in the system is crucial; once drop-outs pass 50% and move towards 100% cost-effectiveness vanishes.

° If student support services are face-to-face and compulsory, cost structures rapidly return toward those of conventional education. Some authors appear to suggest that academic success or reduction of drop-out may be linked to provision of student services.

Within these caveats it is clear that there is now available a comprehensive costing system for distance education. In the final section an attempt will be made to apply these conclusions to the planning of a hypothetical distance system.

## Application

We know from studies by Wagner and Laidlaw - Layard on the OUUK, by Snowden and Daniel on Athabasca University and by Rumble on a series of DTUs, that costs of a distance teaching system have the following characteristics:

° high fixed costs
° low variable costs per student
° design and production costs of materials which depend on the choice of media.

We know that the variable costs per student are dependent on the following variables:

° number of local centres
° number of courses in production

234

° number of students.

The costs of a system can be

° fixed costs if they occur only once (plant, buildings)
° recurrent non-variable costs
° variable recurrent costs (as above).

In accordance with this analysis it is possible to develop a mathematical cost function for a distance education system.

The cost of the system in any year is:

$$T + Z$$

where T = recurrent costs
and Z = fixed costs (plant, buildings)

because $T = F + L\alpha + D\beta + Cy + Sx$

where    T = total recurrent costs

F = recurrent fixed costs

L = number of local centres

$\alpha$ = average costs of a local centre

D = number of courses in production

$\beta$ = cost of design and production of a course

C = number of courses in presentation

y = average cost of presentation of a course

S = number of students

x = average cost per student.

Let us hypothesize that there are

6 local centres (L)
13 courses in development (D)
11 courses in presentation (C)
500 students (S)

and that costs are calculated as follows:

235

|  |  |
|---|---|
| Plant and buildings | $850,000 |
| Fixed recurrent costs | $2,031,200 |
| Average cost of a local centre | $26,073 |
| Average cost of producing a course | $12,033 |
| Average cost of presenting a course | $18,454 |
| Average cost per student | $829 |

In accordance with these data the costs of the system for a full year are:

Fixed costs

Z = $850,000

Recurrent costs

F = $2,031,200

$\alpha$ = $26,073 x 8 = $156,440

$\beta$ = $12,033 x13 = $156,429

y = $18,454 x11 = $203,000

x = $829 x 500  = $414,650

Thus total system costs Z + T = $3,811,719

| | | |
|---|---|---|
| Fixed costs (Z) | = | 850,000 |
| Fixed recurrent costs (F) | = | 2,031,200 |
| Centres (L) | = | 145,330 |
| Development (D) | = | 1,458,000 |
| Presentation (C) | = | 203,000 |
| Students (S) | = | 414,650 |
| | | $3,811,719 |

and total annual costs (T)  = $2,961,719

In addition one can analyse the costs of a system if it has an increased level of activity.

For example let us assume that there are now:

○   8 local centres
○   60 courses in presentation
○   10 courses that are remade each year or that
    each course is remade once every 6 years or
    that 10 courses are produced each year.
○   500 or 1,000, or 5,000, 10,000 or 20,000
    students.

Then total cost (T) is:

| | |
|---|---|
| Fixed | $2,021,200 |
| 8 Local centres | $ 208,586 |
| 60 courses in presentation | $1,107,272 |
| 10 courses in production | $ 120,330 |

and there are

| | |
|---|---|
| 500 students | $ 414,650 |
| 1,000 students | $ 829,399 |
| 5,000 students | $4,146,500 |
| 10,000 students | $8,293,000 |
| 20,000 students | $16,586,000 |

Therefore total system costs for different student
levels are:

| Number | Total costs | Average cost per student |
|---|---|---|
| 500 | $ 3,881,650 | $ 7,763 p.a. |
| 1,000 | $ 4,296,300 | $ 4,296 p.a. |
| 5,000 | $ 7,613,000 | $ 1,522 p.a. |
| 10,000 | $11,760,000 | $ 1,176 p.a. |
| 20,000 | $20,053,000 | $ 1,002 p.a. |

Finally Rumble has provided us with graphs for
demonstrating the comparative costs of distance
and conventional students.

Assuming that a certain distance system has
fixed costs which are three times those of a conventional system, and that its variable costs are
one-third of those of a conventional system, then
at a certain point the distance system becomes
cheaper per capita than the conventional system.

Figure 12.1 (Rumble 1982:222) shows that fixed
costs are constant for campus-based and distance
learning systems and are always higher for the
distance system. Variable costs on the other hand
start lower for the campus-based system but quickly

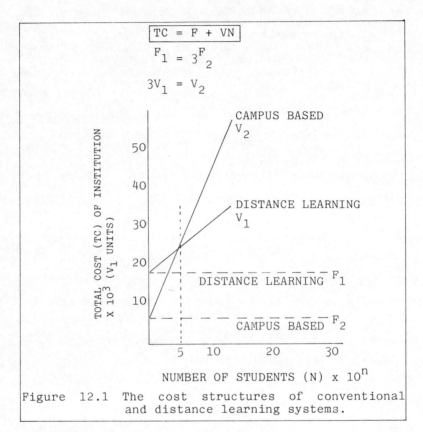

Figure 12.1 The cost structures of conventional and distance learning systems.

Note copyright approval.

reach a breakeven point from which stage on, costs are always higher for the conventional system.

When student numbers and unit costs are compared in conventional and distance learning systems (Rumble 1982:223) in Figure 12.2 it is seen that the cost curve quickly favours the distance system but that as students numbers annually increase beyond the 30,000 mark, the curve tends to flatten out and remains permanently parallel to and significantly below the costs of a conventional system.

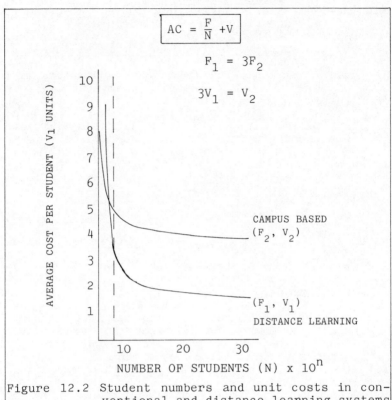

Figure 12.2 Student numbers and unit costs in conventional and distance learning systems

References

Carnoy, M. and Levin, H. (1975) Evaluation of educational media: some issues. _Instructional Science_, 4, 385-406.
Carter, C.F. (1973) The economics of the OU: a comment. _Higher Education_, 1, 285-288.
Daniel, J. and Stroud, M. (1981) Distance education

- a reappraisal for the 1980s. <u>Distance Education</u>, 2, 1, 35-51.

Ehmann, C. (1981) Reflections on Otto Peters' research. <u>Distance Education</u>, 2, 2, 228-233.

Eicher, J-C. et al. (1977, 1980, 1982) <u>The economics of new educational media</u>. Paris: UNESCO.

Karow, W. (1979) <u>Privater Fernunterricht in der Bundesrepublik Deutschland und in Ausland</u>. Berlin: DIBB.

Keegan, D. and Rumble, G. (1982) Characteristics of the distance teaching universities. In Rumble, G. and Harry, K. (eds) <u>The distance teaching universities</u> London: Croom Helm.

Laidlaw, B. and Layard, R. (1974) Traditional versus OU teaching methods: a cost comparison. <u>Higher Education</u>, 3, 439-468.

Lumsden, K. and Ritchie, C. (1975) The Open University: a survey and cost analysis. <u>Instructional Science</u>, 4, 237-261.

Mace, J. (1978) Mythology in the making: is the OU really cost effective? <u>Higher Education</u>, 7, 295-309.

McIntosh, N. (1976) <u>A degree of difference</u>. Guildford: SRHE.

McKenzie, O. and Christensen, E. (1968) <u>Correspondence instruction in the United States</u>. New York: McGraw Hill.

Neil, M., Rumble, G. and Tout, A. (1979) Some aspects of modelling for recurrent cost budgeting and forecasting in distance learning systems. In Dörfert, W. (ed) <u>Fernstudien an Universitäten</u>. Klagenfurt: UVD.

Perraton, H. (1982a) <u>The cost of distance education</u>. Cambridge: IEC.

Perraton, H. (1982b) <u>Alternative routes to formal education</u>. Washington: World Bank.

Rumble, G. (1976) Management and costing models for distance teaching. In Hakemulder, J. (ed) <u>Distance education for development</u>. Bonn: German Foundation for International Development.

Rumble, G. (1981) The cost analysis of distance teaching: Costa Rica's UNED. <u>Higher Education</u>, 10, 375-401.

Rumble, G. (1981) Economics and cost structures. In Kaye, A. and Rumble, G. (eds) <u>Distance teaching for higher and adult education</u>. London: Croom Helm.

Rumble, G. (1982) The cost analysis of learning at a distance. Venezuela's UNA. <u>Distance Education</u>, 4, 2, 101-131.

Schramm, W. (1977) Big media, little media. London:
    Sage.
Snowden, B. and Daniel, J. (1980) The economics
    and management of small, post-secondary dis-
    tance education systems. Distance Education,
    1, 1, 68-91.
Swift, B. (1980) Analysis of OU graduates. Teaching
    at a Distance, 17, 21-29.
Wagner, L. (1972) The economics of the Open Uni-
    versity. Higher Education, 2, 159-183.
Wagner, L. (1973a) The OU and the costs of expanding
    higher education. Universities Quarterly,
    21-29.
Wagner, L. (1973b) The economics of the OU: a reply.
    Higher Education, 3, 21-27.
Wagner, L. (1977) The economics of the OU revisited.
    Higher Education, 6, 359-381.
Weinstok, N. (1975) Les cours par correspondance
    du secteur privé en Belgique. Brussels: Centre
    National du Droit.
White, M. (1975) Correspondence courses in the
    U.S. Report to the University of Syracuse,
    mimeograph.

# CHAPTER THIRTEEN

## APPRAISAL OF SELECTED SYSTEMS

The problem is that we have been so dominated by the technical problems of our technological age that we tend to be satisfied by purely technical solutions. Those tend to be mass solutions; they may or may not be solutions to our own problems; they may distract our attention from leading us to see this or that aspect with which a given technology can cope, and ignoring the wholeness, the manifold reality of our own situation. Stephen Kemmis, 1980.

## Introduction

Writing on educational evaluation in recent years shows attempts to advance from models that measured the extent to which performance of students exposed to a certain treatment corresponds to the developer's intentions. The writings of Dressel, Eisner, Partlett and Hamilton; show various attempts to cope with 'the wholeness', 'the manifold reality' of the educational situation to be evaluated. These ideas have been adapted for distance education by McIntosh (1975), Gooler (1979), Rumble (1981) and Keegan and Rumble (1982).

## McIntosh

McIntosh was for many years head of the statistical research department of the OUUK. She emphasises (1974:43) that financial penalties for bad decisions are greater in the evaluation of multi-media distance education systems than in conventional programmes. Multi-media distance systems are set up with both educational and social objectives and hence semi-economic and semi-political factors are implied. She made a strong case for evaluation based on survey research linked to institutional decision making rather than the prevailing experimental and psychometric nature of evaluative research.

The major areas of concern for the evaluation of open and innovative systems are listed as:

1. Is the course aimed at an open or closed student population, or both?
2. Is the learning system direct or via an intermediary?

3. Is the course to be repeated, or is it to be run once only?
4. What is the relationship of the cost of the course to the cost of possible evaluation procedures?
5. Does the course have an assumed entry behaviour or not? If yes, then is it known, and if so, by whom?
6. If the course has an assumed entry behaviour, is it desirable to measure it or not?
7. Is the performance of the student to be assessed, or not?
8. What combinations of media are to be used, and in what ways?
9. Is the course to be evaluated unit-by-unit, (week by week), or as a whole, or both? (1974: 56).

## Gooler

Gooler (1979:43-55) views evaluation as an attempt to determine worth or value and to provide useful information to decision makers. He provides these criteria for evaluating distance education pro-grammes:

1. Access. Access is discussed and compared with equality of opportunity but Gooler seems undecided as to whether it is a criterion or not.
2. Relevancy to needs. Relevancy is accepted as a criterion but cautions are expressed as shifts of needs and priorities occur: what may be relevant to the needs of one group in the community, may be irrelevant to others.
3. Quality. It is suggested that the 'face validity' or general acceptability of the product together with technical analysis, plus an analysis of the delivery system, might enable an evaluation of quality to be made.
4. Learners' outcomes - the extent to which learn-ers achieve the goals set by the institution, their own personal goals and unanticipated outcomes.
5. Cost-effectiveness - comparability of costs and comparability of effectiveness. The prob-lems of this evaluation are spelled out:

> Another difficulty is the problem of matching or relating cost to effective-ness. Since cost analysis schemes vary,

243

and since effectiveness measures are not consistent, relationships of cost to effectiveness (and subsequent comparisons of these relationships across programmes) are tenuous. Consequently, most people use only cost comparison data in their evaluations of programmes, rather than the comparison or ratios of cost to effectiveness across programmes. (pp:50)

6. Impact - the impact of the programmes on society or on other programmes, institutions and individuals. What happens in distance education programmes may cause a re-examination of our assumptions about how adults learn, who wants to learn, what they want to learn, and the ways in which they learn best.
7. Generation of knowledge - programmes might be deemed a success to the extent that the study of them contributes to a better understanding of the broader phenomenon.

The concluding part of his presentation gives a plan for evaluation and a guideline for action and for the allocation of resources to evaluation.

| ELEMENTS OF AN EVALUATION PLAN | |
|---|---|
| Purposes: | Why evaluate? |
| Audiences: | Who is the evaluation for? |
| Issues: | What questions should the evaluation address? |
| Resources: | What resources are available for evaluation? |
| Evidence: | What evidence should be collected? |
| Data-gathering: | How is the evidence to be collected? |
| Analysts: | How can evidence be analysed? |
| Reporting: | How can evaluation findings be reported? |

It is suggested that in carrying out the valuation, policy issues should be distinguished from operating issues and that those interested in promoting distance education programmes must learn to gather and report data which adequately tell the distance education story. Well-planned evaluations may be helpful in telling the story.

Rumble

Rumble of the OUUK has published comprehensive evaluations of a number of distance systems, notably those in Costa Rica and Venezuela. He insists on evaluations of both the effectiveness and efficiency of educational systems (1981:70). He sees evaluation as the activity of examining and judging the value, quality, significance, quantity or condition of an institution or system. Both qualitative and quantitative judgments are needed in the context of a benchmark or ideal against which actual performance can be compared. He requires a two-tiered evaluation structure comprising judgments on the effectiveness of the system as a whole and the efficiency of its internal operations.

To measure effectiveness and/or efficiency he proposes four levels of analysis:

1.  The response time test: how long does it take to produce a graduate? A series of nine factors for analysis related to the number of credits in the study pattern and the ratio of success to failure in achieving these.
2.  The output-input ratio: the number of graduates as a proportion of the number of students admitted. Both quantitative and qualitative data collection is recommended here, with the latter trying to measure satisfactorily the value added to the student as a result of his studies from a consideration of:

    °   previous educational qualifications
    °   number of years elapsed since end of schooling
    °   regional distribution of students
    °   psychological preparedness of students
    °   physical condition in which students live and study.

3.  The correctness of output: does it correspond to system's goals, needs and demands of the community and the students? It is suggested that data be collected on:

    °   needs and expectations
    °   extent to which needs are being satisfied
    °   extent to which students achieve aims.

4.  Cost efficiency and cost effectiveness:

      °    average cost per student per year
      °    average cost per student credit per year
      °    average cost per student study-hour
      °    average cost per student credit completion
          per year
      °    average cost per graduate.

Overall cost-effectiveness of a distance education system is difficult to evaluate because it is a measure of a nation's investment in a distance system of education as opposed to allocating revenue from taxes to conventional forms of education or other forms of social service.

The cost efficiency of autonomous distance education systems depends for Rumble on three factors: the number of students that can be enrolled in the system, the number of students that can be retained in the system and the media that are utilized. To measure the internal efficiency of a system Rumble suggests data gathering on six items:

the students
the design of the curriculum
course materials and tutorial support
student administrative and support services
institutional coordination and decisions-making
institutional logistics and resource provisions (1981:78).

## Keegan and Rumble

In their appraisal of the success or failure of the distance teaching universities (DTUs) Keegan and Rumble (1982) used a four-point evaluation scheme of their effectiveness - they did not deal with internal efficiency. This four-point external evaluation is recommended here as suitable for the overall evaluation of any distance teaching system.

Evaluation should be focused on:

the quantity of the learning achieved
the quality of the learning achieved
the status of the learning achieved
the relative cost of the learning achieved.

## The quantity of the learning achieved

Under this heading are considered:

     °    The success of the DTUs in widening access, not just in terms of absolute numbers, but in attracting specific target groups,

     °    Drop-outs,

     °    The quantity of the output relative to the input (the output: input ratio),

     °    the time it takes to produce the output,

     °    the DTU's success in satisfying national, local and individual needs.

The time taken to produce a graduate - or whatever way the output is defined - and the quantity of the output as a ratio of the input (Rumble's first two criteria) are included here as is Gooler's focus on the evaluation of access and relevancy to needs. Evaluation of access requires a brief consideration because it seems clear that a number of evaluators of distance systems would include it as a major area for evaluation, of equal importance to the four chosen for this analysis. Some argue that 'access' should be rated as a separate criterion for evaluation because the raison d'être of distance systems as opposed to conventional ones, is to increase access. In this study it is maintained that a distance system is a necessary component of a national education system and in this context, therefore, access is not separated out as a separate criterion for evaluation but is treated under the heading 'quantity of provision'.

Access and relevancy are to be rejected if they lead people to almost automatic educational failure, or if the quality and/or status of the learning achieved in the programme is unacceptable. To receive a satisfactory evaluation the institution is required to achieve measurable success in:

(i)   the avoidance of avoidable drop-out
(ii)  the number of successful students as a proportion of the number of students admitted
(iii) the time it takes for students to achieve successful outcomes.

It is clear that many distance systems fail this test. No one has yet attempted a meta-analysis of drop-out studies but many published studies cite a large number of drop-outs from many distance systems. Keegan and Rumble (1982:228) insist that one compares like with like in these studies, i.e. full-time distance students with full-time on-campus students; university distance students in the U.K., with university students in the U.K. and not in Spain or the Federal Republic of Germany - but even when this is done there seems to be clear statistical evidence that the drop-out from some distance systems is often unacceptably high.

## The quality of learning achieved

Under this heading is grouped the gathering of data for the evaluation of:

° the quality of the learning materials provided by the DTUs,
° The extent to which distance teaching is a suitable vehicle for educating students in certain subjects.
° The extent to which education is provided as opposed to instruction,
° The effectiveness of learning at a distance,
° The 'intersubjectivity' of learning at a distance.

We are concerned here with Gooler's requirements that quality, personal goals, unanticipated outcomes and long-term effects of involvement in a distance programme be evaluated and certain aspects of Rumble's test on the correctness of output. The quality of the learning materials of an institution can be evaluated against the aims and curriculum for which they were designed. The structuring of content will be more important here than the physical production, being more closely linked to effective student learning. Boring materials can be analysed and condemned from an evaluation of student reaction but it is more difficult to establish evaluation mechanisms for materials which tend to stereotype or limit student response. Other aspects for consideration are the extent to which materials contribute to the students' freedom of choice within the structure of a distance course and the ability of learning materials to cope with divergent student reactions. The effectiveness of learning at a distance and the possibility of a distance system providing education, as opposed to instruction, especially at university level are themes that have been debated for a century. They need to be faced again in the evaluation of each distance system and the arguments have recently been re-presented by Escotet (1979) from Latin America and Carnoy and Levin

(1976) from the United Kingdom. Much of what happens in a lecture theatre, whether it be good or bad, is quite clearly irreproducible at a distance.

Examples of lecture procedure that cannot be reproduced at a distance include:

° the brilliant excursus of a professor on recent drama, literature or cinema that can be linked to a course

° the daily contact with an outstanding professor as he develops his research at international level

° the atmosphere in French/Italian lecture theatres as a professor reads the text of his lectures to hundreds of students who read silently with him from their copy of the lecture notes he has already published.

° the electric atmosphere, reaching occasionally to fisticuffs, as a professor provokes discussion on the subject of his lectures to a committed group of students

° the explanation of a professor of the context, time, atmosphere and personal cost of research accomplished.

Much of what occurs in the lecture theatre cannot be reproduced at a distance: it is the challenge of distance systems especially at university level to achieve quality of education in spite of this.

## The status of the learning achieved

Indications of the status accorded the learning achieved by distance students come from:

° The extent to which other educational institutions recognise the studies for credit transfer purposes.

° The acceptance of the degrees and diplomas awarded as qualifying students to go on to higher level studies.

° The recognition of the awards by employers.

° The esteem in which the distance teaching institutions and their awards are held in the community at large.

Under this heading are grouped the preoccupations of Gooler for an evaluation of the impact of distance programmes on society and the generation of knowledge about the phenomenon of non-traditional learning strategies.

The status of distance programmes can be measured and data collected for evaluation on the extent to which other educational institutions recognise the studies for credit transfer; the acceptance of the distance degrees for higher level studies; the recognition of the awards by managers in competitive interviews for employment. There is little point enrolling in a distance system, studying for a month, or a year or a period of years and then finding that the qualifications offered at the end of the study are not acceptable.

## The relative cost of the learning achieved

Keegan and Rumble were concerned here with:

° The cost-efficiency of distance universities relative to conventional universities or to other modes of internal operation which the distance universities could adopt. The more cost-efficient system is the one that is the cheapest means of accomplishing a defined objective, or which provides maximum value for a given level of expenditure. The assumption here is that the quality of the output is the same.

° The cost-effectiveness of distance universities relative to conventional universities. The concept of cost-effectiveness tries to weigh the relative value of the outputs in qualitative terms.

° The cost benefits of distance and traditional university education, in which the costs of the education provided and the benefits (direct and indirect, financial and social) to the individual and society are taken into account.

° The opportunity cost of education at a distance.

It has been said that teaching at a distance should cost more than conventional education; things at a distance usually do. However, the history of proprietary correspondence schools had shown the way to mass education by demonstrating how large numbers of students could be enrolled in distance programmes at a lower average cost, once the initial capital outlay in the development of learning materials had been undertaken. Studies by Wagner and others showed that similar patterns were achievable by government sponsored distance teaching universities.

It is clear that a major attraction to those governments in developing and developed countries which have considered setting up distance systems in the last two decades has been the reputation of distance education systems for cost-efficiency relative to conventional institutions. Of the five basic institutional models identified in this study, only one (Type 5 - the Australian integrated mode of the University of New England) does not generally propose lower costs than conventional education as one of its characteristics. Yet a major factor in the success of a number of systems (especially Type 2 'distance teaching universities', Type 4 'The consultation model' as well as Type 5) has been the extent to which they have provided facilities for student interaction, with the system or with other students. There is a limit, therefore, to what can be provided without undermining the cost advantage of the distance system or reducing distance students' freedom and flexibility.

## Three case studies

In conclusion three institutions are evaluated in accordance with the criteria presented. One institution is from Type 1 (correspondence schools and colleges) the French Centre National d'Enseigne-ment par Correspondance (CNEC). The evaluation focuses on the section of the institution at Vanves, Paris and, as has been pointed out above, it has many of the characteristics of a Type 2 institution. The second institution, the Open University of the United Kingdom (OUUK) is an example of a dis-tance teaching university (Type 2) whilst the third is from the Australian Type 5 the integrated mode of the University of New England (UNE) at Armidale, New South Wales.

The institutions chosen are diverse in many respects. They cover, for example, a wide range of levels of teaching. The CNEC is a multi-level autonomous distance teaching institution with courses at every level from primary schooling to the equivalent of post-graduate university work. The OUUK is an autonomous, multi-media distance teaching university offering programmes at at least four levels: 70% primary degrees: B.A. (Open), B.A. (Hons) (Open), 20% continuing education courses; the remaining 10% is split between lower level courses (mother and child education) or ad-vanced programmes for M.A./MSC, advanced and post-graduate diplomas, and B.Phil, M.Phil and Ph.D research degrees at a distance. UNE teaches both internally and externally with external enrolments representing 60% of its activity. In 1982 it offered five Masters degrees, seven Bachelors degrees and eleven post-graduate diplomas (Smith, 1983).

The institutions have been chosen to represent quite different national educational structures. France has a centralized controlled model, Australia a federal structure with much responsibility for education resting with the states and the UK has a decentralized model, with, however, growing centralized control in recent years. Australia has a population density of two persons per square kilometre, France 150 and the U.K. 250. Education is a high social and political priority in France, of medium importance in the U.K., and has a lower social and political profile in Australia. Both Australia and the U.K. belong to a group of nations whose pattern of educational ideals is based on behaviouristic-philosophies, quantitative evaluation and innovation. France, on the other hand, belongs with other Latin countries, to a grouping which sees successful progress in education as more traditional than innovative, with less emphasis on technological and behaviouristic philosophies and more interest in qualitative evaluation (Ardagh, 1975).

The assessment systems of the three institutions chosen are quite disparate too. The CNEC at all levels is locked into a national, government-organized, competitive examination structure. The OUUK validates its own degrees, using the British system of visiting examiners (usually professors from other U.K. universities) as a criterion. UNE external students sit for the same examinations at the same time as the internal students and follow all the other assessment procedures for internal students. CNEC graduates receive a national government award, indistinguishable from that of conventional students; OUUK graduates receive an OUUK degree; UNE external students receive the same degree or diploma as their conventional colleagues.

## The Open University of the United Kingdom (OUUK)

1.  Access and needs. The OUUK has done an excellent job of increasing access to university education:

| Table 13.1 Applications to enrol at OUUK 1970-1983. | | |
|---|---|---|
| Year | Applications to enrol for a degree by correspondence | Provisional registration of new students |
| 1970 | 40,817 | 24,220 |
| 1971 | 34,222 | 20,501 |
| 1972 | 30,414 | 16,895 |
| 1973 | 34,017 | 14,976 |
| 1974 | 49,550 | 20,045 |
| 1975 | 51,546 | 17,159 |
| 1976 | 48,252 | 20,097 |
| 1977 | 42,833 | 21,000 |
| 1978 | 40,235 | 21,140 |
| 1979 | 45,125 | 19,448 |
| 1980 | 42,273 | 20,332 |
| 1981 | 45,667 | 25,311 |
| 1982 | 43,332 | 25,513 |
| 1983 | 31,395 | 20,300 |
| | 579,678 | 286,937 |
| Source: OUUK Academic Planning Office | | |

Since its inception in 1971 the OUUK has permitted no less than 600,000 U.K. citizens officially to apply for enrolment for a university degree. It has discovered an extremely large population of adults for whom the offerings of other U.K. universities was inaccessible or unimportant. Many of these students would never have enrolled in a conventional university and 40% of all students enrolled did not have the requisite number of O or A levels for entrance to a conventional U.K. university.

The OUUK has also contributed to improving the relatively unqualified teaching force of the U.K. in 1971 and the fact that only 11% of each age cohort participated in higher education. Some hesitancy has been encountered in representatives of lower social classes enrolling and OUUK statistics when compared with those of the other U.K. universities show a marked difference in occupations of

OUUK students' parents rather than the students themselves. (McIntosh et al.; 1980:107).

2. <u>Drop-outs</u>. The OUUK has largely solved the drop-out problem that has plagued other distance education systems and has today no drop-out problem. The sceptics who claimed at the foundation of the OUUK that no more than 10% of any intake would eventually graduate have been resoundingly answered. The following table shows that at least 50% of every cohort will always graduate, unless there is an abrupt change of statistical pattern.

Up to 45% of each year's cohort is graduating in a highly acceptable time scale of six years. Of these students only 11.7% were 'at home/not working' in 1971 (rising to 26% in 1981).

3. <u>Quality of materials</u>. The OUUK broke new ground in distance education by the quality, complexity and comprehensiveness of its learn-materials, both print and non-print. The A4 profile layout with the OU logo became an easily recognised standard, not only for the OU's students, but in bookshops throughout the U.K.; and on the reading lists of many conventional universities. The materials were characterised by careful structuring and sequencing of content together with sophisticated lay-out and design.

4. <u>Education or instruction</u>? Carnoy and Levin (1975), Mace (1975) and others have queried the OUUK's claims that its degree is the equivalent of an on-campus degree. Against this judgement can be cited the general transferability of the OUUK degree within the U.K. system (Swift, 1980) and the clear design of the OUUK system to provide education at a distance and not just information giving (Keegan, 1979). Evidences of this are:

    ° the continuity of concern for students studying at a distance (Sewart, 1978)
    ° the structuring of the system for the avoidance of avoidable drop-out
    ° the identification of students who are at risk
    ° the wide range of student support services including compulsory residential schools

Table 13.2 OUUK Ordinary graduates by cohort 1972/82

| Year | 1971 | 1972 | 1973 | 1974 | 1975 | 1976 | 1977 | 1978 | 1979 | 1980 | 1981 | 1982 | Total BA Ordinary Graduates | Total Students |
|---|---|---|---|---|---|---|---|---|---|---|---|---|---|---|
| 1971 | 888 | | | | | | | | | | | | 888 | 19581 |
| 1972 | 3318 | 322 | | | | | | | | | | | 3640 | 31902 |
| 1973 | 2636 | 2292 | 252 | | | | | | | | | | 5180 | 38424 |
| 1974 | 1649 | 1743 | 1859 | 217 | 1 | | | | | | | | 5469 | 42636 |
| 1975 | 1259 | 1349 | 1495 | 1693 | 229 | 2 | | | | | | | 6027 | 49358 |
| 1976 | 561 | 1123 | 1068 | 1251 | 1814 | 177 | 5 | | | | | | 5997 | 50994 |
| 1977 | 323 | 549 | 881 | 790 | 1365 | 1423 | 193 | 10 | | | | | 5534 | 55397 |
| 1978 | 198 | 285 | 449 | 833 | 1083 | 1102 | 1707 | 161 | 17 | | | | 5835 | 58778 |
| 1979 | 127 | 207 | 303 | 463 | 1110 | 904 | 1260 | 1536 | 176 | 5 | | | 6091 | 60579 |
| 1980 | 88 | 145 | 171 | 227 | 571 | 1029 | 1075 | 1236 | 1730 | 207 | 24 | | 6503 | 61007 |
| 1981 | 85 | 99 | 127 | 158 | 365 | 536 | 1205 | 1038 | 1207 | 1468 | 125 | 27 | 6440 | 59968 |
| 1982 | | | | | | | | | | | | | | 63119 |
| Total Graduates by cohort 71-82 | 11142 | 8114 | 6603 | 5632 | 6538 | 5173 | 5445 | 3981 | 3130 | 1680 | 149 | 27 | 57614 | |
| Graduates as % of finally registered students in cohort | 56.90 (19581) | 51.63 (15716) | 52.07 (12680) | 49.68 (11336) | 44.09 (14330) | 42.29 (12231) | 35.95 (15146) | 25.48 (15622) | 21.07 (14854) | 11.98 (14022) | 1.03 (14410) | | | |

56% of cohort A (19581) had graduated up until 1982. Source: OUUK Academic Planning Office

    &deg;      provision of a personal tutor counsellor and a variety of optional or compulsory contact activities.

5. <u>Status</u>. The OUUK quickly shed its correspondence image and sought to insert itself within its first decade into the fabric of British educational and political life. This was achieved partly through an astute usage of contact with the British Broadcasting Corporation and partly through a series of measures which are worth listing as a guideline for other distance university systems:

    &deg;      the calibre of the authors who agreed to write the first units

    &deg;      the immediate international reputation of the UKOU

    &deg;      the number of qualified academics who joined its full-time staff

    &deg;      the number of U.K. academics who applied, unsuccessfully, for positions at the OUUK

    &deg;      the political diplomacy of Perry, the first Vice-Chancellor and Christodoulou, the first Secetary

    &deg;      the winning of a series of national research awards

    &deg;      the winning of positions on national educational and governmental committees

    &deg;      the cohesiveness of the system, especially concerning the evaluation of students' study.

6. <u>Costs</u>. The OUUK is not cheap. In 1983 it cost the British taxpayer £60m with small additional funds coming from student fees and sales of materials.

    Dey (1984) presents the 1983 costs as illustrated in table 13.3.

    The cost structures of the OUUK are now well known and have been referred to extensively in Chapter 12. It spends large amounts of monies on broadcast television and this has been critisized by Mace (1975) on economic grounds and queried by Bates (1981) in terms of educational effectiveness. It also spends large amounts of money on regional and student support services and this has been queried also. Defenders of this expenditure (Sewart, 1981) claim that this is the only way to keep

Table 13.3 Costs of OUUK in 1982

Open University students pay their own fees and
other costs and a typical picture is presented
by 1983 figures.

1983 Costs to Students

| | |
|---|---|
| Summer School | £ 83.00 |
| Tuition and Materials | £127.00 |
| Set Books | £ 25.00 |
| Miscellaneous | £ 15.00 |
| | |
| Total | £250.00 |

It is interesting to compare these figures with
1983 Open University expenditure.

1983 Expenditure

| | |
|---|---|
| Central Academic | £ 12.9m |
| Academic Support | £ 2.9m |
| Local Tuition | £ 7.2m |
| TV & Radio | £ 10.0m |
| Central Administration | £ 9.2m |
| Regional Administration | £ 9.0m |
| Course Materials | £ 3.8m |
| Operations | £ 4.9m |
| Estates | £ 5.3m |
| | |
| Total | £ 65.2m |

(Dey, 1984)

students in the system and to provide university education rather than instruction.

Up to December 1983 the evaluation by
all the criteria chosen is highly positive.
In 1984 a series of articles (Whitehead, 1984)
evidenced a difficult period ahead as the
new proposed changes of government funding
structures placed in jeopardy a number of
the criteria put forward in this study.

## The University of New England, Armidale, New South Wales

1. Access and needs. When the university was inaugurated in 1955 it immediately taught both internally and externally. The external provision was principally to meet the needs of the shortage of graduate teachers in New South Wales. In 1964 82% of the 2263 external enrolments were teachers; by 1983 the proportion had fallen to 28%.

   Today UNE gives external access to bachelor degrees, postgraduate diplomas and masters degrees for 27 separate awards in a wide range of disciplines. Over 300 full-time academic staff in 35 departments teach part of their student load externally and the other part of their students in lecture theatres. They are supported by a Director of External Studies and 38 administrative and clerical staff. The external studies department provides for the needs of a student body who are 90% in New South Wales and 10% in the rest of Australia (the obligation and cost of travelling to Armidale for the compulsory summer schools being a deterrent to many interstate enrolments), over 40% of the students coming from metropolitan Sydney where there are three major conventional universities. Students are 50% female with an average age of 33.

   In 1982 the student population of UNE was:

   Table 13.4: Enrolment at UNE (1982)

   | | |
   |---|---|
   | Full-time students | 2,263 |
   | Post-time students | 356 |
   | External students | 6,280 |
   | Total students | 8,899 |

2. Withdrawal rates trend. Smith comments on the withdrawal rates in Figure 13.1:

   > Withdrawal rates are based on the number of students still enrolled at the time of the November examination period compared with the total intake at the

beginning of the academic year in early March. If one allowed a month or two for students to settle down to study during some period of provisional registration as is done at the Open University in Britain, then the withdrawal rate could be reduced by between 7-10%, the proportion of students (mainly new ones) who now withdraw early in the year before having made a serious start. Secondly, there is a significant difference between withdrawal rates of new students and continuing students. Although about 35% of each intake of new students is lost each year, only about 10%-12% of continuing students withdraw or suspend studies each year. It is evident that once a student has been successful in a course, ability and determination to maintain studies is improved immeasurably. Thirdly, about 10% of the total enrolment consists of resuming students who take up their studies after a temporary interruption to them.(1983:17)

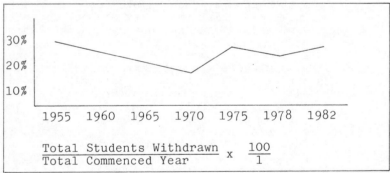

Figure 13.1 Withdrawal rates of external students at UNE 1955-1982.

As external and internal students sit for the same examination, are prepared by the same full-time lecturers and are examined by the same examiners, it is easy to compare the records of both types of students. The external studies department is particularly proud of the number of external students who achieve distinctions and the number of mature-age non-matriculants who graduate despite having no qualifications to enter the university.

3.  Quality of materials. UNE provides printed
    learning materials plus audio and some video
    cassettes.   To these are added face-to-face
    tuition at weekend and residential schools
    and telephone contact. The materials are writ-
    ten by the academic lecturers, who teach the
    same subjects face-to-face and are printed
    by the university printery.   UNE materials
    are functional, not gaudy, and frequently
    reflect their origin in the lecture notes
    for on-campus students.

4.  Education or instruction? Intersubjectivity.
    It is clear that the rather functional and
    often cheaply presented UNE distance learning
    materials cannot account fully for the success
    of its external students vis-a-vis the uni-
    versity's normal students.   Both Sheath and
    Smith pride themselves on the university's
    student support services and Smith comments:

    > If academic staff are to be heavily com-
    > mitted to a dual system of teaching,
    > it is essential that they are not diverted
    > from this demanding role by administrative
    > and organisational responsibilities that
    > are rapidly generated in an educational
    > system where students are widely scattered
    > across a continent.   External studies
    > will not operate effectively just by
    > offering carefully prepared courses and
    > marking assignments. All too many systems
    > at home and abroad bear testimony to
    > this with catastrophic withdrawal and
    > failure rates. (1979:35).   The notion
    > of a university as a community of scholars
    > is still important and whilst it may
    > seem a contradiction in terms to talk
    > about a community of scholars studying
    > as external students, no such contradic-
    > tion need exist at all.   Indeed, at the
    > University of New England we believe
    > that teaching and learning in the external
    > studies system should be based on the
    > premise that although most study will
    > be done in an independent way, there
    > should also be a significant element
    > of personal interaction. (1979:39).

In practical terms this means:

°     compulsory residential summer schools for each unit
°     the obligation for externals to see their university and enjoy a brief period of traditional university life as a full-time student in residence (1979:38)
°     optional weekend seminars
°     visits by full-time faculty to student groups or to individuals on farms
°     externals being brought into contact with the best brains in the university, not part-time staff.

5.   Status. The status of qualifications from the UNE external programmes is similar to the status of the UNE degrees and diplomas on-campus. When interviewing for educational positions in Australian schools and colleges one frequently encounters candidates with UNE Graduate Diplomas in Educational Administration or similar fields. One suspects that these qualifications were probably won at a distance but one normally grants parity of esteem without checking and evaluating whether it was an internal UNE degree or diploma or an external one.

6.   Costs. The university provides a fixed ratio of lecturing staff appointments for both internal and external students. For 1981 UNE received $Austr. 23m. in recurrent funding from the government on the agreed formula of $Austr. 4,000 per whole student enrolment. Of this the Department of External studies' budget was $Austr. 400,000 for clerical staffing and $Austr. 180,000 for equipment and maintenance. Salaries of academic staff are not distinguished between external and internal teaching and do not come within the external studies costs.

Conclusion

Again the evaluation in terms of student learning and achievement is highly favourable. Despite doubts expressed in recent years (Ortmeier 1979, Shott 1983) about (i) the peripheral relationship of the external studies department to university planning and budgeting, (ii) the quality of the learning materials and (iii) the compulsory residential schools; the UNE external students maintain a high quantity, quality and status of learning at very reasonable costs.

## The Centre National d'Enseignement par Correspondance, France

1.  Access and needs. The invasion of France led to the creation of the CNEC by a government decree of 2 December 1939 to meet the needs of school children dislocated by war. Shortly before the liberation it was reconstituted as a Lycée by a decree of 30 May 1944. When the war was over the CNEC went through a difficult period when its necessity was questioned but by May 1950 its future was assured. It was about 1950, too, that the first adults were enrolled by the provision of access to underqualified teachers (as in many other national systems).

    The official government provision of distance education in France has been marked with rapidly accelerating student numbers:

Table 13.5 Enrolment at CNEC 1940-1983.

| Year | Student enrolments |
|------|--------------------|
| 1940 | war years |
| 1945 | 1413 |
| 1950 | 8300 |
| 1955 | 30000 |
| 1960 | 61000 |
| 1965 | 109000 |
| 1970 | 146000 |
| 1975 | 180000 |
| 1980 | 197000 |
| 1983 | 220000 |

Source: Renseignment statistiques

In 1971 the name of the CNEC was changed to Centre National de Télé-enseignment par correspondance, par radio et par télévision (CNTE - National Centre for Distance Education - by correspondence, radio and television) but reverted to CNEC in 1979 (decree of 1.1. 1980). When the annual enrolment at the CNTE in Paris reached 150,000 in the early 1970s a major structural change was achieved.

Administrative control of programmes was divided to six centres: Paris, Grenoble, Lille, Lyon, Rouen and Toulouse. A seventh centre at Rheims was added in 1982. The division of responsibilities in the early 1980s was thus:

Table 13.6 Administrative distribution of CNEC programmes 1982.

| C.N.E.C Centre | Programmes | |
|---|---|---|
| | Children | Adults |
| | Electronics Certificates | |
| Grenoble | Secondary education | Teacher education |
| Lille | | Public Service education |
| | Secretarial, accounting certificates | |
| Lyon | | Nursing<br>Public service<br>  qualifications<br>Technical teachers |
| Rouen | Primary education | C.A.P.E.S. (Teacher education) |
| Toulouse | Secondary education | Basic education<br>Teacher education |
| | Industrial Certificate | |
| | Matriculation | |
| | Advanced Industrial and commercial certificate | |
| Vanves, Paris | | Adult education<br>Modern Languages<br>Continuing teacher<br>  education (in service)<br>D.E.U.G. (two year<br>  university degree)<br>C.A.P.E.S. - C.A.P.E.T.<br>  (post-graduate teacher<br>  education)<br>Agrégation = (M.Phil?) |

Source: Renseignements statistiques

263

15% of today's enrolment of over 220,000 represents the original mandate of primary and secondary schooling. Access is provided throughout the world, as it is a French tradition that French government or business officials who are working overseas enrol their children in the full French school programme at the CNEC for the years in which the family is outside France. As a result the 1983 CNEC statistics include enrolments from 107 countries. 85% of the students are adults, enrolled in every possible level from post-literacy and numeracy to the equivalent of post-graduate university level courses.

2.    Drop-outs. For students in compulsory education aged 6-16 drop-out is not a phenomenon. Students pass easily from classroom education to correspondence and back. Those students resident in France receive a two-hour visit from a CNEC teacher to their house (or hospital etc.) once a week. Students overseas receive comprehensive correspondence tuition from a personal tutor-counsellor assigned to them.

For an analysis of drop-outs at CNEC for adults the French national education system provides excellent possibilities of control. All awards in France are the result of competitive examinations: all adult students sit for the same national government examinations whether they studied conventionally or at a distance. Before the examinations the number of candidates is known, as is the number of passes available in that particular year. The researcher can establish from government statistics the number of candidates (étudiants admissibles) who studied at the CNEC and the number who studied face-to-face. When the results are published the researcher can establish the number and percentage of successful students who studied at a distance and the number and percentage of successful (étudiants reçus) students who studied face-to-face.

In what follows this is done for the CAPES and agrégation courses in 1982. The prerequisites for CAPES or agrégation may be stated as follows: after high school matriculation (Baccalauréat) at least three years full-time study is needed for the Licence (Bachelor's degree), this is followed by one year full-time study for either the maitrise (Master's degree) or CAPES (post-graduate diploma). A further one year's full-time study is necessary after either a maitrise or a CAPES for agrégation. For the CAPES Anglais (post-graduate diploma for teachers of English) the figures are for 1982:

| Table 13.7 CAPES Anglais statistics 1982 | |
| --- | --- |
| CNEC | CONVENTIONAL INSTITUTIONS |
| Enrolled at CNEC 1480<br>Present at exam-<br>  inations 734<br>Qualified (admissible) 287<br>Successful (reçus) 118 | Enrolled for concours 4555<br>Present at exam-<br>  inations 3200<br>Qualified (admissible) 733<br>Successful (reçus) 360 |

Thus CNEC students won 32.7% of all positions in the 1982 CAPES anglais national examinations and competitions: a highly significant proportion.

3.   Quality of materials. CNEC printed materials are functional. An A4 portrait format with a typeface that gives an average of 22 words per line and over 40 lines per page gives a density of presentation that is relieved only rarely by line drawings. Margins are minimal (average 1.5cm on both sides) and use of headings, and other layout devices is sparse. One is reminded, however, that until quite recently the publication of books in France, and especially academic texts, followed also a closely packed print format and one had frequently to cut the pages oneself.

    On the other hand the quality of CNEC's audio materials is uniformly excellent and a model for other distance institutions because of the quality achieved in a recording studio with quite modest equipment. The 'symphony on three glass tumblers' in the CAPES music course must be a classic in distance education materials both from the pedagogical structuring of the content and the realisation. Language tapes at all levels and in languages as diverse as Russian and Chinese make up an audio component of extensive quantity and quality.

The CNEC no longer uses television broadcasting nor video cassettes.

4.  Education or instruction? Intersubjectivity. The main teaching strategies of the CNEC for preparing its students for the national French examinations, once the audio and printed materials have been distributed, is correspondence tuition from a tutor-counsellor, often a full-time staff member, and occasional, voluntary face-to-face sessions. The CNEC represents the transition to national, government distance education provision of a range of didactic strategies that were developed by the proprietary correspondence schools. It is the world's major government sponsored example of the personal tutor-counsellor assigned to an adult student to provide student support services.

5.  Status. A national, competitive examination system works well for distance education institutions and students who study at a distance. The status of the qualification is guaranteed by government and employment is guaranteed for the graduates of the distance system if they are successful in winning a place in the quota of successful candidates, as the CNEC students do. At school level the status of children who re-enter or leave the normal school system is accepted without question, whether they have spent the intervening year or years in France or overseas.

6.  Costs. Most of the CNEC budget goes on salaries of full-time staff. The full-time staff of 1,900 are all employed by the Ministry of Education on the same terms as ordinary teachers in French schools. The difference is that many of them have been assigned to the CNEC for reasons of some physical or psychological disability and could not be transferred back to the face-to-face system for this reason. In addition 1,000 staff are employed for technological and higher education subjects. Many of these staff work full-time from their own homes, thus saving enormously on plant and buildings.

## Conclusion

The 45 years provision of distance education by the French national system of the CNEC has been little studied. It is practically unknown in the English-speaking world and as an organ of the Ministry of Education is not cited in studies of higher education in France and unrecognised within the French university system.

Certain elements of its structure are of importance for distance education and have recently been reproduced in one of the English-speaking distance systems, the Open Learning Institute of British Columbia. Salient points for consideration by those planning distance systems in both developed and developing countries are:

  ° the official national provision of distance education
  ° an autonomous (Type 1 / Type 2) institution designed specifically for distance education
  ° a multi-level institution with divisions which cover, at least, university level education at a distance, college and further education at a distance, adult basic education at a distance, primary and secondary schooling
  ° the provision of full-time staffing for designing distance teaching materials
  ° the provision of full-time staffing for student support services, with each student being linked to a personal tutor-counsellor at least for the length of one course
  ° a media mix with print dominating, a sophisticated use of audio-cassettes and telephone, and an absence of broadcasting.

This 45-year tradition is in many ways a fundamental model for distance systems; more recent foundations of distance or open universities risk the danger of not being able to attract the volume of annual enrolments necessary for an autonomous institution at the level of university provision but the combination of all levels of adult provision in the one distance institution can provide the volume required.

## References

Ardagh, J. (1975) The new France. Harmondsworth: Penguin.
Bates, A.W. (1981) Towards a better framework for

evaluating the effectiveness of educational media. British Journal of Educational Technology, 12, 215-233.

Carnoy M. and Levin, H. (1975) Evaluation of educational media; some issues. Instructional Science, 17, 21-34.

Dey, I. (1984) L'amministrazione della Open University di Inghilterra. In Keegan, D. e Lata.F. (ed) L'università a distanza. Riflessioni e proposte per un nuovo modello di università. Milano: Angeli.

Escotet, M. (1980) Tendencias de la Educación Superior a Distancia. San José: Editorial UNED.

Gooler, D. (1979) Evaluating distance education programmes. Canadian Journal of University Continuing Education, 6, 1, 43-55.

Keegan, D. (1979) The Regional Tutorial Services of the Open University: a case study. ZIFF Papiere 29, Fernuniversität,Hagen.

Keegan, D. and Rumble, G. (1982) The DTUs: an appraisal. In Rumble, G. and Harry, K. (eds) The distance teaching universities. London: Croom Helm, 222-250.

Kemmis, S. (1980) Programme evaluation in distance education: against the technologisation of reason. Open Campus, 2, 11-29.

Mace, J. (1975) Mythology in the making: is the OU really cost-effective? Higher Education, 7, 295-309.

McIntosh, N. (1975) Institutional research: needs and uses. Teaching at a Distance, 2, 33-48.

McIntosh, N., Woodley, A. and Morrison, V. (1980) The Open University - the first eight years. Distance Education, 1, 1, 99-111.

Ortmeier, A. (1979) Die Fernunterricht an Universitäten und Fachhochschulen Australiens. Tübingen: DIFF.

Rumble, G. (1981) Evaluating autonomous multimedia distance learning systems; a practical approach. Distance Education, 2,1, 64-90.

Sewart, D. (1978) Continuity of concern for students studying at a distance. ZIFF Papiere 18, Hagen: Fernuniversität.

Shott, M. (1983) An analysis of the Australian integrated mode. Aspesa Newsletter, 17, 6-10.

Smith, K. (1979) External studies at New England: a silver jubilee review. Armidale: UNE.

Smith, K. (1983) The integrated New England model:

how well has it stood the test of time? Paper at UNED Congress of Open and Distance Teaching Universities, Madrid, October 24-28.

Swift, B. (1980) Outcomes of Open University studies. Milton Keynes: OU Survey Research Department paper.

Whitehead, P. (1984) The Open University - a dream deferred? The Listener, 17 May, 24 May.

# CHAPTER FOURTEEN

## CONCLUSION

Distance education is a little-studied area of education which is growing in importance annually. As a more industrialised form of educational provision it is well adapted to the developments of new communications technologies and brings to education many of the strengths and dangers of industrialisation. It is also adapted to the growth of privacy in post-industrial societies which focuses many of the functions of living on the individual's residence with a concomitant loss of the sense of community in society.

The conclusions from the study are many and varied but are not put forward here as judgements which are to be considered normative for practice. Rather they are put forward as suggestions for research by other scholars and invitations to others to contribute to our knowledge of the theory and practice of distance education.

Among the most important are:

- °     distance education is a coherent and distinct field of educational endeavour.
- °     distance education is a distinct field of education, parallel to and a complement of conventional education. It has its own didactic laws, administrative procedures and characteristic buildings and plant.
- °     distance education is a needed component of many national education systems.
- °     the correct term for this sector of education is 'distance education'.
- °     it is possible to propose a coherent definition of distance education which distinguishes it from other areas of educational activity.
- °     distance education institutions can be classified into five major groupings.

   °     an institutional model of great importance
is the autonomous distance institution teaching
at a number of levels as exemplified by the
Centre National d'Education par Correspondance,
France.

   °     distance systems can be cheaper but this depends on a complex range of factors, some
of which may affect the quality of provision.

   °     distance systems have inherent difficulties
with the quantity, quality and status of provision.

   °     cohesive and competently administered systems
can solve the problems of quantity, quality
and status of provision. Three examples are
given of institutions which appear to have
achieved acceptable solutions.

   °     distance education is a legitimate field of
academic enquiry.